LEARNING

READING STRATEGIES
Comprehension Skills

**Study Guide
HA 1-20**

Second Edition

www.steck-vaughn.com

1-56260-714-6

Copyright © 1997 Steck-Vaughn Company. All rights reserved. No part of this publication may be reproduced, or utilized in any form or by any means, electronic or mechanical, including photocopying, recording or by any information storage and retrieval system, without permission in writing from the copyright owner. Requests for permission to make copies of any part of this publication should be mailed to: Copyright Permissions, Steck-Vaughn Company, P.O. Box 26015, Austin, TX 78755. Printed in the United States.

3 4 5 6 7 8 9   DBH   05 04 03 02

CONTENTS

	Lessons: Story Titles and Skill Topics		Page
1	Revenge of the Bugs 101	Scanning	2
2	Jake	Substitutions	10
3	Mysterious Talents	Context Clues	18
4	The Greatest Bronc Buster Who Ever Lived	Inferences	26
5	The Weed Killer That Kills People	Main Ideas	34
6	Athletes on Drugs	Types of Supporting Details	42
7	The Trials of Edith Cavell and Jomo Kenyatta	Comparisons	50
8	Introducing the Mom and Pop Supermarket	Sequence	58
9	The Return of the Puffins	Cause and Effect	66
10	Job Opportunities in Health Care	Problem and Solution	74
11	A Woman's Icy Struggle	Summarizing	82
12	The Greatest Adventure	Fact and Opinion	90
13	When Will Companies Become Family-Friendly?	Recognizing Bias/Author's Viewpoint	98
14	War Propaganda	Persuasion	106
15	Letters from the Past	Judging Relevance/Finding Proof	114
16	The Man Who Put Up at Gadsby's	Setting/Tone/Theme	122
17	The Necklace—Part One	Character and Feelings	130
18	The Necklace—Part Two	Plot	138
19	A Gray Sleeve	Sensory Images/Figurative Language	146
20	To Build a Fire	Qualities in Literature: Suspense	154

Extension Activities _____ 162

How to Score for Mastery _____ 166

Progress Chart _____ 167

Answer Key _____ 168

Skill Review Activities _____ 176

Skill Review Activities

This edition of the Reading Strategies Study Guide contains a Skill Review Activity for each lesson that reinforces the reading skill taught in the lesson. These Skill Review Activities can either be used as a follow-up activity or as a posttest immediately after the lesson has been taught, or for review and reinforcement after some time has lapsed. Skill Review Activities begin on page 176.

HA-1 SCANNING
REVENGE OF THE BUGS 101

 GETTING READY

How do you feel when you look at the picture above? If you feel somewhat uneasy, you're not alone. Many people are anxious around insects, and some have a real fear of them. This is why filmmakers have used insects to make our skin crawl in horror movies. What are some horror movies you have seen that involve insects? What effect have these movies had on you? Why do you think you responded this way?

This selection explains how a college professor who studies insects came up with a unique way of getting people to find out more about the creatures: she started an Insect Fear Film Festival. When you read "Revenge of the Bugs 101," you'll find out just how successful this festival is.

VOCABULARY BUILDING

Study each key word to make sure you know its pronunciation and definition. Then study the way the word is used in the sentence based on the story.

accumulated (ə kyü′ myə lāt id) Gathered little by little. *McClelland has accumulated information on some of the more extreme forms of anxiety caused by insects.*

browse (brouz) To look at in a casual way. *They browse through exhibits of live specimens in cages and under glass.*

distribution (dis′ trə byü′ shən) Act of giving some of to each. *Graduate students are responsible for the distribution of crispy insect treats like deep-fried crickets.*

emotions (i mō′ shəns) Feelings. *Why do insects cause such strong emotions?*

immersed (i mėrst′) Involved deeply. *Enthusiastic fans of creepy thrills are immersed in the insect theme.*

indifferent (in dif′ ər ənt) Having or showing no interest or attention. *Almost without exception, the rare good film is still indifferent to the principles of good science.*

inflict (in flikt′) Cause to have or suffer. *Extreme forms of anxiety insects inflict on humans include an unreasonable fear that can produce panic attacks and flight.*

intruder (in trüd′ ėr) One who comes unasked and unwanted. *In The Fly, Jeff Goldblum played a scientist accidentally changed into a king-sized version of the household intruder.*

obscure (əb skyür′) Not well known. *An obscure but not uncommon related fear is one in which people become convinced that bugs are living in their hair or burrowing under their skin.*

prestigious (pre stij′ əs) Honored; respected. *Since then, the festival has been written up in prestigious newspapers.*

Now choose a word that fits in each of the following sentences. Write the best word for each sentence.

1. Many customers come into my store not to buy, but to _____ .

2. When Carmen became famous, she moved from a poor neighborhood to a more _____ address.

3. I was so _____ in the book that I didn't hear the doorbell.

4. Over the years Bob has _____ a wonderful collection of modern painting.

5. The company president showed she was _____ to her workers by refusing to listen to their complaints.

6. Many people have not read the works of the _____ poet.

7. I called the police when I thought that an _____ had entered the house.

8. I helped with the _____ of food at the homeless shelter.

HA-1

9. I had mixed _____ about leaving my home and making a fresh start elsewhere.

10. A broken marriage can _____ pain on the children as well as on the couple breaking up.

Check your answers with the key.

SPECIAL WORDS

ecosystem (ē' kō sis' təm) A physical environment with the community of various animals and plants that live there. *Insects are critical to the planetary ecosystem.*
entomology (en' tə mol' ə jē) The study of animal life dealing with insects. *Founder, host, and entomology professor May Berenbaum is a champion of her trade—and a practical person.* An **entomologist** is a person who studies entomology; **entomological** means having to do with entomology.

 ## PREVIEW

Read the first paragraph and the first sentence of each of the other paragraphs to discover what you will learn from the story. Do this now.

Did you notice that the story gives you certain information about insects and the Insect Fear Film Festival? A list of topics that may or may not be discussed in the story follows.

Based on what you have learned from previewing the story, write *yes* if you think the topic might be discussed. Write *no* if you think the topic will not be discussed.

11. _____ What happens at the festival

12. _____ Why people fear insects

13. _____ How to get rid of insects

14. _____ Why insects are important

15. _____ Films about killer plants

Check your answers with the key.

 ## READING

Now read the story to find out more about the Insect Fear Film Festival.

REVENGE OF THE BUGS 101
by Frank Kuznik

"Take a seat, or we'll turn the roaches loose!"

Those are no ordinary roaches University of Illinois entomologist May Berenbaum is threatening to unleash. They're 4-inch Madagascar hissing roaches, just the sort of vile brutes to scare an audience into its seats—and to set the proper tone for the Insect Fear Film Festival, an annual evening-long showcase of films featuring all manner of entomological disasters. Giant grasshoppers, wasp women, bee girls, human flies: Name any of Hollywood's most outrageous insect villains, and chances are the festival has screened them.

The festival has become a full-blown insect spectacular in the dead of winter. Enthusiastic fans of creepy thrills are immersed in the insect theme. They browse through exhibits of live specimens in cages and under glass. Graduate students are responsible for the distribution of crispy insect treats like deep-fried crickets. There are insect costumes, rubber insect door prizes, insect cartoons and, of course, Insect Fear T-shirts and sweatshirts for sale.

For all that, the festival is at heart a well-disguised science lesson. Founder, host, and entomology professor May Berenbaum is a champion of her trade—and a practical person. "You catch more flies with honey, to use an entomological phrase, than you do with vinegar," she says. "The films draw a big audience that would never ordinarily attend a lecture on entomology. We try to pick films that illustrate some basic point about insects, and if you're having a pleasant experience, then you'll remember the point."

Generally, the films illustrate a point by being wrong about it, leaving Berenbaum to sort out fact from fiction in her witty and informed introductions. But no matter how bad the science, films like *Mothra* (in which an enormous moth terrorizes Tokyo) and *Empire of the Ants* (giant ants put Joan Collins and other human captives to work in a sugar factory) are dead-on in one respect: They reflect the fear humans have of insects.

Why do insects cause such strong emotions? "There's quite a range of theories," says Tad Hardy, an entomologist with the Louisiana Department of Agriculture and Forestry. "One of the most obvious is they're just very different. They look so alien compared to what we're used to." That, says Berenbaum, is the primary reason insects remain fright-film favorites. "It's great from a filmmaker's point of view," she says. "Take a picture of an insect up close, and you've got a horrible creature."

Insects are also unpredictable, and they can be fast. Worse for nervous humans, many can fly. And their size gives them a disturbing advantage. Jokes Berenbaum, "If you had porcupines in your basement, it would be a little strange, but you'd know where they were. If you have roaches in the basement, they could be anywhere. That's unsettling; people don't like things to be out of their control."

Certainly no creatures are more out of our control than insects, which make up about 70 percent of all animal species. There are nearly 900,000 known species of insects. Estimates of the number yet to be discovered range as high as 35 million. Insects have been around since before the dinosaurs and have proved amazingly hardy; throw a poison at them, and they simply adapt.

Aside from the sheer creepiness factor, there are several good reasons to be wary of insects. Some, like mosquitoes, are bloodsuckers and agents for spreading disease. Crop pests can do in a food supply. The most common bug health threat is from stinging insects such as wasps and bees.

"Our society constantly presents unfavorable images of insects," says Andy McClelland, an entomologist at the University of California, Davis. "Look at the pest-control commercials on TV, where the message is 'The only good bug is a dead bug.'" Indeed, the *Wall Street Journal* has estimated that getting rid of insects is a $3.5-billion-a-year business.

McClelland has accumulated information on some of the more extreme forms of anxiety insects inflict on humans, including an unreasonable fear that can produce panic attacks and flight. An obscure but not uncommon related fear is one in which people become convinced that bugs are living in their hair or burrowing under their skin. For the more common fears, knowledge is often an effective remedy. Once people start to learn about insects, their fears are often replaced by a growing fascination.

Insects are critical to the planetary ecosystem. They are vital to plant growth, and enormous numbers of birds and fish depend on them for food. Insects allow air to penetrate the soil, consume vast amounts of garbage and dead vegetation, and produce goods valued by humans, such as honey and silk. Insects are also starting to attract attention for their possible value to medicine.

"Insects are a tremendous source of chemical information," says Cornell entomologist Thomas Eisner, who has found possible heart and nerve drugs in insects. Though a leader of insect-chemistry studies, Eisner says what fascinates him most is basic bug behavior. "What goes on in the insect world is just so startling," he marvels. "I'm very sorry that no one emphasizes their incredible entertainment value."

Berenbaum had a similar thought in 1980, when she became a professor at the University of Illinois' Champaign-Urbana campus. The Insect Fear Film Festival came into being four years later. Since then, the festival has been written up in prestigious newspapers and featured on television and radio.

Almost without exception, the rare good film is still indifferent to the principles of good science. The well-regarded 1986 remake of *The Fly,* for example, featured a riveting performance by Jeff Goldblum as a scientist accidentally changed into a king-sized version of the household intruder. "And it still had the same scientific nonsense that every giant-insect film has ever had," says Berenbaum. "If you're 6 feet tall, you cannot walk on the ceiling, even if you look like a fly. Gravity still works on you."

The release of *Arachnophobia*[1] (poisonous spider terrorizes a California town) in 1990 raised Berenbaum's hopes that a golden age of insect-fear films had arrived. Alas, that movie too turned out to be full of scientific errors. But maybe it was better that way; the sillier the films, the more the audiences seem to like them.

---
[1] Extreme and unreasonable fear of spiders

COMPREHENSION CHECK

Choose the best answer.

CAUSE/EFFECT

16. Why does May Berenbaum hold the Insect Fear Festival?
    a. She loves horror movies.
    b. She wants to make money.
    c. She wants to teach people about insects.
    d. She would like to get over her fear of insects.

COMPARISONS

17. What do all the films have in common?
    a. They involve giant insects.
    b. They reflect the fear humans have of insects.
    c. The insects always get the better of humans.
    d. They are scientifically accurate.

CAUSE/EFFECT

18. Which of these are reasons why humans fear insects? (Choose all the correct answers.)
    a. Most insects are poisonous.
    b. Insects look alien.
    c. Insects are fast, with many being able to fly.
    d. The size of insects gives them a disturbing advantage.

TYPES OF SUPPORTING DETAILS

19. One paragraph begins "Aside from the sheer creepiness factor, there are several good reasons to be wary of insects." Which of the following paragraph patterns does it use?
    a. Generalization
    b. Enumeration
    c. Opinion/reason
    d. Question/answer

FACT/OPINION

20. Which of these sentences is an opinion?
    a. The only good bug is a dead bug.
    b. Insects make up about 70 percent of all animal species.
    c. Mosquitoes are agents for spreading disease.
    d. McClelland has accumulated information on some of the more extreme forms of anxiety insects inflict on humans.

PROBLEM/SOLUTION

21. What is one solution mentioned in the story to combat fear of insects?
    a. Viewing horror movies involving them
    b. Killing them
    c. Avoiding them
    d. Finding out more about them

INFERENCE

22. Which of the following accurately describes Thomas Eisner's view of insects?
    a. They are boring to work with.
    b. They are a necessary evil.
    c. They are important to scientific research.
    d. They are frightening creatures.

SEQUENCE

23. The remake of *The Fly* came out
    a. after the first Insect Fear Film Festival.
    b. before May Berenbaum became a professor at the University of Illinois.
    c. after the release of *Arachnophobia*.
    d. at the same time as *Arachnophobia*.

SUBSTITUTIONS

24. Read the following sentence from the last paragraph: "Alas, that movie too turned out to be full of scientific errors." The phrase "that movie" refers to
    a. *Mothra*.
    b. *Arachnophobia*.
    c. *The Fly*.
    d. *Empire of the Ants*.

MAIN IDEA

25. This selection is mainly about
    a. how insects are used for medicinal purposes.
    b. the Insect Fear Film Festival and general information about insects.
    c. how to make an insect horror movie.
    d. why people fear insects and what they can do about this.

Check your answers with the key.

HA-1

SKILL PRACTICE
SCANNING

Scanning is a special kind of reading that you do when you are looking for certain information. When you scan, you only read as much as you need to find the information.

Some information stands out on the page. If you need to find a date, a time, or a measurement, look for a number on the page. If you need to find a name of some kind, look for capital letters as you scan. Here's an example:

> In what city does the film *Mothra* take place?

The answer, the name of a city, begins with a capital letter. If you scan the fifth paragraph of the story, you'll find the answer, *Tokyo*.

Sometimes the question itself suggests words to look for as you scan. Here is an example:

> What is one type of insect that is a bloodsucker and agent for spreading disease?

As you scan, look for these target words: *bloodsucker, agent,* and *spreading disease*. If you scan the ninth paragraph of the story, you'll find the answer: *mosquitoes*.

Sometimes the target words stated in the question don't appear in the selection. Instead, a target work triggers sub-topics you should look for. For example, suppose that you are looking for information about the climate of a certain area. You are likely to find sub-topics of the word *climate* in the selection. Sub-topics such as "temperature," "rainfall," "seasons," and "humidity" act as signals that you are close to the information you seek.

In the following exercise, you will scan the story to find answers to the questions. As you scan, remember to look for items that stand out on the page or look for target words from the question itself. Also, think about the words you are likely to find as signals that you're close to the information you want.

Scan to find the answer to each question. Write the answer.

26. How many known species of insects are there?

27. During what time of year is the Insect Fear Film Festival held?

28. In what way do the films illustrate a point about insects?

29. In what movie did Jeff Goldblum play a huge household pest?

30. In what year was *Arachnophobia* released?

31. Which newspaper estimated that getting rid of insects is a $3.5-billion-a-year business?

32. What reason does Tad Hardy present for the human fear of insects?

33. What symptoms can be caused by intense fear of insects?

Check your answers with the key.

VOCABULARY REVIEW

Choose the best answer.

34. Which of these is a **prestigious** event?
    a. Falling in the mud
    b. Eating dinner
    c. Being late for work
    d. Winning an award

35. What could one person **inflict** on another?
    a. Joy
    b. Pain
    c. Smiles
    d. Candy

36. John **accumulated** postcards. This means John
    a. acquired postcards.
    b. sold postcards.
    c. burned postcards.
    d. wrote postcards.

37. If a sign in a store says that you are welcome to **browse**, that means you can
    a. ask for help.
    b. eat a sandwich.
    c. just look around.
    d. bring a friend.

38. Who would be an **intruder**?
    a. An unwelcome guest
    b. A beloved family member
    c. The family pet
    d. The mail carrier

39. If you're **immersed** in a television show, then the show
    a. has your complete attention.
    b. is boring.
    c. is on in the evening.
    d. is a comedy.

40. Which of the following is an example of a **distribution**?
    a. A child going to school
    b. A woman walking her dog
    c. A car stopping for a red light
    d. A man handing out pamphlets

41. If they were **indifferent** to our problem, then they
    a. helped us solve it.
    b. felt sorry for us.
    c. blamed us for it.
    d. didn't care about it.

42. If a certain book is **obscure**, then there are not many
    a. characters in the book.
    b. exciting events in the book.
    c. people who know about the book.
    d. pages in the book.

43. An example of one of your **emotions** is
    a. laziness.
    b. fear.
    c. energy.
    d. respect.

Check your answers with the key.

HA-2 SUBSTITUTIONS
JAKE

ⓐ GETTING READY

Not everyone feels the same way about pets. Some people treat their pets as part of the family, while others feel that a pet is just an animal and nothing more. Which way would you feel about your pet?

As you can see from the picture above, this story is about a hunting dog. His name was Jake, and the author of the story, who is a hunter, loved him very much.

Jake was a bird dog, a special kind of dog that is trained to locate game birds for a hunter. After the bird is shot, the bird dog brings it back to the hunter. Dog and hunter work together as a team.

When you read "Jake," you will find out why Jake was a better hunter than the author, and what the author learned from Jake.

b VOCABULARY BUILDING

Study each key word to make sure you know its pronunciation and definition. Then study the way in which the word is used in the sentence based on the story.

awry (ə rī′) Toward one side; not in order. *I think of how Jake often looked, with his head tilted into the breeze, his whiskers lifted up a little awry.*

droll (drōl) Amusing; charmingly humorous. *Maybe Jake saw himself as being droll rather than serious.*

fracas (frā′ kəs) Noisy fight; violent confusion. *The others in his litter were the usual madmen—knocking each other witless. Jake would always be off to one side, waiting for the fracas to calm down.*

homily (hom′ ə lē) A saying that gives advice. *Jake was always reminding me that time is money, or some such homily.*

perfection (pər fek′ shən) Being without fault. *Jake always expected no less of me than perfection, and it always made me nervous.*

pompous (pom′ pəs) Exaggerated dignity, trying to be serious and very important. *Jake was a little pompous, and I was often tempted to tell him so, but it just wasn't his style to kid around.*

professorial (prō′ fə sôr′ ē əl) In the manner of a professor or other teacher. *Maybe Jake saw himself as being amusing rather than professorial.*

reminiscing (rem′ ə nis′ ing) Thinking or telling about past events. *I can never drive by a group of elm trees without fondly reminiscing about the bird dog I once served under.*

reprimand (rep′ rə mand) A serious scolding. *He always seemed to be about to give me some sort of reprimand, and he made sure I wasn't fooling around.*

verged (vėrjd) Inclined toward. *The way he always looked at me verged on some sort of scolding.*

Now choose a word that fits in each of the following sentences. Write the best word for each sentence.

1. He was so lonesome, his expression _____ on tears.

2. My mother assumed a _____ manner when she was teaching the honor students.

3. Ellie practiced the songs on the piano over and over, trying for _____ .

4. Alfie is usually serious, but he has a _____ sense of humor.

5. Ben's clothes were all _____ after he fell down.

6. Grandfather had an appropriate _____ for almost every situation.

7. The two kittens began to hiss at each other and the other cats quickly joined the _____ .

8. If you are late for work again, the boss will _____ you.

HA-2

9. Santo is a very fine actor but inclines to be _____ when he gives an interview.

10. It was fun _____ with my friend Chris about the old days in Maine.

Check your answers with the key.

SPECIAL WORDS

cover (kuv′ ər) Small trees, shrubs, that shelter game and wild animals. *I can never drive by an elm cover without fondly reminiscing about the bird dog I once served under.*

pointer (poin′ tər) A type of hunting dog that indicates, by "pointing," where wild game is located. *Jake was physically on the small side for a pointer puppy.*

shells (shelz) Metal or cardboard holders for gunpowder which are used in a shotgun. *I put a couple of empty shells with him because he always seemed to like the way they smelled.*

c PREVIEW

Read the first two paragraphs to find out how the story begins. Do this now.

Did you notice that the author says a lot about his feelings for Jake in the first two paragraphs? Below are some statements about the author and Jake.

Based on what you learned from previewing the story, write *true* for each true statement, and write *false* for each false statement.

11. _____ The author believed that Jake wasn't serious enough.

12. _____ The author felt that Jake was a little pompous.

13. _____ The author felt that Jake should join the Army.

14. _____ The author felt that Jake spent too much time digging for arrowheads.

15. _____ The author felt that Jake was trying to teach him.

Check your answers with the key.

d READING

Now read the story to find out the kind of relationship Jake and the author had.

JAKE
by Gene Hill

I can never drive by an elm cover without fondly reminiscing about the bird dog I once served under.

Jake was a very serious dog. He was never one for a lot of horseplay or funny stories. The way he always looked at me verged on some sort of reprimand, and every so often he paused and looked back over his shoulder to make sure I wasn't fooling around with my pipe, or poking for arrowheads, or generally playing around. Jake was always reminding me that time is money, or some such homily. He should have been an army sergeant or a schoolmaster. Actually, Jake was a little pompous, and I was often tempted to tell him so, but it just wasn't his style to kid around.

As Jake instructs, we weave our way across the hillside. Jake has figured out some sort of grid—thorough and mathematical—and I plod along like a slow schoolboy being drilled in the multiplication tables. Jake stops, and I can see him ahead, looking over his shoulder at me. Then, knowing I'm under orders, he straightens up, holds his head high in the air, and waits a little less than patiently for me to come up and walk in past him.

Jake always expected no less of me than perfection, and it always made me nervous. But this time, the bird soars up to the left through a small clearing and into my gun sight. I pull the trigger; Jake carefully works his way over, knowing full well that there might be another bird on the way to the fallen one. I stay put as instructed—he doesn't like me messing up his bird field unless it is absolutely necessary.

Jake never made a remark when I missed a bird. After two shots were fired and the gun was reloaded, he would watch the bird for another second or so. Then, satisfied that there was nothing to be done except try again, he would lope off without so much as dignifying my performance in any way. It was as if nothing at all had happened. I had come up with the wrong answer and he would patiently try again. When he was younger, he would sometimes shrug his shoulders at being with such a partner, as if to say, "Well, that's life." But eventually he quit that little gesture and just kept trying to teach me.

Jake was physically on the small side for a pointer puppy, and I think that had a lot to do with his attitude. The others in his litter were the usual madmen—knocking each other witless, standing in the food pan, trying to chew each other's ears and legs off. Not Jake. He would always be off to one side waiting patiently for the fracas to calm down. When he was first home with me, I'd bring him in the house and offer him squeaky toys and bones, and roll around on the floor trying to make him play. He gave all this foolishness an honest effort, but it really wasn't his style. He'd take the bones and toys back into his kennel to please me, and sometimes I'd think I heard a tiny whistle from a rubber mouse; but when I cleaned out his house, there they would all be, as good as new, pushed back into one corner.

But he loved the hunting and all that went with it. At the sight of a shotgun, he'd prance around as if he couldn't help himself, and as if to prove how much he appreciated me taking him out, he insisted on always riding in the front seat of the car. If I had someone with me, Jake would squeeze over in the middle, and if he was very tired, he'd sometimes slide his head very quietly into my lap and fall asleep. I think he took my love completely for granted and did his best to show me that he didn't need any presents or games to prove our relationship. I was the hunter and he was the hunting dog. That was enough.

When you tell a story about your dog, it has to have an ending.

I really don't exactly know what happened.

It was late summer and Jake and I had been out for our usual walk—Jake had a strong feeling of property and was along to see that things were running smoothly before we went to bed.

The next morning Jake didn't seem to be feeling too well, and I left him in the kennel while I did some chores around the lawn. Later that afternoon when I visited him again, he was gone to wherever bird dogs go. He left his life as he had lived it, by himself, with dignity and calm.

Jake always seemed fond of his little hunting bell, so I put that with him, along with a couple of empty shells, because he always seemed to like the way they smelled. In the fresh earth I stuck a small white pine. I like to think that Jake would have approved of the tree. It is a more natural reminder than a stone would be. Now that the tree has grown a bit, I sometimes see the wind lift one side of its branches and I think of how Jake often looked, with his head tilted into the breeze, his whiskers lifted up a little awry, and his eyes rolling back at me to make sure I was there.

I've been thinking about Jake a lot lately; you tend to do that with a dog who left before he told you all that he wanted you to know. Maybe I was wrong about him. Maybe Jake saw himself as being droll rather than professorial. Maybe he thought that he'd set an example for me, and when I came around a little, he could afford to relax a bit—you never really know about these things. Now I've become concerned about the white pine. It's too late to do much about the tree now. But I'm beginning to lean toward putting a small stone under the pine—nothing to it, just a plain stone. Just because he wasn't sentimental doesn't mean I can't be.

COMPREHENSION CHECK

Choose the best answer.

TONE
16. The mood of this story is
    a. happy.
    b. scary.
    c. depressing.
    d. sentimental.

INFERENCE
△ 17. The author adopted Jake when Jake was
    a. sick.
    b. a puppy.
    c. a fully trained dog.
    d. left alone.

INFERENCE
△ 18. The author has
    a. a serious outlook on life.
    b. a love for all living things.
    c. love and respect for his dog.
    d. a need to make jokes all the time.

FIGURATIVE LANGUAGE
△ 19. What does the author mean when he says, "I plod along like a slow schoolboy being drilled in the multiplication tables"?
    a. He is trudging along, practicing his multiplication tables.
    b. He is trudging along, having difficulty following the dog's expert lead.
    c. He is trudging along, daydreaming.
    d. He is trudging along, resenting the dog being in charge.

SCANNING
20. Where did Jake live?
    a. In the author's house
    b. With the other dogs in his litter
    c. In his kennel
    d. In the author's car

CHARACTER / FEELINGS
21. How did the author feel about Jake? (Choose all the correct answers.)
    a. He felt Jake was always giving orders.
    b. He felt Jake was too noisy to be a hunting dog.
    c. He felt Jake wasn't serious enough.
    d. He felt Jake was a good hunting dog.

COMPARISON
22. Which of these does the author compare Jake to? (Choose all the correct answers.)
    a. A horse
    b. An army sergeant
    c. A teacher
    d. A rubber mouse

CAUSE / EFFECT
23. Why did the author bury Jake's hunting bell and some empty shells with Jake?
    a. Because the author gave up hunting
    b. Because the author couldn't bear to see those things anymore
    c. Because the author was playing a joke
    d. Because Jake liked them

CAUSE / EFFECT
24. Whenever the author drives by an elm cover, he
    a. looks for birds to hunt.
    b. remembers his dog.
    c. stops to rest.
    d. plants a tree.

MAIN IDEA
○ 25. This selection is mainly about
    a. how a dog taught a man to hunt birds.
    b. the special relationship between a man and his dog.
    c. how a man treated his dog after the dog died.
    d. how a man's life was changed by his dog.

Check your answers with the key.

SKILL PRACTICE
SUBSTITUTIONS

A **substitution** is a word that stands for or refers to another word or words.

Here is an example:

> Maria and Juan bought a grocery store last year. **They** have worked very hard **there** since **then.** They both enjoy working in **their** store.

The word *they* is a substitute for *Maria and Juan*. The word *there* refers to *a grocery store*. The word *then* refers to *last year*. And the word *their* is a substitute for *Maria and Juan*.

The substitutions *they* tells "who" and *there* indicates "where." The substitutions *then* tells "when" and, in the last sentence, *their* tells "whose."

There are other kinds of substitutions that state the general category for a word already used, as in this example:

> Juanita was born in Tulsa. She left **that city** when she was five years old.

The words *that city* tell you the larger group to which *Tulsa* belongs. In the following paragraph are two different kinds of substitutions:

> Everyone should have a sensible diet, regular exercise, and an enjoyable job. **That** is the way to good health. **So** is getting enough sleep and having regular checkups.

The word *that* refers to the three things mentioned in the previous sentence: *good diet, exercise, and an enjoyable job*. The word *so* is a substitute for *the way to good health*.

In "Jake" you read some substitutions such as those in the examples above.

Look at the chart below. For each example, find the numbered line in the story and the substitution in that line. Write the word or words each substitution refers to.

	Line Number(s)	Substitutions	Word(s) Substitution Refers to
26.	15	so	
27.	28	it	
28.	48–49	that little gesture	
29.	52	others	
30.	61	this foolishness	
31.	66	there	
32.	81	that	
33.	82	it	
34.	96	his	
35.	101	it	
36.	110	that	

Check your answers with the key.

VOCABULARY REVIEW

Choose the best answer.

37. Which of these might make your hat go **awry**?
    a. Bad news
    b. A gust of wind
    c. A waiter
    d. A clap of thunder

38. A **droll** storyteller makes you
    a. laugh.
    b. cry.
    c. sleep.
    d. nervous.

39. After you receive a **reprimand,** you should
    a. celebrate.
    b. change your behavior.
    c. spend it.
    d. eat it.

40. A **pompous** man would probably
    a. be very humble.
    b. think he was inferior to others.
    c. be very popular.
    d. think highly of himself.

41. Which of these is a **homily**?
    a. Wish you were here.
    b. Live and let live.
    c. Leave me alone!
    d. What time is it?

42. A woman who is **professorial** would probably give you
    a. a home-baked pie.
    b. a fancy sports car.
    c. a serious book.
    d. a haircut.

43. If your guests say that your dinner was absolute **perfection,** they mean
    a. it was excellent.
    b. it was a big surprise.
    c. it didn't look very good.
    d. it was not cooked enough.

44. If you find yourself in the middle of a **fracas,** you may get
    a. your shirt torn.
    b. a sunburn.
    c. a new jacket.
    d. a new pet.

45. If your behavior **verged** on rudeness, you
    a. liked being rude.
    b. were very rude.
    c. came close to being rude.
    d. disliked being rude.

46. If Jan is **reminiscing,** she is thinking about
    a. the past.
    b. today.
    c. tomorrow.
    d. eternity.

Check your answers with the key.

HA-3 CONTEXT CLUES
MYSTERIOUS TALENTS

a GETTING READY

What talent or talents do you have? Do you think you were born with this ability, or did you work at developing it? Do you think perhaps it was a combination of both? Explain.

There are some people in the world who have been gifted with amazing abilities in one area, one in which they've had little or no training. Often they are talented in only this area and have average or below-average abilities in others.

This story is about Alonzo Clemons, who has a remarkable ability to sculpt lifelike animal figures. What is especially unusual about Alonzo is that although he has this remarkable talent, his other abilities are very limited. He cannot learn normally. He cannot work like an adult. He even has trouble speaking. Yet he is a genius at making animal figures.

There are many other people like Alonzo Clemons. When you read "Mysterious Talents," you will learn what scientists have discovered about people such as Alonzo—and what is left to discover.

VOCABULARY BUILDING

Study each key word to make sure you know its pronunciation and definition. Then study the way in which the word is used in the sentence based on the story.

administrator (ad min′ ə strā′ tər) Manager; director. *Jim Graves is the administrator at the home where Alonzo lives.*

extraordinary (ek strôr′ də ner′ ē) Very unusual; remarkable. *Some people with limited mental ability have extraordinary skills.*

functions (fungk′ shənz) Normal actions or uses; purposes. *The phenomenon may be related to the division of functions between the left and right hemispheres of the brain.*

intellectual (in′ tə lek′ chü əl) Having to do with intelligence. *As a result of some fault in their intellectual capability, they shut out the kinds of distractions that affect other people.*

mentality (men tal′ ə tē) Mental capacity, power, or activity. *Some people with a limited mentality have remarkable skills.*

perceptual (pər sep′ chü′ əl) Having to do with knowledge gained through one of the five senses: sight, hearing, touch, taste, smell. *People with artistic skills score higher on tests measuring perceptual abilities than do people with musical skills.*

phenomenal (fə nom′ ə nəl) Amazing; remarkable; outstanding. *Alonzo has emerged as a sculptor of phenomenal skill and talent.*

psychologists (sī kol′ ə jists) Experts in the branch of science dealing with the actions, feelings, thoughts, and other mental or behavioral processes of people. *Psychologists say that Alonzo shares some of the skills and abilities of an exceptional group.*

retarded (ri tär′ did) Slow in mental development. *Mentally retarded since early childhood, Alonzo would sit silently for hours shaping the clay into tiny animals.*

verbal (vėr′ bəl) Expressed in spoken words; oral. *Many of Alonzo's verbal and social skills are those of a child.*

Now choose a word that fits in each of the following sentences. Write the best word for each sentence.

1. Angela is a very good speaker; she has strong _____ skills.

2. Roger gets great satisfaction from teaching mentally _____ children.

3. After the flood, many people met with _____ to talk about their fears.

4. The word from the list that has almost the same meaning as *extraordinary* is _____ .

5. Her performance was _____ .

6. The new work schedule for the hospital must be approved by the hospital _____ .

7. A bat's hearing is its greatest _____ ability.

8. Bruce learns quickly and easily because he has a high _____ .

9. This machine can perform several _____ at once.

10. A genius is a person with great _____ ability.

Check your answers with the key.

SPECIAL WORDS

cerebral (sə rē′ brəl) Of the part of the brain that controls thought and certain muscle movements. *The phenomenon may be related somehow to the division of functions between the left and right cerebral hemispheres.*

I.Q. (intelligence quotient) Measure or rating of a person's intelligence. (The average I.Q. is 100.) *Most of these people tended to fall within an I.Q. range of 50 to 75.*

 ## PREVIEW

Read the first sentence of each paragraph to discover what you can learn from the story. Do this now.

Did you notice that the information in the story is organized in certain ways? Below are some statements about the way the story is organized.

Based on what you learned from previewing the story, write *true* for each true statement and write *false* for each false statement.

11. _____ The story begins with a particular case and then talks about general ideas.

12. _____ The story discusses some theories about retarded people with mysterious talents.

13. _____ The story presents the life stories of several mentally retarded people.

14. _____ The story gives facts and figures about mentally retarded people with special abilities and admits that no one knows why this happens.

Check your answers with the key.

 ## READING

Now read the story to find out more about people with limited mental abilities who possess extraordinary talents.

MYSTERIOUS TALENTS
by William E. Schmidt

As a teenager at the state training school in western Colorado, the one thing that Alonzo Clemons wanted to do more than anything else was to work with modeling clay. Mentally retarded since early childhood, he would sit silently for hours shaping the clay into tiny animals.

At one point, in fact, staff members at the school concluded that Alonzo's devotion to his clay was causing him to fall behind in learning other skills. So they took the clay away, hoping to use it as a reward for better performance in his speech and school lessons.

That's when they first discovered the streaks of tar in his bedding. Later, on the floor beneath the bed, the staff found the tiny group of sticky, black animals. At night, when others were sleeping, Alonzo went to work. Using the tar he had scraped from the school pavement, he shaped the creatures that continued to crowd his mind.

It is a story that is recalled often these days by people who know Alonzo. Now 25 years old, he is a resident in a private home for the mentally retarded in Boulder, Colorado. Although many of his verbal and social skills are those of a child, Alonzo has emerged as a sculptor of phenomenal skill and talent.

In Colorado, professional artists who have seen his hand-worked wax models of bulls and horses and antelope say he is very good. "Not long ago a local artist came here to see Alonzo," said Jim Graves, the administrator at the home where Alonzo has lived for the last four years. Alonzo's prodigious output of sculptures fill his room to overflowing. "When the man left," continued Mr. Graves, "there were tears running down his face. He simply couldn't believe what he saw as he watched Alonzo work." Last May, a gallery in Denver presented the first public exhibition of Alonzo's work. Many of the animals are cast in bronze. A series of charging bulls are being sold for $950 apiece.

Just how much of all this Alonzo understands is unclear, as he has difficulty speaking. So, if you ask him how he is able to shape such wonderfully exact figures of animals, without the benefit of models or photographs, he just smiles broadly and slowly taps the side of his head with his finger.

Those who have worked with Alonzo say that he shares some of the skills and abilities of an exceptional group of gifted retardates. Psychologists refer to them as savants, people of limited mentality with extraordinary skills which would be unusual even in more normal individuals.

It is now estimated that about one of every 2,000 mentally retarded people displays savant-like skills. And the incidence of the syndrome is more common in men than in women by 3 to 1.

There is also a growing realization that among savants in general, there is a great deal of individual diversity. This variety occurs both in special skills they develop and in their underlying mental abilities.

According to a paper presented to the Eastern Psychological Association in Baltimore least year, most savants tended to fall within an I.Q. range of 50 to 75. But those with artistic skills score higher on tests measuring perceptual abilities than do savants whose skills are musical. And those with musical skills, in turn, tend to do better on verbal tests than do the artists.

Richard Wawro, a 30-year-old artist from Edinburgh, Scotland, is nearly blind and also mentally retarded. By placing his face barely two inches from the canvas, and using thick artist's crayons, he is able to produce extraordinary landscapes.

And still others have multiple skills, as opposed to a single skill. Dr. Bernard Rimland, director of the Institute for Child Behavior Research in San Diego, is a leading authority on so-called "savant" abilities. He tells of a mentally disabled boy who can calculate square roots in his head, play the piano by ear, and compose songs.

Dr. Rimland and others agree that scientists are unable to explain how or why these people are able to do what they do.

Most savants, Dr. Rimland says, suffer from a disorder known as autism. Autistic people are almost totally withdrawn from social contact from birth. Though they appear physically normal, they rarely make eye contact with others, much less talk. Many sit for hours in one place, rocking back and forth, unaware of events around them.

Dr. Rimland believes that 1 in 10 autistic people display some of the abilities connected with the savant syndrome. Some theories have suggested that the abilities might be explained by some unusual development of nerve cells within the brain. Others have speculated that the phenomenon is related somehow to the division of functions between the left and right cerebral hemispheres of the brain.

Dr. Rimland says he believes the key to understanding the savants is what he calls their power to concentrate. That is "to shut out completely, as a result of some fault in their intellectual capability, the kinds of distractions that affect other people. Instead, they are able to devote 100 percent of their mental energy to the task at hand."

The result, says Dr. Rimland, is that the mind of the savant is something like a "little electronic calculator or camera." It captures the particular details of a picture, or the notes of a song, or the order of a mathematical process, allowing it to be played back, as it were, with astounding constancy.

Despite their remarkable skills, savants usually fail to transfer their abilities into other areas. The result is that they remain unable to function normally in the outside world.

Science still does not understand how savants come by their special abilities. Dr. Rimland believes that advances in brain science—and even computer technology—will eventually lead to some understanding of how savants are able to focus such tremendous concentration on the tasks at which they shine.

COMPREHENSION CHECK

Choose the best answer.

SEQUENCE
15. Which happened last?
    a. A gallery in Denver exhibited Alonzo's work.
    b. Alonzo sculpted figures of clay.
    c. Tar sculptures were found under Alonzo's bed.
    d. School staff members took the clay away from Alonzo.

CHARACTER / FEELINGS
△ 16. How do you think Alonzo feels about his sculptures?
    a. Ashamed
    b. Proud
    c. Sad
    d. Angry

INFERENCE
△ 17. If you wanted to collect sculptures made by Alonzo Clemons, you would need
    a. to know Alonzo's teachers.
    b. to be a psychologist.
    c. to talk to Alonzo.
    d. to have a lot of money.

INFERENCE
△ 18. Which one of these figures would Alonzo probably make?
    a. Boy
    b. Skyscraper
    c. Cloud
    d. Zebra

SCANNING
19. What do all savants have in common?
    a. They can all do sculpting.
    b. They are all physically disabled.
    c. They are all mentally retarded.
    d. They can all do math problems.

COMPARISON
20. Dr. Rimland compares the brain of a savant to a
    a. piece of sculpture.
    b. calculator or camera.
    c. landscape painting.
    d. computer.

CAUSE / EFFECT
21. What is one result of the ability of a savant to concentrate?
    a. They always keep their eyes closed.
    b. They sing songs to themselves.
    c. They can devote all their mental ability to what they are doing.
    d. They can converse at length with many people to use up their energy.

CAUSE / EFFECT
22. Why is it difficult to find out from Alonzo about his abilities?
    a. Because he has difficulty speaking.
    b. Because he cannot hear.
    c. Because he cannot remember anything.
    d. Because he likes to shape clay animals at night and sleep all day.

FACT / OPINION
23. Which of these sentences from the story are opinions? (Choose all the correct answers.)
    a. The abilities of the savants might be explained by some unusual development of nerve cells within the brain.
    b. The mind of the savant is something like a "little electronic calculator or camera."
    c. Despite their remarkable skills, savants usually fail to transfer their abilities to other areas.
    d. Last May, a gallery in Denver presented the first public exhibition of Alonzo's work.

MAIN IDEA
○ 24. This selection is mainly about
    a. how scientists have discovered many new things about savants in recent years.
    b. why scientists do not know what causes some mentally retarded people to be savants.
    c. how most mentally retarded people can work at developing amazing skills.
    d. how some mentally retarded people have amazing skills in one or more areas.

Check your answers with the key.

HA-3

SKILL PRACTICE
CONTEXT CLUES

Sometimes when you are reading, you come across a word you don't know. Often an author will give clues in the same sentence or paragraph to let you know the meaning of a difficult word. These clues are called **context clues.**

How do you go about finding these context clues? Sometimes it's easy because the author directly states the definition. Look at the example below:

> Tomorrow the soldiers will begin their furlough. This leave of absence will enable them to visit their families.

The definition of *furlough* is given in the second sentence—"leave of absence."

Sometimes you can use what you already know to figure out the meaning of a new word, as in this example:

> The walls were dingy, so I painted them a bright color.

You can tell that *dingy* means "dull or dirty-looking," because I changed the walls and made them bright instead.

Sometimes a difficult word sums up the ideas in a paragraph. The ideas may come before or after the difficult word. In this example, the ideas come after the difficult word:

> The party invitation said, "conspicuous outfit." So Arlene wore green tights, a red sweater with hearts on it, striped pants, and a feathered hat.

You can tell from the colorful description of Arlene's outfit in the rest of the paragraph that the word *conspicuous* means "easily seen" or "attracting attention."

Sometimes you can figure out the meaning of a new word by comparing it to a word or an idea that you already know. Look at the example below:

> Franco treats people very rudely. He obviously feels he is superior to everyone else. His only friend Carlos is just as arrogant.

You can tell from the comparison of Carlos with Franco that *arrogant* means "rude" and "feeling superior."

Choose the best definition for each of these words from the story.

25. The word prodigious on line 35 of the story means
    a. made of wax.
    b. having to do with animals.
    c. having to do with sculpture.
    d. very large.

26. The word savants on line 54 of the story means
    a. mentally retarded people.
    b. psychologists who study mentally retarded people.
    c. mentally retarded people with remarkable talents.
    d. people with unusual talents who aren't retarded.

27. The word syndrome on line 60 of the story means
    a. a set of unusual skills.
    b. the history of a mentally retarded person.
    c. a small number of people within a group.
    d. a group of symptoms of a mental disorder.

28. The word diversity on line 65 of the story means
    a. variety.
    b. individual.
    c. realization.
    d. ability.

29. The word multiple on line 83 of the story means
    a. countable.
    b. many.
    c. unusual.
    d. arithmetic.

30. The word autistic on line 95 of the story means
    a. the majority of people.
    b. the study of mental conditions.
    c. a certain mental condition.
    d. of eyes and ears.

Check your answers with the key.

VOCABULARY REVIEW

Choose the best answer.

31. If your piano teacher says your musical talent is **phenomenal,** it means you
    a. are very talented.
    b. are an average piano player.
    c. can only play easy songs.
    d. are wasting your time trying to learn to play the piano.

32. If Pat is mentally **retarded,** he
    a. is good at sculpting.
    b. is able to do math problems quickly.
    c. is below average in intellectual abilities.
    d. is shorter than the average person his age.

33. The **function** of the heart is to
    a. pump blood through the body.
    b. help you digest your food.
    c. beat loudly and quickly.
    d. allow you to fall in love.

34. Cynthia gave a **verbal** promise to complete the project in one week. She
    a. signed a contract promising to finish in one week.
    b. said she would finish in one week.
    c. sent a message promising to finish in one week.
    d. was reluctant to promise to finish in one week.

35. If there are people in outer space with a highly developed **mentality,** they are
    a. smart.
    b. slow.
    c. heavy.
    d. forgetful.

36. How can you increase your **perceptual** abilities?
    a. Practice jumping rope.
    b. Look and listen carefully.
    c. Study the sciences.
    d. Get some job training.

37. Which of these things might an **administrator** do?
    a. Decide on how to use money.
    b. Sweep the floors of the building.
    c. Type letters for other people.
    d. Teach people how to swim.

38. People with **intellectual** interests probably like to
    a. go bowling.
    b. do magic tricks.
    c. play baseball.
    d. read books.

39. If a baseball player has an **extraordinary** ability to hit home runs, that means he
    a. never hits home runs.
    b. hits many home runs.
    c. would like to hit home runs.
    d. used to hit home runs.

40. If you went to see a **psychologist,** she would listen to your
    a. heartbeat.
    b. watch.
    c. problems.
    d. breathing.

Check your answers with the key.

HA-4 INFERENCES

THE GREATEST BRONC BUSTER WHO EVER LIVED

ⓐ GETTING READY

Have you ever pitted yourself against someone or something, determined that you would be the winner? This is what rodeo riders do when they climb up on the wild horses they ride.

What do you think it would be like to ride a wild horse? What kind of person do you think enjoys riding wild horses?

The man in the picture above is trying to make a wild horse accept a rider on its back. He is a bronco buster, or bronc buster. (The word *bronco* comes from a Spanish word meaning "rough" or "rude" and became a word to describe a wild horse in the Old West.)

The man in the picture is Manuel Airola, a famous bronc buster. He was so good at staying on a wild horse that he drank a bottle of soda during his wild rides! When you read "The Greatest Bronc Buster Who Ever Lived," you will find out more about this amazing man and why he is remembered still.

VOCABULARY BUILDING

Study each key word to make sure you know its pronunciation and definition. Then study the way in which the word is used in the sentence based on the story.

annals (an' lz) History. *Manny Airola is a legend in the annals of great bronc busters.*

contempt (kən tempt') Scorn; the feeling that something is worthless. *As if in contempt for the bloody sign of his mortality, Manny would drink the soda through bloody lips.*

dominant (dom' ə nənt) Controlling; most powerful. *All these qualities seem to have fused into the single, dominant, and powerful will of the superb rider.*

enhanced (en hansd') Made greater in importance. *Early death enhanced the legend, leaving him forever fixed in the history of great bronc busters.*

evoked (i vōk'd) Brought forth; called out. *Manny's ability to stay on a bucking horse evoked the awe of the crusty old punchers.*

exploits (ek' sploits) Daring acts. *He was really the perfect cowboy, whose exploits on bucking broncs are still remembered.*

flailing (flāl' ing) Thrashing; swinging. *Kicking and flailing, The Stallion lost his footing and crashed to the ground.*

flair (fler) Talent. *He rode with a flair for the dramatic without any sign of self-consciousness.*

frenzy (fren' zē) Violent excitement; frantic condition. *The smell of Manny's blood drove The Stallion into a frenzy. He bucked across the arena.*

unassuming (un' ə sü ' ming) Modest and humble. *Manny was quiet and unassuming.*

Now choose a word that fits in each of the following sentences. Write the best word for each sentence.

1. The clown's ridiculous act _____ much laughter from the audience.

2. Arturo has a _____ for designing exciting women's clothing.

3. Have you ever heard about the amazing _____ of the early fliers?

4. For millions of years, dinosaurs were the _____ animals on earth.

5. Cara is very _____ , even though she is rich and famous.

6. The swimmer was _____ his arms and yelling for help.

7. The judge said, "I have only _____ for liars and thieves."

8. The gray sharks went into a _____ when they attacked the school of fish.

9. The colorful sunset _____ the beauty of the mountains.

10. Who is the most famous astronaut in the _____ of space travel?

Check your answers with the key.

HA-4

SPECIAL WORDS

bronc buster (brongk′ bus′ tər) Person who breaks wild horses to the saddle. *He was the greatest bronc buster who ever lived. "There was never no rider like Manny," said one old-timer.*

grandstand (grand′ stand′) Seating area for people at rodeos or other outdoor activities. *He would hold up the empty bottle and then toss it toward the grandstand.*

roan (rōn) Horse with a reddish-brown color. *Manny is best remembered for his battle with a killer-roan-stallion.*

stirrups (stėr′ əps) Rings of metal that hang from a saddle and hold a rider's feet. *The Stallion went across the arena in great, stiff-legged jumps. Manny took the landings in the stirrups.*

PREVIEW

Read the first paragraph and the first sentence of each of the other paragraphs to discover what you will learn in the story. Do this now.

Did you notice how the author organized the story? The first part of the story deals in a rather general way with Manny Airola's career as a bronc buster. In the second part of the story, the author details one instance when Manny tried to ride a horse called The Stallion.

Below are two lists of information—one under the heading **First Part** and the other under the heading **Second Part**.

Based on what you learned from previewing the story, write *yes* if you think the information will be included in that part of the story. Write *no* if you think the information will not be included in that part of the story.

First Part

11. _____ Why Manny was considered a great bronc buster

12. _____ How Manny met his wife

Second Part

13. _____ What The Stallion was like

14. _____ Other horses that Manny rode

15. _____ How Manny broke The Stallion

Check your answers with the key.

READING

Now read the story to find out why Manny Airola was such a great horseman that he is still remembered today.

28

THE GREATEST BRONC BUSTER WHO EVER LIVED
by Jack Burrows

I never saw him ride. He was before my time. But I have spoken to a score or more of old-timers who knew him and saw him ride and rode with him. They were of one mind. He was the greatest bronc buster who ever lived. "There was never no rider like Manny," said one old-timer quietly and with finality. "Nowhere. Never."

"Manny" was Manuel Airola, born in 1888 near Angels Camp in California's Mother Lode country. Manny was born to the horse. A little over average height, slim, with boyish good looks, he was quiet and unassuming. He was really the perfect cowboy, whose exploits on bucking broncs are still remembered and talked about up in the hill country, more than fifty years after his death. I learned from old-timers that Manny had powerful legs ("if he went up, he took the horse with him"); that he rode for the love of riding, not for the winning of prizes; that he respected the broncs he rode but never feared them; and that he rode with a flair for the dramatic without any sign of self-consciousness. All of these qualities seem to have fused into the single, dominant, and powerful will of the superb rider they believed him to be.

It was not the winning of prizes that evoked the awe of these crusty old punchers. It was what Manny would do on a bucking horse—the imaginative, the impossible things. He would come bursting out of the chute on a wild-eyed, bawling bronc. With his high-crowned cowboy hat jammed down on his head, he would wave a full bottle of strawberry soda for the crowd to see. Then, while the horse bucked and shook himself, Manny would drain the bottle at a single pull and "never spill a drop." He would hold up the empty bottle and then toss it toward the grandstand. In an instant a dozen or more small boys would tumble into the arena and wrestle for the bottle in a swirling cloud of dust.

Nobody remembered when Manny commenced bleeding. It was probably late in his career, in the early 1920s. It seemed then as if he had always bled, and he rarely finished a ride without the blood starting to come. Sometimes the blood came in bright spurts that flashed in the sunlight. When the blood began spurting, the crowd was in turn frenzied by his reckless courage in continuing to ride despite the blood. As if in contempt for this sign of his mortality, Manny would drink the bottle of strawberry soda through bloody lips. He would toss the empty bottle toward the grandstand where it rolled to a stop, caked with blood and dust. The small boys scrambled into the arena as always, but they would not wrestle for the bottle. They stood and stared at it, then edged uneasily back toward the grandstand. They did not pick up the bottle.

Beyond what became known as the "blood and bottle ride," Manny is best remembered for his battle with a killer-roan-stallion known only as The Stallion. Nobody would try to ride him. His owner said he was going to have the horse shot and give the meat away. Someone told Manny about The Stallion, and Manny came to have a look at him. "I'll ride him," Manny said to the owner.

"You're welcome to him," the owner said, "but he'll kill you."

"I don't think so," Manny replied.

Manny rode The Stallion on a bright, blue June day at the fairgrounds in Angels Camp. The grandstands were packed, and the betting was high. Most of the bets, I am told, were on The Stallion.

When The Stallion was in the starting gate, Manny began talking softly to the horse. He smoothed a blanket over The Stallion's back and set the saddle down, tugging hard at the strap to tighten it. Then Manny edged carefully along the fence, holding the bridle so it did not jingle. While another man pressed the horse's nostrils shut, Manny slipped the bit into the horse's gasping mouth and fastened the bridle. Then, he slid quickly into the saddle.

The Stallion twisted his head and rolled one eye back to look at Manny. An electric shiver went through his body, and his muscles rolled and swelled. He growled deep in his barrel. This time Manny did not fetch the bottle of strawberry soda. He nodded, the lock was released, and the gate flew open.

The Stallion smashed into the side of the chute coming out. He rose into the air and came down stiff-legged. Manny raised and took the jolt in his legs. Then, Manny began to bleed. The smell of his blood drove The Stallion into a frenzy. He bucked across the arena and tried to smash Manny against the fence.

The Stallion went across the arena in great, stiff-legged jumps. Manny took the landings in the stirrups. Now great spurts of blood pumped from his nose, masking his face. Moans swelled in waves out of the crowd as they viewed the red mask.

Whether from impulse or to reassure the crowd, Manny suddenly leaned forward and stripped off the bridle. He circled the bridle, flashing in the sun, above his head and sent it sailing across the arena. The crowd came to its feet yelling, "Manny, Manny!" Freed of the bridle, The Stallion went crazy. Kicking and flailing, he lost his footing and crashed to the ground. When The Stallion fought his way back up, Manny was still in the saddle.

The Stallion was lathered and blowing foam. The fall had knocked the wind out of the wild animal. He made a bucking and wobbling run across the arena and blindly butted his head into the fence. There was blood on his nose. He staggered and nearly fell. Manny swung down. His face was black with dust and blood.

The Stallion had to be dragged away, still trying to buck. Two months later another man tried to ride him. The Stallion threw him just outside the chute and turned and tried to stomp him. He had to be driven off by two horsemen. His owner had him shot as originally planned.

Manny Airola died in 1925. He was thirty-seven years old and free of the ruins of time. Early death enhanced the legend, leaving him forever fixed in the annals of great bronc busters: The lone rider aboard a bucking bronc, drinking strawberry "sodie pop" through the bloody proof of his mortality.

COMPREHENSION CHECK

Choose the best answer.

SCANNING
16. How did the author get the information for the selection?
    a. He talked to Manny Airola.
    b. He talked to the people who had watched Manny Airola.
    c. He read about Manny Airola in reference books.
    d. He hired detectives to find other bronc busters.

SCANNING
17. When was Manny Airola born?
    a. About 100 years ago
    b. About 50 years ago
    c. About 37 years ago
    d. About 25 years ago

COMPARISON
18. How was Manny different in the saddle from the way he was out of it?
    a. He was kind out of the saddle and cruel in it.
    b. He was quiet out of the saddle and dramatic in it.
    c. He was serious out of the saddle and funny in it.
    d. He was friendly out of the saddle and unfriendly in it.

FIGURATIVE LANGUAGE
△ 19. What is the red mask?
    a. The blood covering Manny's face
    b. The strawberry soda Manny drank
    c. The horse Manny rode
    d. Part of Manny's outfit

CAUSE / EFFECT
20. How did the crowd react when Manny began to bleed?
    a. They became very excited.
    b. They began to cry.
    c. They got a doctor.
    d. They left the grandstand.

SEQUENCE
21. Which happened last?
    a. Manny began to bleed.
    b. The Stallion ran straight into the fence.
    c. Manny took off the bridle.
    d. The Stallion fell down.

PROBLEM / SOLUTION
22. How did Manny solve the problem of getting on The Stallion's back?
    a. He gave the horse a bottle of soda.
    b. He blindfolded the horse first.
    c. He scared the horse by shouting.
    d. He moved quickly and quietly.

CAUSE / EFFECT
23. Why did The Stallion try to smash Manny against the fence?
    a. Because Manny was drinking strawberry soda.
    b. Because Manny was kicking him.
    c. Because the smell of Manny's blood made him frantic.
    d. Because Manny was laughing.

CHARACTER / FEELINGS
24. Which of the following describe Manny? (Choose all the correct answers.)
    a. He was very courageous.
    b. He was overly cautious.
    c. He was easily frightened.
    d. He was a dramatic rider.

MAIN IDEA
○ 25. This selection is mainly about
    a. why bronc busting is so dangerous.
    b. why the stories about cowboys grow into legends after they die.
    c. why Manny Airola is considered to be the best bronc rider ever.
    d. why Manny Airola refused to give up riding.

Check your answers with the key.

SKILL PRACTICE
INFERENCES

An **inference** is a conclusion you reach from your reading even though the information is not directly stated. As you read this paragraph, think about an inference you can make about Will Rogers:

> In the 1920s Will Rogers was world famous for his jokes and comments concerning important issues of his day. While making his remarks, he used a tool from his earlier working days—a lasso. He was most famous for telling jokes and poking fun at politicians while he was doing rope tricks. While he looped, twirled, and threw his lasso, he entertained the audience with observations that poked fun at many pompous public figures.

One inference that you can make from this paragraph is that Will Rogers had been a cowboy when he was younger. The paragraph states that Will Rogers used a lasso from his earlier working days. You also know from your general knowledge that the people who work with lassos are usually cowboys. Therefore you can combine this information and figure out that Will Rogers had been a cowboy.

Use the information in the story to help you figure out the best answer to each question below.

26. Late in his career, when Manny would throw the empty soda bottle toward the grandstand, why wouldn't the boys pick up the bottle anymore?
    a. It was empty, and that made them angry.
    b. It was full of dust, and that disgusted them.
    c. It had Manny's blood on it, and that frightened them.
    d. It was too close to the bucking horse, and that scared them.

27. Why didn't anyone try to ride The Stallion before Manny?
    a. They were too sick.
    b. They thought he was too big.
    c. They thought he was too valuable.
    d. They thought he was too dangerous.

28. Why did Manny want to ride The Stallion?
    a. For the money
    b. For the prize
    c. For the challenge
    d. For the love of the horse

29. As he prepared to ride The Stallion, why didn't Manny get a bottle of soda?
    a. He wasn't thirsty.
    b. He knew he had to give all his attention to the ride.
    c. He didn't want to scare The Stallion by splashing him with soda.
    d. He didn't expect to stay on The Stallion.

30. Which statement about The Stallion is true?
    a. He could never be broken.
    b. He could never be caught.
    c. He could never be saddled.
    d. He could never be hurt.

31. How did Manny's early death enhance his legend?
    a. His death made people feel sorry for him and talk only about his good side.
    b. He remained forever the powerful and fearless rider of his youth.
    c. His death made it possible to lie about him and exaggerate his exploits.
    d. He never achieved greatness, and people wondered what he could have done.

Check your answers with the key.

VOCABULARY REVIEW

Choose the best answer.

32. The **dominant** person at work is usually
    a. the janitor.   c. the boss.
    b. the secretary.   d. the bookkeeper.

32. If you write the **annals** of your city, you tell
    a. what has happened.
    b. what will happen.
    c. what you wish had happened.
    d. what you wish will happen.

34. Which of these are **exploits**?
    a. Cooking dinner and washing the dishes
    b. Your car breaking down and blocking traffic
    c. Shouting at people and pushing them around
    d. Wrestling a bear and climbing a mountain

35. If I have **contempt** for something, I
    a. am afraid of it.
    b. am scornful of it.
    c. want a lot of it.
    d. have respect for it.

36. If you saw a man **flailing** his arms in a swimming pool, he might be
    a. floating on a raft.
    b. swimming underwater.
    c. diving.
    d. drowning.

37. A woman who is **unassuming** would probably
    a. not tell about her accomplishments.
    b. brag about her accomplishments.
    c. not have any accomplishments.
    d. expect you to already know about her accomplishments.

38. A person who has a **flair** for painting
    a. is good at painting.
    b. doesn't like to paint.
    c. likes to talk about painting.
    d. thinks painting is silly.

39. Jenny used makeup because it **enhanced** her good looks. What did the makeup do?
    a. Made her look plainer
    b. Made her look older
    c. Made her look funny
    d. Made her look prettier

40. Which of these would probably send a cat into a **frenzy**?
    a. Getting fed
    b. Being petted
    c. Falling asleep
    d. Getting chased by a dog

41. A movie that **evoked** sad feelings might make you
    a. stop crying.
    b. start crying.
    c. forget about crying.
    d. think it is silly to cry.

Check your answers with the key.

HA-5 MAIN IDEAS
THE WEED KILLER THAT KILLS PEOPLE

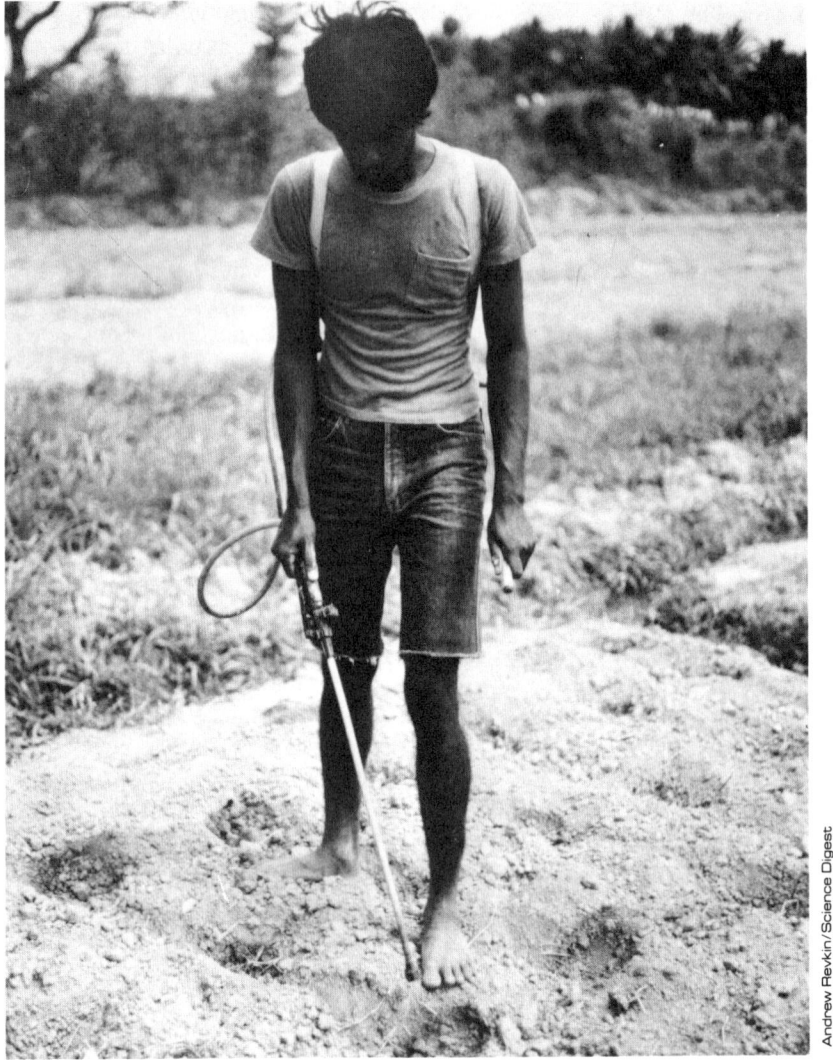

ⓐ GETTING READY

Have you ever seen pictures on television of crops being sprayed? What do you suppose is being sprayed on the crops? Do you think it might be dangerous? In order to prevent weeds from choking their crops, farmers often spray weed killers over them. To prevent insects from destroying crops, farmers spray pest killers.

The man in the picture above is using a very dangerous weed killer. He should not breathe in any of the weed killer or allow any of it to touch his skin. Do you think the man is dressed properly for the job? Why or why not? What do you think he should be wearing?

If weed killers are so dangerous, why do state and federal authorities allow them to be used? When you read "The Weed Killer That Kills People," you will learn why one particular weed killer is so popular—and so deadly.

34

VOCABULARY BUILDING

Study each key word to make sure you know its pronunciation and definition. Then study the way the word is used in the sentence based on the story.

antidote (an′ ti dōt) Something that acts against poison; anything that stops the action of poison. *There is no known antidote for this type of poison.*

disregard (dis′ ri gärd′) Not giving attention to; not caring about. *This disregard for the unseen effects of the weed killer is widespread.*

inhaled (in hāld′) Breathed in. *This weed killer can kill a person if small amounts are swallowed, inhaled, or spilled on the skin.*

lethal (lē′ thəl) Deadly; levels sufficient to cause death. *Lethal doses of this weed killer have not been accurately determined.*

organic (ôr gan′ ik) Of or obtained from animal or vegetable matter. *The plants and weeds form a layer of rotting material. This organic carpet provides a fine seedbed.*

pervasive (pər vā′ siv) Tending to be widely existing or generally practiced. *Lack of attention to the unseen effects of this weed killer seems pervasive.*

registration (rej′ ə strā′ shən) The act of assembling a written or printed list or record. *The system of registration, review, and regulation has grown complicated.*

suffocation (suf′ ə kā′ shən) Lack of ability to breathe; a smothering. *She finally died of suffocation—her lungs useless sacks of scar tissue.*

versatile (vėr′ sə təl) Able to do a number of things well. *Farmers know this weed killer as one of the most versatile tools in agriculture.*

violators (vī′ ə lāt rz) Those who break a law or rule. *Although users of this weed killer are supposed to follow certain rules, there is no way to keep track of violators.*

Now choose a word that fits in each of the following sentences. Write the best word for each sentence.

1. The campers _____ the delicious smell of bacon cooking.

2. Amy uses _____ fertilizer for her crops because she dislikes chemical fertilizer.

3. Astronauts would have to wear space suits on Venus because the atmosphere is _____ to humans.

4. Juanita is so _____ that she can sing, dance, and play three musical instruments.

5. Tom is going to help with voter _____ right before this year's election.

6. Clarence got a speeding ticket because of his total _____ of the speed limit.

7. Have the scientists found an _____ for this poison?

8. The smell of gasoline is _____ throughout the garage.

HA-5

9. The new law takes effect today, and all _____ will be arrested.

10. George was afraid the baby would die from accidental _____ if she was allowed to play with the plastic bag.

Check your answers with the key.

SPECIAL WORDS

herbicides (hėr′ bə sīdz) Chemical substances used to kill plants, especially weeds. *This weed killer is one of the most effective herbicides.*

paraquat (par′ ə kwot) A very poisonous weed and vegetation killer. *Farmers know paraquat as one of the most versatile tools in agriculture.*

pesticide (pes′ tə sīd) Any chemical used to kill pests, such as insects. *People will not read the labels before using a pesticide—increasing the "chemical dependency" of world agriculture.*

c PREVIEW

Read the first paragraph and the first sentence of each of the other paragraphs to learn about a herbicide named paraquat. Do this now.

This story discusses some of the advantages and disadvantages of using paraquat.

Based on what you learned from previewing the story, list at least two advantages and three disadvantages of using paraquat.

Advantages

11. _____

12. _____

Disadvantages

13. _____

14. _____

15. _____

Check your answers with the key.

d READING

Now read the story to find out why paraquat is a great benefit to farmers—and a horrible danger to humanity.

THE WEED KILLER THAT KILLS PEOPLE
by Andrew C. Revkin

A   The girl is weak and very sick. She is rushed to the hospital. She has been vomiting for hours. The doctors examine and test her. The father pulls out a bottle half full of a brown liquid that clings like syrup to the glass. Paraquat.

B   The course of the girl's poisoning is textbook, just like the 150 her doctor's seen before. For 40 more hours she vomits. Her yellowing eyes say her liver is failing. Her mouth and throat fill with sores, and she can no longer swallow. The doctors hear rumbling in her chest.

C   Then, for a couple of days, things look better. She sits up, eats, and talks. But the doctors aren't fooled by her progress. The next day, her breathing becomes labored. The doctors stand by helplessly, able only to kill the pain. She finally dies of suffocation—her lungs useless sacks of scar tissue, a victim of paraquat poisoning.

D   Farmers, however, know paraquat as one of the most versatile tools in agriculture. It is used to control weeds and speed the harvest on more than 10 million acres of American crops. And paraquat is replacing the plow as the standard method of preparing a field for planting in what is called no-till farming.

E   When a field is sprayed with paraquat, the plants and weeds will droop and shrivel within hours, compacting down into a layer of rotting material. This organic carpet will hold the soil and reduce evaporation, providing a fine seedbed and protecting the crop to come.

F   This is, basically, no-till farming. It takes very little labor, does not disturb the soil, and requires only spraying and planting.

G   Paraquat is uniquely suited to no-till because it is the most effective of the so-called hit-and-run herbicides. It is immediately rendered harmless by clay particles in the soil, with which it forms an almost unbreakable bond. It thus leaves the soil safe for the emerging crop.

H   But while paraquat is probably the most effective herbicide on the Earth, it is also one of the world's worst poisons. Although lethal doses have not been accurately determined, paraquat can kill even if only small amounts are swallowed, inhaled, or spilled on the skin. If swallowed, as little as a teaspoonful of the liquid form can kill.

     A list of cases reveals a grim picture of this popular herbicide. A woman made salad dressing, mistakenly using paraquat that her husband had stored in an unmarked jar. After several tastes, she decided the salad was no good. Three weeks later she died. In another case, the owner of a fruit grove sipped some from a container he thought held water. Although he told his doctor he had spit it out before swallowing any, he soon died. The list goes on—victims of circumstance or ignorance, accident or suicide.

J   There is no known antidote for paraquat poisoning. The closest thing to one is a sort of clay milkshake that is given to the victim. Any paraquat still in the stomach forms nearly unbreakable bonds with the clay particles just as it does in the field, and so cannot be absorbed by the body.

K   But any clay treatment, whether improvised on the spot or applied in a hospital, is useless once the paraquat has entered the bloodstream. And because telltale symptoms do not appear for days, a correct diagnosis often comes too late.

L   When asked how many people have died from paraquat poisoning, most medical experts and industry spokespersons recite figures between 600 and 1,000. And about half of those were suicides. Considering the worldwide popularity of the herbicide and its 20-year history, the experts say this is a very small number. But a review of the medical literature and personal interviews with physicians and scientists around the world indicate that the reported death rate has been greatly underestimated.

M   Physicians insist that paraquat must be strictly controlled. Says a doctor who dealt with a triple paraquat poisoning, "Paraquat should certainly not be put in the hands of the general public—ever."

N   But many claim that paraquat is already out of control and that the situation is rapidly getting worse. There are strong indications that the agencies charged with regulating paraquat and other herbicides are unable to do so. There are too many chemicals and users, too little basic information on health effects, and too few people to enforce the regulations the agencies make.

O   In the United States, the Environmental Protection Agency has the responsibility for weighing the agricultural benefits of extremely poisonous chemicals like paraquat against the human and environmental risks. The system of registration, review, and regulation has grown so complicated that even ten-year veterans of the agency complain that they get "lost and confused."

P   Paraquat, because of its deadly characteristics, is a limited-use herbicide. Only one form is available without a permit. The EPA requires that the users of all other varieties be licensed by the states and that paraquat be used only for approved purposes.

Q   But officials from Florida to California admit that these laws are all but unenforceable. Technically, the licensed user does not have to be present during use of the herbicide; the spraying is often done by untrained laborers.

R   According to Bruce Miller, administrator of pesticide enforcement for the state of Florida, there is no way to keep track of violators. "There are approximately twenty-two thousand licensed users in Florida; we have eight people in our enforcement section here."

S   Even licensed users often don't use the required protective clothing and face masks. The liquid is easily mishandled or spilled, and during spraying operations, particularly aerial sprayings, the paraquat can drift.

T   This disregard for unseen effects seems pervasive. People do not read the labels before they use a pesticide—from the least dangerous to the most toxic, so the increasing "chemical dependency" of world agriculture, which is producing record crops and growth now, may yield a bitter harvest of unforeseen dangers in the future.

U   There are bottles and jars and cans of paraquat that sit in homes and farms—some labeled, some not, some in knowledgeable hands, some not. Who will be the next victim of this blessed-cursed chemical age?

ⓔ COMPREHENSION CHECK

Choose the best answer.

SCANNING
16. How long ago was paraquat invented?
    a. About 5 years ago
    b. About 10 years ago
    c. About 20 years ago
    d. About 30 years ago

CAUSE / EFFECT
17. Why does a correct diagnosis of paraquat poisoning often come too late for the clay treatment to be of any use?
    a. There are not many doctors located in the areas where paraquat is used.
    b. The telltale symptoms do not appear for days after the poisoning.
    c. The doctors perform the wrong tests.
    d. There is a delay in getting the patient to the hospital.

SCANNING
18. You can get paraquat poisoning from doing which of the following? (Choose all the correct answers.)
    a. Drinking it
    b. Touching it
    c. Seeing it
    d. Breathing it

INFERENCE
△ 19. A clay milkshake may cure paraquat poisoning if it is taken
    a. in large doses.
    b. immediately after paraquat is swallowed.
    c. with a lot of vegetables and other foods.
    d. over a period of several days.

CAUSE / EFFECT
△ 20. Paraquat is called a hit-and-run weed killer because
    a. it causes instant death in people.
    b. paraquat poisoning has no known cure.
    c. it kills weeds and quickly becomes harmless.
    d. it kills all the plants it touches.

SCANNING
21. What is no-till farming?
    a. A method of preparing the soil for planting without using plows
    b. A way of planting seeds before the snow has melted
    c. A method of growing crops in water
    d. A method of harvesting crops without using machines

PROBLEM / SOLUTION
22. The misuse of paraquat is a big problem. What solutions have been tried? (Choose all the correct answers.)
    a. People who use paraquat must register with their state government.
    b. People who use paraquat must take a course on how to prevent paraquat poisoning.
    c. Paraquat is allowed to be used only for certain purposes.
    d. Paraquat is given out only in small amounts.

FACT / OPINION
23. Which of these sentences from the story are facts? (Choose all the correct answers.)
    a. Paraquat should certainly not be put in the hands of the general public—ever.
    b. Paraquat is probably the most effective herbicide on earth.
    c. Paraquat is a limited-use herbicide.
    d. Paraquat is used to control weeds and speed the harvest.

CAUSE / EFFECT
24. Why can't the government enforce the rules on the use of paraquat?
    a. The enforcement agencies don't really care about the problem.
    b. There are too many users and too few enforcement people.
    c. The manufacturers of paraquat refuse to register with the government.
    d. The users of paraquat die from paraquat poisoning.

MAIN IDEA
○ 25. This selection is mainly about
    a. the carelessness of people who use paraquat.
    b. the problems paraquat poisoning causes for doctors.
    c. the deadly effects of paraquat on humans.
    d. the changes paraquat made in farming.

Check your answers with the key.

SKILL PRACTICE
MAIN IDEAS

The **topic** of a paragraph, or a section of an article, is what the paragraph or section is about. The **main idea** is the most important thing the paragraph or section says about the topic. If the main idea is stated in a sentence in a paragraph, it is often in the first or last sentence. Look at the example below:

> **Topic:** Airplane mechanics
> **Main Idea:** Being an airplane mechanic requires continual retraining to keep up with the new developments in the aviation industry.

Sometimes, the main idea is not stated. In the following example, the topic is poisonous plants. Read these paragraphs and try to think of the main idea:

> People have known about the useful properties of some poisonous plants for thousands of years. Ancient doctors used very small doses of some poisonous plants to cure diseases.
>
> Even today some poisonous plants are used in making drugs. The berries and roots of one particular poisonous plant, called pokeweed, are used in medicines that treat pain and inflammation as well as blood and skin diseases.
>
> Some poisonous plants are also used in making some of our most effective insecticides. The roots of the cube plant, for example, contain a poisonous substance which is used against grubs, lice, and garden insects.

The unstated main idea of these three paragraphs is *People have discovered ways to use poisonous plants to help others.*

Read the paragraphs indicated in each question. Then choose the main idea of each.

26. What is the main idea of Paragraph D?
    a. Paraquat can be used to prepare fields for planting.
    b. It is used to speed the harvest on more than 10 million acres of crops in America.
    c. Farmers know paraquat as one of the most versatile tools in agriculture.
    d. Paraquat is used to control plant growth on farms.

27. What is the main idea of Paragraphs E, F, and G?
    a. Paraquat becomes harmless when it bonds with clay particles in the soil.
    b. Paraquat is ideal because it turns existing plants into a good seedbed, does not harm the soil, and requires little labor.
    c. Paraquat causes plants to shrivel and droop, then rot, which is good for the soil.
    d. Paraquat is needed by farmers for no-till farming.

28. What is the main idea of Paragraphs H and I?
    a. While paraquat is probably the most effective herbicide on the Earth, it is also one of the world's worst poisons.
    b. The list goes on—people become victims of circumstance or ignorance, accident or suicide.
    c. Doctors have yet to find out how much paraquat is lethal to the human body.
    d. Paraquat is most dangerous when people drink it.

29. What is the main idea of Paragraphs J and K?
   a. The hope for a cure of paraquat poisoning lies in the fact that paraquat bonds with clay.
   b. The paraquat still in the stomach forms bonds with the clay particles and cannot be absorbed by the body.
   c. Because telltale symptoms do not appear for days, a correct diagnosis often comes too late.
   d. The clay treatment is the closest thing to a cure for paraquat poisoning, but it is useless once paraquat has entered the bloodstream.

30. What is the main idea of Paragraphs O through S?
   a. There are not enough officials to enforce the laws regarding paraquat use.
   b. Although the EPA restricts the use of paraquat, those restrictions are widely disregarded and are almost impossible to enforce.
   c. The liquid is easily mishandled or spilled, and during spraying operations, particularly aerial sprayings, the paraquat can drift.
   d. The system of registration, review, and regulation has grown very complicated.

Check your answers with the key.

g VOCABULARY REVIEW

Choose the best answer.

31. If a piano player is **versatile,** she can play
   a. one tune very well.
   b. many kinds of music.
   c. all day without getting tired.
   d. with a delicate touch.

32. Which of these might lead to **suffocation**?
   a. Eating a ten-course dinner
   b. Being scolded for something you didn't do
   c. A child wearing a pair of shoes that are too small
   d. A child becoming trapped in a discarded refrigerator with the door shut.

33. A rat that gets a **lethal** dose of poison
   a. heals quickly.   c. changes color.
   b. loses weight.   d. dies.

34. If you **inhaled** some dust, you
   a. saw it.   c. breathed it.
   b. tasted it.   d. touched it.

35. If you are poisoned but you take the **antidote,** you will probably
   a. die.   c. go blind.
   b. get well.   d. stop breathing.

36. **Violators** are people who
   a. obey laws.   c. interpret laws.
   b. make laws.   d. break laws.

37. If fog is **pervasive** in the town, the fog is
   a. on the hill in back of the town.
   b. thickly covering all the town.
   c. in the part of town near the river.
   d. covering all the roads leading into the town.

38. Fertilizer that is **organic** might be made of
   a. cut grass and dead flowers.
   b. ordinary chemicals.
   c. metal and plastic.
   d. old glasses and rubber tires.

39. If you **disregard** my feelings, you
   a. are very careful not to hurt my feelings.
   b. show respect for my feelings.
   c. sympathize with the way I feel.
   d. don't care about my feelings.

40. **Registration** for swimming classes has begun. That means that people can now
   a. go swimming.
   b. watch people swim.
   c. sign up for swimming classes.
   d. teach swimming classes.

Check your answers with the key.

HA-6 TYPES OF SUPPORTING DETAILS

ATHLETES ON DRUGS

ⓐ GETTING READY

Have you ever been under a great deal of pressure to perform well? How did you handle the pressure? How do you think professional athletes feel when they must repeatedly perform under pressure to win?

Unfortunately, many athletes don't know how to handle this pressure or their newfound fame. They find themselves with a great deal of money, and feel they can take on the world. Some turn to drugs, but they soon learn that drugs can destroy anybody, even a star athlete.

How do you think athletes become hooked on drugs? How does their drug use affect their lives? What effect does it have on professional sports? What can be done to stop this problem?

When you read "Athletes on Drugs," you will find out the answers to some of the above questions.

VOCABULARY BUILDING

Study each key word to make sure you know its pronunciation and definition. Then study the way the word is used in the sentence based on the story.

addict (ad′ ikt) A person who cannot break a habit, particularly of using a drug. *A drug addict, he drifted in and out of drug treatment centers four times.*

diminish (də min′ ish) Become less: decrease. *If athletes don't live up to certain standards, attendance at games will begin to diminish.*

financially (fə nan′ shəl lē) Something that has to do with money. *Many athletes who become drug abusers wind up financially ruined by their habit.*

horrendous (hô ren′ dəs) Horrible. *There are many elements to the horrendous attraction drugs hold for these athletes.*

immature (im′ ə chür′) Not fully developed; not experienced. *Many athletes are young and immature. They don't have enough experience to enable them to resist drugs.*

impervious (im pėr′ vē əs) Not allowing harm; not able to be hurt. *Because of their youth and good health, they feel they're impervious to life-threatening substances.*

integrity (in teg′ rə tē) Honesty. *Athletes who might take bribes are a definite threat to the integrity of sports.*

rigorously (rig′ ər əs lē) Strictly, without letting up. *They train rigorously, even in the off-season, to keep fit.*

stamina (stam′ ə nə) Endurance; strength. *One effect of drug use is decreased stamina.*

vulnerable (vul′ nər ə bəl) Open to temptation. *Athletes with worries about money might be vulnerable to taking bribes.*

Now choose a word that fits in each of the following sentences. Write the best word for each sentence.

1. We were stranded on the roof because of the _____ flooding.

2. A person needs a lot of _____ to run 20 miles.

3. His interest in the contest began to _____ as he listened to the long list of rules.

4. Demond smokes 2 packs of cigarettes a day, but he denies that he is a tobacco _____ .

5. This plastic camera case is so tough that it is _____ to water, cold, and shock.

6. The hungry watchdog was _____ to the offer of meat from the burglar.

7. I do not doubt Rudi's _____ and trust him completely.

8. Rita trained _____ to get ready for the competition.

HA-6

9. She was _____ ruined after her company went out of business.

10. Barry had trouble in his first job because he was too _____ to handle a management position.

Check your answers with the key.

SPECIAL WORDS

alcoholic (al′ kə hô′ lik) Someone addicted to alcohol. *John Lucas is a recovering alcoholic and drug addict.*
cocaine (kō kān′) A dangerous drug derived from dried coca leaves, used to deaden pain. *At a party in his honor, Len Bias used cocaine for the first or second time ever.*
high (hī) Under the influence of a drug. *A cocaine high can make athletes feel on top of the world.*
hyped (hīpt) Artificially roused, as on drugs. *Cocaine can get athletes hyped for a game.*
recovery (ri kuv′ ər ē) A coming back to health or normal condition. *An addict has three choices—jail, cemetery, or recovery.*

c PREVIEW

Read the first sentence of each paragraph to discover what you will learn from the story. Do this now.

Did you notice that the story gives you certain information about athletes who take drugs? Some topics that may or may not be discussed in the story follow.

Based on what you learned from previewing the story, write *yes* if you think the topic might be discussed. Write *no* if you think the topic will not be discussed.

11. _____ Different sports stars who have had substance abuse problems

12. _____ Why athletes turn to drugs

13. _____ How coaches prepare athletes for a big game

14. _____ What athletes risk by taking drugs

15. _____ Why drug abuse by athletes is not a major problem

Check your answers with the key.

d READING

Now read the story to find out why athletes face severe problems with drugs.

44

ATHLETES ON DRUGS
by Daniel J. Domoff and Estelle Kleinman

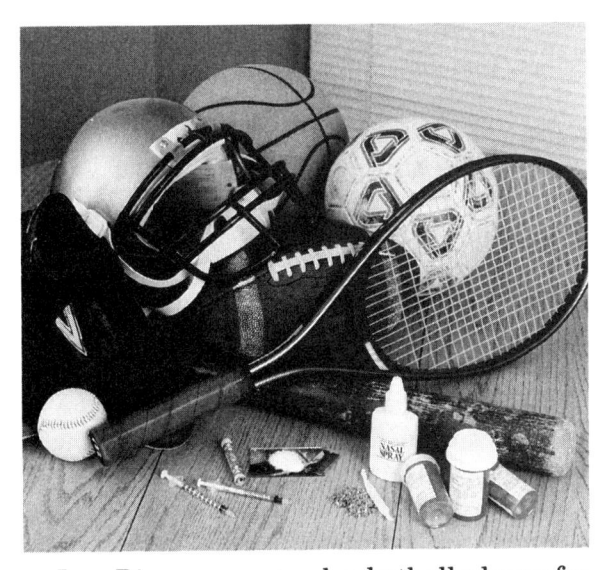

A   Len Bias was a star basketball player for the University of Maryland. Young, healthy, and talented, he was sought by professional teams from all over the country. After signing with the Boston Celtics, he felt everything was going his way. Then, at a party in his honor, Bias used cocaine for the first or second time ever. He died before he could play his first game in a Celtics uniform. If Len Bias were the only athlete to fall prey to drugs, perhaps his story wouldn't matter much. But he's not the only one.

B   The list of sport figures with substance abuse problems includes many celebrated names. The alcohol abuse of baseball great Mickey Mantle went unchecked and seriously affected his health, shortening his life. Other baseball stars such as Dwight Gooden, Darryl Strawberry, and Steve Howe have had their careers damaged by substance abuse. Football stars Carl Eller, George Rogers, and Lawrence Taylor have had trouble with drugs, as have hockey players Mark Heaslip, Don Murdoch, and Derek Sanderson. In basketball, John Drew, Bernard King, and David Thompson have all battled substance abuse problems.

C   There are many elements to the horrendous attraction drugs hold for athletes. First, many are young and immature. They don't yet have enough worldly experience to enable them to resist the appeal of the drug scene. Second, many professional athletes receive extremely high salaries. Expensive drugs such as cocaine are easy for them to buy. Further, many young people, athletes and non-athletes, feel immortal; they think that because of their youth and good health, they're impervious to such life-threatening substances as cocaine, alcohol, and tobacco. Finally, all professional athletes are under great pressure to perform well. The pressure comes from the fans, the team owners, the coaches, teammates, and the newspapers. Players even put intense pressure on themselves. To try to perform better or to seek some relief from this pressure, even for a short while, athletes may turn to drugs. One of the major drugs they turn to is cocaine.

D   Why does cocaine appeal to athletes? One reason is that it can get them hyped for a game. The drug makes athletes feel like they have more energy and confidence, although repeated use can result in quite the opposite effect. Away from the game, a cocaine high can make them feel on top of the world, allowing them to forget their problems and the pressures of the game. Few users consider the prospect of getting hooked on cocaine, which is almost certain in over 50 percent of users, even with limited initial use. The drug can soon become the center of the athlete's life, eventually ruining his or her body.

E   Because a healthy body is an athlete's greatest possession, most professional athletes take good care of their bodies. They train rigorously, even in the off-season. They eat carefully and wisely. They stay away from alcohol, tobacco, and other drugs. By keeping fit, they reduce their chances of being injured, and they can often extend their sports careers by a number of years. Their bodies are their fortunes, and they don't want to waste them. But wasting their fortune is just what drug-using athletes do.

F   Athletes on drugs risk losing much more

than just their fortune. Drug-using athletes lose the respect of people around them, drifting apart from friends and family. Besides losing the respect of others, these athletes lose pride in themselves. They will never know how good they could have been or how far they could have gone. Perhaps the greatest risk for athletes taking drugs is the threat to their health in both the short and long term. Health risks include decreased physical performance, damage to the body's organs, depression, and anxiety. A shortened athletic career, decreased stamina, and loss of concentration are common. And, of course, athletes who take drugs risk the supreme loss: like Len Bias, they might lose their lives.

G In the opinion of many people, if drug use by athletes isn't stopped, professional sports could be ruined. Fans are paying high prices to watch professionals perform. The least they can expect is to see athletes who are under control and giving their best. If athletes don't live up to these standards, attendance at games will begin to diminish. Also, many athletes who become drug abusers wind up financially ruined by their habit. Such financial pressures worry officials, who fear athletes are vulnerable to taking bribes. This is a definite threat to the integrity of sports. Because of this threat, some people are calling for a tougher policy toward drug use in professional sports. Rather than giving athletes chance after chance, they feel that after two strikes the athlete should be out of the game forever.

H Although a tough policy toward drug-using athletes might certainly help, there is enough responsibility to go around. Athletes must develop a game plan to handle pressure and to resist the temptation of drugs. Coaches have to teach players that being the best doesn't necessarily mean doing whatever it takes to win. They must be aware of the drug problem and, above all, be concerned with the welfare and health of their athletes. Society must stop sending the message to athletes that being the best or coming in first is the only thing that counts. In a survey conducted one year at the Olympics, a hundred athletes were asked if they would take a "magic pill" that would guarantee them a gold medal but take their lives; fifty chose winning over living. This is a sad statement of what our performance-driven society has done to our athletes.

One man who knows a great deal about drug abuse is former basketball player John Lucas, the first declared recovering substance abuser to coach a major professional sports team. An alcoholic and cocaine addict, he drifted in and out of drug treatment centers four times. But for over ten years, he has been "clean"—free of drugs—and has been helping other athletes with substance abuse problems. His message is simple: an addict has three choices—jail, cemetery, or recovery. The right choice seems easy; it is tragic that many athletes don't seem able to make it.

ⓔ COMPREHENSION CHECK

Choose the best answer.

SCANNING

16. Which athlete died after using cocaine?
    a. Mickey Mantle
    b. Carl Eller
    c. John Lucas
    d. Len Bias

PROBLEM/SOLUTION

17. According to the story, what problem may prompt a player to turn to drugs?
    a. Too many fans
    b. Not enough money
    c. Too much pressure
    d. Too much traveling

CAUSE/EFFECT

18. Which of the following might cause an athlete to use cocaine? (Choose all the correct answers.)
    a. To get hyped for a game
    b. To forget problems and pressures
    c. To make money
    d. To stop drinking alcohol

CAUSE/EFFECT

19. Most athletes take good care of their bodies because
    a. they want to live to be a hundred years old.
    b. a healthy body is their greatest possession.
    c. they fear being injured.
    d. their coaches make them.

INFERENCE

△ 20. Athletes who take drugs
    a. have the best interests of the team at heart.
    b. don't give enough consideration to the eventual price they will pay.
    c. have carefully thought out their decision.
    d. know they will be able to stop in the future.

SUBSTITUTIONS

21. Read the following sentences from the story: "Fans are paying high prices to watch professionals perform. The least they can expect is to see athletes who are under control and giving their best." The word *they* in the second sentence refers to
    a. fans.
    b. professionals.
    c. athletes.
    d. prices.

PROBLEM/SOLUTION

22. What is one solution to the threat drug-using athletes present to the integrity of sports?
    a. Have athletes watched at all times
    b. Lower the salaries of athletes
    c. Have police look for problems at games
    d. Ban athletes from the game after they have been caught using drugs for the second time

AUTHOR'S VIEWPOINT

△ 23. The author believes that
    a. athletes alone are responsible for their problems with drugs.
    b. drug use by athletes is not a serious problem.
    c. society is partly responsible for causing athletes to turn to drugs.
    d. coaches are not in any way responsible for their players' drug problems.

SCANNING

24. According to John Lucas, what three choices does a drug-using athlete have? (Choose all the correct answers.)
    a. Recovery
    b. Olympics
    c. Cemetery
    d. Jail

MAIN IDEA

◯ 25. This story is mainly about
    a. the problems athletes have with drugs.
    b. how Len Bias fell prey to cocaine.
    c. the pressures that athletes face.
    d. the effects of different kinds of drugs.

Check your answers with the key.

SKILL PRACTICE
TYPES OF SUPPORTING DETAILS

Paragraphs often begin with a statement which establishes the kind of **supporting details** that follow. These paragraphs occur in four different patterns which we'll look at now.

In some paragraphs, the first sentence indicates that the details that come after will be given in the form of a list. Such paragraphs may use signal words such as *first, second, next,* and *finally.* This paragraph pattern is called **enumeration**. Here is an example:

> There are several reasons to rent a car when you visit Ireland. First, trains and buses do not run very often. You could bike or hitch-hike, but it often rains so you might get wet. Finally, Ireland is full of unexpected delights, and having a car enables you to explore them all at your leisure.

In the second type of paragraph pattern, the first sentence is a general statement, or main idea, and the supporting details that follow explain or elaborate on the main idea. The words that might signal this pattern are *for example, for instance, another example.* A sample of this pattern, which is called **generalization**, follows:

> Women's sports are gaining importance, especially in the United States. Many high schools are increasing the amount of money they use for young women's sports programs and equipment. Many professional sports are raising the amount of the prize money for female athletes such as tennis stars.

The third type of paragraph pattern is called **opinion and reason**. This occurs when the author gives an opinion and the supporting details give reasons for the opinion. The signal words *believe, think,* or *feel* are used to indicate this pattern. Here is an example:

> John thinks he would be a good professional basketball player. He has been playing since he was eight years old. He has well-developed skills and handles the ball with ease. In addition, he's very tall and fast.

The fourth and last pattern, which is called **question and answer**, occurs when the paragraph starts off with a question, and the supporting details in the rest of the paragraph help answer the question.

> What is winter like in different states in the United States? In Minnesota, the winters are cold with temperatures that can dip as low as -40 degrees Fahrenheit. In southern Florida, Texas, and California, the winters are warm, and the temperature rarely is below 32 degrees Fahrenheit. Winter is almost the same as summer in Hawaii. In other states, winter temperatures fall between those of Florida and Minnesota.

Reread each paragraph indicated below. Choose the correct pattern for each paragraph.

26. Paragraph C uses
    a. enumeration.   c. opinion/reason.
    b. generalization.   d. question/answer.

27. Paragraph D uses
    a. enumeration.   c. opinion/reason.
    b. generalization.   d. question/answer.

28. Paragraph E uses
    a. enumeration.   c. opinion/reason.
    b. generalization.   d. question/answer.

29. Paragraph F uses
    a. enumeration.   c. opinion/reason.
    b. generalization.   d. question/answer.

30. Paragraph G uses
    a. enumeration.   c. opinion/reason.
    b. generalization.   d. question/answer.

Check your answers with the key.

VOCABULARY REVIEW

Choose the best answer.

31. A car bumper that is **impervious** to dents
    a. is full of dents.
    b. looks as if it has dents.
    c. doesn't get dents.
    d. looks better with dents.

32. Which of these is the most **immature**?
    a. A baby
    b. A ten-year old
    c. A teenager
    d. A middle-aged person

33. If you succeed **financially,** you are
    a. taller.
    b. healthier.
    c. athletic.
    d. wealthy.

34. If the street noises **diminish,** they
    a. get louder.
    b. decrease.
    c. stop.
    d. change.

35. An example of a **horrendous** day would be if you
    a. broke your leg and were fired from your job.
    b. won money in a contest and bought a car.
    c. watched television and went to bed.
    d. took a long walk in the woods.

36. Theresa is a television **addict.** She
    a. never watches television.
    b. repairs television sets.
    c. watches television constantly.
    d. performs for television.

37. If you prepare for a test **rigorously,** you
    a. forget to study.
    b. refuse to study.
    c. worry about studying.
    d. study without letup.

38. If you have the **stamina** to climb a mountain, you have
    a. courage.
    b. guides.
    c. strength.
    d. equipment.

39. If you say I have **integrity,** you mean I am
    a. an athlete.
    b. an addict.
    c. a sports fan.
    d. an honest person.

40. You may be **vulnerable** to disease if you
    a. get a lot of exercise.
    b. don't eat properly.
    c. read books about medicine.
    d. get enough sleep.

Check your answers with the key.

HA-7 COMPARISONS

THE TRIALS OF EDITH CAVELL AND JOMO KENYATTA

ⓐ GETTING READY

Do you like reading about trials or watching them on television? Most people do. Why do you think that people are so fascinated with court-room proceedings?

Of course, trials are of great importance to the parties concerned. But trials can have important effects outside of the courtroom. Keeping in mind that there are many different types of trials—military, political, criminal, civil—what trials are you aware of that have had effects outside of the courtroom? What were these effects?

Today you'll read about the trials of Edith Cavell and Jomo Kenyatta, the people pictured above. These trials occurred at different points in history and involved very different circumstances. What the trials do have in common is that both had an effect on the events of the time. You'll find out how when you read "The Trials of Edith Cavell and Jomo Kenyatta."

50

VOCABULARY BUILDING

Study each key word to make sure you know its pronunciation and definition. Then study the way the word is used in the sentence based on the story.

alternative (ôl tėr′ nə tiv) Choice. *When she saw how the Belgians suffered at the hands of the Germans, Cavell felt she had no alternative: she had to help.*

contrary (kon′ trer ē) In opposition. *Contrary to the pleas of her fellow prisoners, she refused to ask for mercy.*

contrast (kon′ trast) Striking difference. *In contrast to the hatred Cavell's death caused, the words engraved on her statue send a gentle message: "Patriotism is not enough. I must have no hatred or bitterness for anyone."*

dire (dīr) Causing great fear or suffering; dreadful. *Her actions had dire consequences.*

exalted (eg zôlt′ əd) Honored. *After the trial, Kenyatta became even more exalted in the eyes of his people.*

landmark (land′ märk′) Buildings, objects, etc., that have historical importance. *Edith Cavell's statue is a landmark near Trafalgar Square in London.*

minimum (min′ ə məm) Least possible. *The magistrate sentenced Kenyatta to a minimum of seven years at hard labor.*

morale (mə ral′) Mental condition or attitude of a person or group regarding courage, enthusiasm, etc. *During the trial, the morale of Kenyatta and his friends remained relatively high.*

spiritual (spir′ ə chü əl) Religious. *Born in England on December 4, 1865, Edith Cavell, a spiritual woman, was trained in nursing.*

verdict (vėr′ dikt) Any decision or judgment. *Cavell was informed of the guilty verdict on October 11.*

Now choose a word that fits in each of the following sentences. Write the best word for each sentence.

1. We fear the _____ results of an atomic war.

2. _____ to the latest polls, our candidate will win.

3. Most people following the trial did not agree with the not-guilty _____ .

4. After our tent collapsed, the dinner burned, and it began to rain, our _____ was as low as it could be.

5. His dark brown hair is in sharp _____ to his sister's blond hair.

6. Being a _____ person, Irma goes to her house of worship every week.

7. What is the _____ legal driving age in your state?

8. A four-star general holds an _____ position in the U.S. Army.

HA-7

9. Paco has the _____ of holding two jobs or giving one up to attend night school.

10. This _____ was built more than 100 years ago.

Check your answers with the key.

SPECIAL WORDS

magistrate (maj′ ə strāt) A government official who has power to apply the law and put it in force. *There was no jury, just a magistrate.*

prosecution (pros′ ə kyü′ shən) Side that starts action against another in a court of law. *When the prosecution concluded its case, the defense called Kenyatta to the stand.* A prosecutor is the lawyer in charge of the government's side of a case against an accused person.

terrorist (ter′ ər ist) Of or by people who use intentional acts of violence in an organized attempt to overthrow a government. *A growing terrorist movement, known as the Mau Mau, attacked both African opponents and European settlers.*

c PREVIEW

Read the first sentence of each paragraph to discover what you will learn from the story. Do this now.

Did you notice that the story gives you certain information about two trials? You will soon be reading some topics that may or may not be discussed in the story.

Based on what you learned from previewing the story, write *yes* if you think the topic might be discussed. Write *no* if you think the topic will not be discussed.

11. _____ Why Edith Cavell was arrested and put on trial

12. _____ The effects of Cavell's death

13. _____ Why the evidence against Jomo Kenyatta was so strong

14. _____ The effects of the guilty verdict against Kenyatta

15. _____ What the government is like in modern-day Kenya

Check your answers with the key.

d READING

Now read the story to find out how these two trials affected world events.

THE TRIALS OF EDITH CAVELL AND JOMO KENYATTA
by Estelle Kleinman

Throughout time, the public has shown an intense interest in courtroom proceedings. Although today's sensational case will be forgotten tomorrow, many trials will leave their mark on society, sometimes changing outlooks, attitudes, and methods, and sometimes even changing the course of a nation. Two such trials are those of Edith Cavell and Jomo Kenyatta.

Born in England on December 4, 1865, Edith Cavell, a spiritual woman, was trained in nursing. In 1907 a Belgian doctor brought her to Brussels to run his school for nurses, which became a Red Cross hospital after the outbreak of World War I in 1914. On August 20 the German army marched into Brussels. When she saw how the Belgians suffered at the hands of the Germans, Cavell felt she had no alternative: she had to help. So she became one of a growing group which assisted both Belgians and escaped Allied prisoners to cross the border into Holland. Her actions had dire consequences. On August 5, 1915, she was arrested by the Germans.

While held in her cell for several weeks, Cavell supposedly made a full statement of her activities. She and thirty-four others were brought to trial on October 7, 1915. They were tried by a German military court, headed by a lieutenant colonel, and containing two captains and two lower officers. There could be no doubt of Cavell's "guilt" according to her confession. When presented with a list of escapees, she confessed to receiving them into her house, caring for them, and providing them with funds to help them to reach the Allied Army.

On October 8, the prosecutor recommended the death sentence for crimes he said were similar to high treason. The lawyers for Cavell pleaded that she was dedicated to one purpose in life—helping others. She simply wanted to save lives, they argued. Cavell herself refused to make any statement.

Cavell was informed of the guilty verdict on October 11. In the late afternoon, she heard her sentence: death by firing squad. Contrary to the pleas of her fellow prisoners, she refused to ask for mercy. Before dawn the next morning, she was executed.

News of her death created a worldwide stir. Anger against the Germans by the Allied forces increased. The Bishop of London called her execution "the greatest crime in history," and American newspapers used it to rally support for the war effort. In contrast to the hatred Cavell's death caused, the words engraved on her statue, a landmark near Trafalgar Square in London, send a gentle message: "Patriotism is not enough. I must have no hatred or bitterness for anyone."

Jomo Kenyatta was a member of the Kikuyu tribe, the most important tribe in Kenya. In 1928 Kenyatta became leader of the Kikuyu Central Association (KCU), an active group opposing European control of Kenya, which was then a British colony. Kenyatta went abroad in 1929 to study and win support for his cause. Upon returning in 1946, he found that the KCU had been banned. He then became president of a new group, the Kenya African Union (KAU), whose goal was the freedom of Kenya from British rule. Although the KAU advocated change by peaceful means, some saw violence as the only way to obtain freedom. A growing terrorist movement, known as the Mau Mau, attacked both African opponents and European settlers. On October 21, 1952, the British arrested Kenyatta and five other KAU members for secret membership in the outlawed Mau Mau.

The trial began in a schoolroom in the little town of Kapenguria on November 24, 1952. It was then postponed until December 3 to await the arrival of the chief counsel for the defense, D.N. Pritt. There was no jury, just a magistrate. In the prosecutor's opening statements, he charged Kenyatta and the others with managing an unlawful society, but admitted that there was no strong link between them and the Mau Mau.

The trial was a bitter one that lasted almost five months. The British magistrate and Pritt had many sharp exchanges, and a contempt case was even brought against the chief counsel. The official interpreter walked out in a rage when his ability and neutrality were questioned. Despite all this, the trial proceeded, and the morale of Kenyatta and his friends remained relatively high.

When the prosecution concluded its case, the defense called Kenyatta to the stand. Under questioning, Kenyatta stated that the KAU did not believe in violence. In fact, at one public meeting, Kenyatta stated, he asked a large audience to join him in a curse on Mau Mau. Kenyatta handled himself skillfully on cross-examination, avoiding every trap set by the prosecutor. He was questioned on a report of the meeting where he claimed to have cursed the Mau Mau; the report omitted any mention of the curse. Kenyatta simply stated that the report was incomplete. After seven days of cross-examination, the prosecution proposed the theory that Mau Mau was a continuation of the banned KCU, both having the same objective—to drive out the Europeans—and both with the same leader—Kenyatta.

In closing statements, the defense emphasized the weakness of the evidence linking Kenyatta to the Mau Mau. The prosecution argued that an organization such as Mau Mau "can only flourish in an atmosphere of hatred between races." It was Kenyatta and the others, the prosecutor charged, who fueled this hate with anti-European sentiment.

On April 8, 1953, the magistrate brought in his verdict—guilty. When Kenyatta addressed the court, he stated, "We look forward to the day when peace shall come to this land and that the truth shall be known that we, as African leaders, have stood for peace." The magistrate sentenced Kenyatta to a minimum of seven years at hard labor and recommended that he be confined for the rest of his life thereafter.

After the trial, Kenyatta became even more exalted in the eyes of his people. The terrorist activities not only continued, but intensified, making it increasingly difficult for the British to maintain peace in Kenya. In 1961, after the British accepted African self-rule, Kenyatta was released. He became prime minister of Kenya in June 1963, six months before independence, and president in December 1964.

The trials of Edith Cavell and Jomo Kenyatta both affected world events: one spurred the Allies on in their battle against the Germans; the other helped a nation free itself from colonial rule. Only time will tell the broader importance of the trials making today's headlines.

COMPREHENSION CHECK

Choose the best answer.

SEQUENCE

16. Which of the following events happened last?
    a. Edith Cavell was brought to trial.
    b. Cavell went to Brussels to run a nursing school.
    c. Cavell was held in a cell for several weeks.
    d. The German army marched into Brussels.

CAUSE/EFFECT

17. Edith Cavell was arrested by the Germans because she
    a. spied on them for the Allied forces.
    b. helped Belgians and escaped Allied prisoners to cross the border into Holland.
    c. spoke out against them in public meetings.
    d. led terrorist activities against them.

PROBLEM/SOLUTION

18. How did Edith Cavell's lawyers deal with the problem of defending someone who had confessed?
    a. They claimed that the confession was forced.
    b. They pleaded that she just wanted to save lives.
    c. They argued that she was not in her right mind.
    d. They said that the confession was a fake.

CAUSE/EFFECT

19. Which of the following were effects of Edith Cavell's execution? (Choose all the correct answers.)
    a. Anger against the Germans by the Allied forces increased.
    b. Nobody else dared help Belgians escape to Holland.
    c. American newspapers used it to rally support for the war effort.
    d. The nursing school was closed and never opened again.

SEQUENCE

20. Which of the following events happened first?
    a. Jomo Kenyatta became president of the Kenya African Union.
    b. Kenyatta went abroad to study and win support for his cause.
    c. The British arrested Kenyatta for secret membership in Mau Mau.
    d. Kenyatta became leader of the Kikuyu Central Association.

SCANNING

21. What role did D.N. Pritt play in Kenyatta's trial?
    a. Magistrate
    b. Prosecutor
    c. Official interpreter
    d. Chief counsel for the defense

INFERENCE

22. You can tell that at Kenyatta's trial
    a. not everyone spoke English.
    b. the press was not present.
    c. family members could not attend.
    d. the prosecution had strong evidence that Kenyatta was a leader of Mau Mau.

INFERENCE

23. Which of the following can you infer about Kenyatta?
    a. He did not stand up for his beliefs.
    b. He was very wealthy.
    c. He was very clever.
    d. He did not get along with his chief counsel.

SCANNING

24. In what year did Kenyatta become president of Kenya?
    a. 1963
    b. 1961
    c. 1964
    d. 1953

MAIN IDEA

25. This story is mainly about
    a. the quiet courage of Edith Cavell.
    b. two trials that affected world events.
    c. how Jomo Kenyatta became the first president of Kenya.
    d. how both Edith Cavell and Jomo Kenyatta stood up for their rights.

Check your answers with the key.

HA-7

SKILL PRACTICE
COMPARISONS

When you read, you'll often find it useful to **compare** two things to highlight how they are similar and how they are different. Sometimes the author will help you by providing signal words. Words such as *in the same way, like,* and *is similar to* may signal comparisons that show how things are similar. Words such as *although, on the other hand, instead,* and *is different from* may be used to show differences.

Many times, however, the author will not present any signal words. Then it will be up to you to figure out how things are alike and how they are different. This is the case with "The Trials of Edith Cavell and Jomo Kenyatta."

Complete the chart using information from the story. Then use the chart to answer the questions that follow.

	Trial of Edith Cavell	Trial of Jomo Kenyatta
26. Date Started		
27. Tried Alone or with Others		
28. Who Presided?		
29. Length of Time from Start to Verdict		
30. Verdict		
31. Sentence		
32. Was Sentence Completely Carried Out?		

Check your answers with the key.

33. Which trial was presided over by military officers?

34. Which trial lasted longer?

35. Which person received the more severe sentence?

36. Which of the following did both trials have in common? (Choose all the correct answers.)
   a. Both started on the same date.
   b. In both, the person was tried along with others.
   c. In both, a guilty verdict was given.
   d. After both, the sentence was completely carried out.

Check your answers with the key.

⑨ VOCABULARY REVIEW

Choose the best answer.

37. Which of the following is an example of **dire** circumstances?
   a. A family is trapped in a burning building.
   b. A woman receives a promotion and a raise.
   c. A picnic is cancelled due to rain.
   d. A police officer arrests a bank robber.

38. Which has an **exalted** position?
   a. A baby
   b. The President of the United States
   c. A factory worker
   d. A hiker

39. Which of the following pairs suggests a **contrast**?
   a. Candy and sugar
   b. Day and night
   c. Rabbits and hares
   d. Cars and engines

40. Who would reach a **verdict**?
   a. A child
   b. A singer
   c. A jury
   d. A football team

41. Which of these is a **landmark**?
   a. A new trail up a mountain
   b. A stone fort that is 200 years old
   c. A part of the forest recently destroyed by fire
   d. A newly painted fence

42. Which of the following might be an **alternative** to taking pills for high blood pressure?
   a. Risking stroke or heart disease
   b. Side effects that include dizziness or nausea
   c. Controlling your blood pressure with diet and exercise
   d. Eating fatty foods loaded with salt

43. You would most likely get **spiritual** guidance
   a. in school.
   b. in a church or temple.
   c. at work.
   d. in a hospital.

44. If your **morale** is low, you are
   a. discouraged.
   b. amazed.
   c. underweight.
   d. eager to work.

45. If your taste in music is **contrary** to mine, then you
   a. like to listen to the same music that I do.
   b. don't like the same music that I do.
   c. have better taste in music than I do.
   d. don't know as much about music as I do.

46. If you paid the **minimum** price for a radio, you
   a. were cheated.
   b. paid more than the average price.
   c. cannot return the radio.
   d. got a good deal.

Check your answers with the key.

HA-8 SEQUENCE

INTRODUCING THE MOM AND POP SUPERMARKET

ⓐ GETTING READY

How would you feel if your neighborhood supermarket suddenly closed? What problems would this present for you and your family? How do you think the workers in the store would feel? What kind of problems might they face? If they needed their jobs in order to support themselves, what could they do once the store closed?

This story is about some workers in an A&P supermarket who lost their jobs when the company closed down the store. These workers found an unusual solution to their problem. With help from their union, they bought the recently closed supermarket and rehired themselves!

When you read "Introducing the Mom and Pop Supermarket," you will discover some of the changes the new owners made in the old store. You will also learn how the community feels about the new store and how it changed the lives of the new Owner/Operators.

VOCABULARY BUILDING

Study each key word to make sure you know its pronunciation and definition. Then study the way the word is used in the sentence based on the story.

advisers (ad vī′ zərz) People who give advice. *The O&O Fund would help by providing business advisers and low-interest loans.*

citing (sīt′ ing) Referring to; giving as an example. *She says her own change in attitude was not confined to the store, citing a lesson learned during a workshop on "quality of the workplace."*

coalition (kō′ ə lish′ ən) Combination; union. *"Mom and Pop" in these ventures is a coalition of clerks, cashiers, butchers, and managers.*

divorced (də vôrsd′) Legally, permanently separated from one's husband or wife. *She was recently divorced, with a baby daughter to support by herself.*

ethnic (eth′ nik) Having to do with various racial or cultural groups of people. *Since we're small, we can handle special requests, such as orders for ethnic foods.*

flexible (flek′ sə bəl) Easily adapted to fit different situations. *Because their operations are flexible, they have been able to re-enter a field they were once forced out of.*

inability (in′ ə bil′ ə tē) Lack of ability, means, or power. *Because of her inability to find work before, she dreaded that happening again.*

investment (in vest′ mənt) Giving money to a project that may return a profit. *For an investment of $5,000 each, the workers could set up their own company.*

lease (lēs) Rent for an agreed-upon length of time. *The workers could lease the store and run it themselves.*

refurbished (rē fėr′ bishd) Fixed up again. *The new Owner/Operators swung open the doors on the refurbished supermarket.*

Now choose a word that fits in each of the following sentences. Write the best word for each sentence.

1. We can't afford to buy a house, so we will _____ an apartment.

2. The _____ office has new carpets, new curtains, and new lights.

3. Ever since Yvonne and her husband were _____ last year, her career has taken a definite upturn.

4. With the new _____ job schedule, employees can choose their own work hours.

5. My favorite _____ music is Greek.

6. Sandra decided to make an _____ in real estate.

7. Bob said we need a traffic light at Sixth and Willoughby, _____ several accidents there as evidence.

8. I had a good time at the party in spite of my _____ to dance because of a broken toe.

HA-8

9. The agricultural _____ told the farmers which crops to plant.

10. A _____ of walkers, bikers, and drivers demanded that the county fix the roads.

Check your answers with the key.

SPECIAL WORD

laid off (lād ôf) Put out of work for a while. *Union officials met with the soon-to-be laid-off workers to find ways to save jobs.*

ⓒ PREVIEW

Read the first three paragraphs to discover how the story begins. Do this now.

Did you notice that the first and third paragraphs compare Jane Thorpe's old job with her new one? Use the information in those paragraphs to help you answer the questions below.

Write the answers to the questions.

11. Name three ways in which Jane Thorpe's new job is different from her old one.

12. Name two ways in which Jane Thorpe's new job is the same as her old one.

Check your answers with the key.

ⓓ READING

Now read the story to find out how Jane Thorpe's job—and those of the other A&P workers—was transformed.

60

INTRODUCING THE MOM AND POP SUPERMARKET
edited by Gerri Hirshey

Twenty hours a week, and for any extra time she could get, Jane Thorpe stood in the chilly back room of an A&P in Roslyn, Pennsylvania, weighing, wrapping, and pricing cuts of meat. She was young and recently divorced, with a baby daughter to support by herself. The hours weren't nearly enough, the work was uninspiring, and there were rumors that the store was in trouble. In February, 1982, the expected bad news came: A&P was closing 15 area stores. Over 2,000 people, Jane among them, would be out of work in an area already suffering from increased unemployment.

"When the store closed in March, there were no jobs around," Jane recalls. "I had no college education, no other marketable skills, and no reason for hope."

Within months of the closing, Jane found herself back in the same store, working forty hours a week, plus a lot of unpaid overtime. She is still wrapping meat, but she has also learned nearly every other job in the store. She spends nearly as much time in the front office as she does behind the meat counter, and she is happy to do it all.

Now, Jane owns the store she used to work in part-time. Along with 24 partners, all former A&P employees, she is part of a daring experiment. When they swung open the doors on the refurbished O&O Supermarket on the morning of October 13, 1982, Jane and her partners made history with the country's first worker-owned supermarket. The Roslyn O&O and a second sister O&O store nearby are doing quite well, and so are the Owner/Operators who run them. "Mom and Pop" in these ventures is a coalition of clerks, cashiers, butchers, and managers. And because these operations are small and flexible, the Owner/Operators have been able to re-enter a field they were once forced out of. So far, it's working beautifully.

"My daughter and I have a future now," Jane says. "Becoming a partner was an agonizing decision, but it's changed my life."

The reversal began when union officials met with the soon-to-be laid-off workers to find ways to save jobs. The situation was desperate, and the union proposal was a bold one. For an investment of $5,000 each, the workers could lease the store, set up their own company, and run it themselves. They would have to learn many more aspects of the business than the specialized jobs they had held. They would work hard for many months, with no guarantee. The union was behind them, and a new, nonprofit organization, the O&O Investment Fund, would help by providing business advisers and low-interest loans.

"It all made sense," Jane says. "Faced with unemployment, or even welfare, we'd knock ourselves out to make it work."

All summer long, interested workers met three times a week at the union hall. Though A&P reopened most of their closed stores under a new name, two locations were available for employee takeover. As plans were finalized, Jane was elected to the new board of directors for the Roslyn store.

"To be chosen by people I had worked side by side with was a real vote of confidence," she says. "I don't know what we would have done without each other."

Left alone, she guesses she would have ended up on unemployment. She had already moved in with her parents to make ends meet. Her inability to find work for 18 months following the birth of her daughter, Carol Ann, was still a painful memory, and she dreaded that happening again.

"It was awful to be out there with no prospects at all. What kept me going to those meetings all summer was a feeling of unity. We kept saying 'It will be *ours*; we won't be working for somebody else.'"

Despite the general goodwill, it was a tough decision to apply for the $5,000 personal loan needed to join the O&O operation.

"Nobody in my family had ever been in debt," Jane says. "To me, it was a desperate step. And 24 other people had a lot of sleepless nights. But we had to make it work for ourselves and for our families."

At last, with the help of the O&O Fund and its advisers, the Small Business Administration approved the group's bank loan, and they were on their way.

"I remember, it was August when we got the keys to the store," Jane says. "It was a great day."

Leaving Carol Ann with her parents, Jane met her partners at the market. The big store was dark and empty but in good shape. They cleaned the shelves and hung the new O&O signs. By the end of September, they started restocking the shelves. One day while Jane was unloading cartons, she noticed some activity in the parking lot.

"People were coming up and knocking on the windows. They told us that they were glad to see us, that the neighborhood needed a supermarket."

"WE'RE HERE!" heralded a newspaper announcement. Opening-week ads offered competitive sale prices, but the store's most appealing new feature was increased personal service.

"Since we're small and we know the neighborhood, we can handle special requests," Jane explains. Thus, customers can order salt-free products and ethnic foods. The extra service doesn't cost a thing—two recent surveys have found O&O prices to be the lowest in the area.

"When people started stopping clerks and managers to tell us how friendly everyone was, we realized how much our attitudes had changed," Jane says.

She says her own change in attitude was not confined to the store, citing a lesson learned during a workshop on "quality of the workplace." The adviser suggested that the way O&O workers spoke to the customers and to one another was very important. He advised them to use "I" instead of "we." "I" assumes responsibility. It's direct and more honest.

"It works," Jane says. "*I* think, *I* hope, *I* want. Talking that way to one another made this a trusting place to work. And I took the advice home."

Carol Ann Thorpe has just started first grade, and although she sees less of her mother these days, their time together is brightened by a new optimism.

"*I*'ve wanted a home of our own for five years," Jane says. "Now *I*'m making plans."

ⓔ COMPREHENSION CHECK

Choose the best answer.

CAUSE / EFFECT

13. What happened when the A&P closed?
    a. The workers lost their jobs.
    b. The workers were hired by other A&P stores.
    c. The workers demanded that the store be reopened.
    d. The union bought the store and rehired the workers.

INFERENCE

△ 14. In the story, what does "Mom and Pop" mean?
    a. People who have children
    b. People who belong to a small union
    c. People who own and run a small neighborhood store
    d. People who babysit

INFERENCE

△ 15. What did the supermarket workers do in the meetings held during the summer? (Choose all the correct answers.)
    a. Learned how to set up a business
    b. Elected a board of directors
    c. Earned $5,000 each
    d. Fixed up the store

SCANNING

16. How much money did each Owner/Operator invest in the new supermarket?
    a. $1,000
    b. $2,000
    c. $5,000
    d. $10,000

CHARACTER / FEELINGS

17. How did the neighborhood people feel about the workers reopening the store?
    a. They resented the workers.
    b. They were suspicious.
    c. They were happy.
    d. They worried that the store would close again.

COMPARISON

18. How is the new O&O different from the old A&P? (Choose all the correct answers.)
    a. Prices are higher.
    b. Service is more personal.
    c. Workers' attitudes have changed.
    d. The store is larger.

INFERENCE

△ 19. The new O&O Supermarket is probably
    a. not charging enough for special orders.
    b. charging higher prices than other stores.
    c. selling more meat than before.
    d. making a profit.

COMPARISON

20. What is the biggest change in Jane Thorpe's life?
    a. She felt helpless before, and now she is in charge of her life.
    b. She has better job skills now.
    c. She works longer hours for less pay now.
    d. She sees less of her daughter now.

SCANNING

21. Why does Jane use "I" instead of "we" when she talks about her business?
    a. Because she is the only owner.
    b. Because she doesn't like all the other owners.
    c. Because using "I" is more friendly than using "we."
    d. Because using "I" makes her responsible for her statements.

MAIN IDEA

○ 22. This selection is mainly about
    a. how the supermarket business is changing.
    b. how a group of workers took over a supermarket and are successfully running it themselves.
    c. how a group of workers learned to take responsibility for their company.
    d. how a group of workers was able to improve the community by starting a business.

Check your answers with the key.

HA-8

SKILL PRACTICE
SEQUENCE

It is important to understand the order, or **sequence**, of events in a story. For example, in the story Jane became an Owner/Operator of the O&O after the A&P closed.

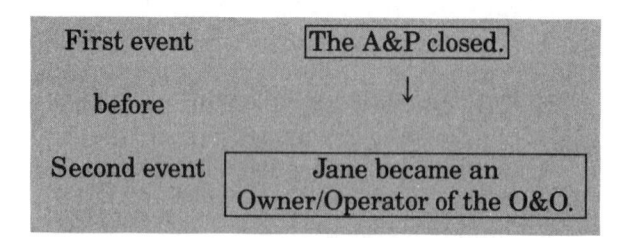

First event	The A&P closed.
before	↓
Second event	Jane became an Owner/Operator of the O&O.

Sometimes a story may talk about the present, and then go into a **flashback**—a return to an earlier time. To understand sequence when a flashback is used, look for signal words, such as *then, now, before, earlier,* and *ago*. You should also be aware of any dates that are mentioned. Verb tenses can help, too. If verb tenses switch from the present to the past, you know that the selection is going back in time.

Look for clues to the sequence in the paragraph below:

> I'm walking again now. But I'll never forget how I broke my leg. Three months ago today I slipped and fell on the ice. I had to wear a cast for two months.

You can put the events in the proper sequence by using a diagram like this one:

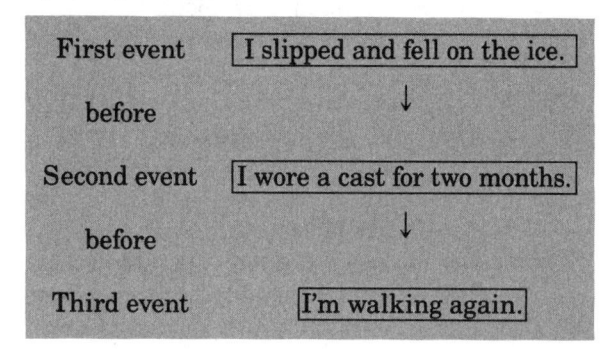

First event	I slipped and fell on the ice.
before	↓
Second event	I wore a cast for two months.
before	↓
Third event	I'm walking again.

Read these events from the story. Then look back at the story to find the events in each example. Decide which event happened first and number it 1. Continue to number all the events in the order in which they happened.

If necessary, use a sequence diagram to help you.

23. a. _____ Jane worried that she would lose her job.

    b. _____ The store closed.

    c. _____ Jane got divorced.

    d. _____ Jane had no prospects for a new job.

    e. _____ A&P announced the closing of the store.

24. a. _____ Jane lost her job.

    b. _____ The new owners got the keys to the store.

    c. _____ The new store offered personal service.

    d. _____ The new owners reopened the store.

    e. _____ The union helped the workers take charge of the store.

25. a. _____ Jane borrowed $5,000 to invest.

    b. _____ The Small Business Administration approved the group loan.

    c. _____ The new owners restocked the store.

    d. _____ Ads in newspapers announced sale prices.

    e. _____ The new owners began to fix up the store.

Check your answers with the key.

VOCABULARY REVIEW

Choose the best answer.

26. If you **lease** an apartment, you
    a. buy it.
    b. sell it.
    c. lend it.
    d. pay to use it.

27. If Carla is **divorced,** she
    a. is married.
    b. has never been married.
    c. is no longer married.
    d. is a widow.

28. If your plans are **flexible,** you
    a. could change them.
    b. refuse to change them.
    c. hope to earn money.
    d. need advice from experts.

29. **Ethnic** food is
    a. always hot and spicy.
    b. from a certain culture or country.
    c. delicious but expensive.
    d. usually fried and fattening.

30. Because of my **inability** to swim, I
    a. enjoy swimming laps.
    b. give swimming lessons.
    c. don't go into deep water.
    d. entered the diving contest.

31. If you are part of a **coalition,** you
    a. always work alone.
    b. work in a coal mine.
    c. belong to a group formed for a certain purpose.
    d. provide services to local people.

32. If you make an **investment** in a company, you
    a. work for the company.
    b. put money into the company.
    c. borrow money from the company.
    d. find partners and take over the company.

33. A **refurbished** car
    a. has been restored.
    b. is brand new.
    c. is old and dusty.
    d. has just been bought.

34. If you met with some **advisers,** they would
    a. give you money.
    b. like your ideas.
    c. take your advice.
    d. give you advice.

35. If you are **citing** a fact in a certain book, you are
    a. reading the book as fast as you can.
    b. talking about the book to prove a point.
    c. drawing pictures for the book.
    d. trying to buy the book cheaply.

Check your answers with the key.

HA-9 CAUSE AND EFFECT

THE RETURN OF THE PUFFINS

GETTING READY

Suppose that one kind of bird had almost totally disappeared from the area where you live. Would you want to help save the birds? Why or why not? Do you think it's important to prevent them from disappearing? Why or why not?

The birds in the picture above are seabirds that used to live in large numbers along the coast of Maine. You can tell from the title of the story that these odd-looking birds are called puffins. In the early 1900s the puffins almost completely disappeared from Maine's coastline.

A young man named Steve Kress decided to try to bring the puffins back. He spent years trying to encourage puffins to nest in one particular place in Maine. When you read "The Return of the Puffins," you will discover what techniques he used and whether or not he succeeded.

VOCABULARY BUILDING

Study each key word to make sure you know its pronunciation and definition. Then study the way the word is used in the sentence based on the story.

aggressive (ə gres′ iv) Attacking; bold. *Terns breed rapidly and are especially aggressive against gulls, thus they are a puffin ally.*

avidly (av′ id lē) Eagerly and enthusiastically; greedily. *Puffins were unable to recover from the abuse they suffered from humans when they were avidly hunted.*

diversity (də vėr′ sə tē) Variety. *It was a conscious desire to increase the diversity of Maine seabirds.*

excessive (ek ses′ iv) Exceeding a reasonable amount; more than necessary; too much. *Laws were passed to protect puffins and other birds from excessive hunting.*

extinct (ek stingkt′) Gone from the earth. *By the 1880s, puffins were practically extinct along the northern New England coast.*

hindrance (hin′ drəns) Obstacle; something that gets in the way. *The gull colonies were a major hindrance because gulls are among the puffins' enemies.*

inhibit (in hib′ it) Hold back or limit. *Frequent inspection of the boulders where the puffins might nest would inhibit mating.*

plight (plīt) A condition or situation, usually sad or dangerous. *The story of the disappearance of puffins from the coast of Maine illustrates the plight of other seabirds.*

predators (pred′ ə tərs) Animals that live by hunting other animals for food. *Gulls are predators of puffins.*

transplant (tran splant′) Relocate; take from one place to another. *Since no puffins were on Eastern Egg Rock, Kress would have to transplant puffin chicks from Newfoundland, Canada, where they thrived.*

Now choose a word that fits in each of the following sentences. Write the best word for each sentence.

1. The deep snow is a _____ to our walking.

2. Zebras will run away from lions and other _____ .

3. The hungry bird's _____ got worse as the snow cover deepened.

4. At the museum we saw the bones of many _____ animals.

5. Pat likes the city because of the _____ of people there.

6. Next week, I plan to _____ the seedlings outdoors.

7. Our pet dog becomes _____ when a stranger knocks on our door.

8. Juan spent an _____ amount of time on the phone.

9. The sight of a police car on the road will usually _____ speeding by motorists.

10. The hungry athlete ran _____ to the dinner table.

Check your answers with the key.

HA-9

SPECIAL WORD

terns (tėrns) Seabirds similar to gulls. *They began an effort to attract terns by playing tape recordings of bird calls.*

ⓒ PREVIEW

Read the first sentence of each paragraph and the whole last paragraph to discover what you will learn from the story. Do this now.

Did you notice that the events are organized in sequence? Here are some sentences adapted from the selection. They describe some of the major events of Steve Kress's story.

Based on what you learned from previewing the story, number the events in the order in which they occurred.

11. ____ A puffin flew overhead and landed in the water nearby.

12. ____ Puffins returned to the island in increasing numbers.

13. ____ The team set out puffin decoys to attract the real birds.

14. ____ The team dug burrows on Eastern Egg Rock.

15. ____ Puffins were again nesting at Eastern Egg Rock.

Check your answers with the key.

ⓓ READING

Now read the story to find out how Steve Kress persuaded puffins to make their homes once again on Eastern Egg Rock Island on the Maine coast.

THE RETURN OF THE PUFFINS
by Ron Winslow

A   A puffin is a small seabird with a black back, snow-white breast, short orange legs, and webbed feet. As early as the 1880s, puffins were practically extinct along the northern New England coast. They were the victims of fishermen who, in search of meat and eggs, stretched huge herring nets over the rocks at night on such islands as Eastern Egg Rock. These nets covered the crevices where puffins made their nests and cared for their young.

B   By 1900 the birds were so scarce that both state and federal laws were passed to protect them and other birds from excessive hunting. But it was too late for the puffin along Maine's coastline. The state's entire puffin population was reduced to a couple of breeding pairs on Martinicus Rock. By 1970 that island's population had increased to about 50, but no new puffin colonies had been established along the coast.

C   Steve Kress decided to change that. "It was simply a conscious desire to increase the diversity of Maine seabirds," he says.

D   Kress chose puffins for two main reasons. First, their story most dramatically illustrated the plight of seabirds. It was a bird that was clearly unable to recover from the abuse it suffered from humans when it was avidly hunted in the 19th century. Then there's just the bird's special appeal. "The puffin looks like a little clown," Kress says.

E   Kress's puffin project is keyed to this fact: young puffins, after spending two to three years at sea, generally return to the place where they were born in order to find a mate. Since no puffins were on Eastern Egg Rock in 1970, Kress would have to transplant puffin chicks from Newfoundland, Canada, where they thrived.

F   He selected Eastern Egg Rock Island as the real-life laboratory where techniques to restore the bird would be tested.

G   While it had once been home to puffins, the island's most recent inhabitants were seagulls. The thriving gull colonies were a major hindrance to Kress because gulls are among the puffins' predators. So when Kress decided to reestablish a puffin colony on Eastern Egg Rock, he also decided to drive the gulls off the island. It took a couple of years to clear the island of most of the gulls.

H   Getting the puffin chicks to the island was a major problem. Each June for eight years, Kress loaded crates, made specially for transporting the chicks, onto a rented plane and flew to Newfoundland. He picked up week-old chicks and raced to make the 1,000-mile journey back to Eastern Egg Rock within a day.

I   But that was the easy part. Kress and his research assistants had to make nests for these puffins. "The puffin in Maine makes its nest in rock crevices," explains Kress. "In other areas, it digs a nice burrow in the soil."

J   Partly because Eastern Egg Rock is mostly rock, and partly because the researchers were to be parents to these chicks and needed access to them, Kress decided to make rock burrows from cement blocks. But when he realized that ferrying all that cement to the island would be a problem, he changed his mind.

K   In 1975 the team dug burrows in what soil they could find on Eastern Egg Rock. A week or so after they had transplanted chicks into the burrows, it rained for three days straight. Many chicks nearly drowned because the holes wouldn't drain.

L   Finally, in 1976, they found the solution. They built burrows in blocks of sod. Each burrow was L-shaped, a required feature for happy puffins, Kress learned. Because the burrows were built in sod, the chicks could scratch away at the sides and shape their homes to their taste.

M   After four or five weeks the puffin chicks would get restless in their burrows, often refusing to eat. That usually meant they were ready to fledge—that is, to leave their nests to survive in the wild on their own.

N Once the young birds fly or stumble into the sea, the researchers await their return. In later years, even while they were caring for the current year's class of chicks, they eagerly scanned the skies and the rocks for signs that the earlier years' classes had returned.

O Finally, on June 12, 1977, as Kress was rowing ashore, a puffin flew overhead and landed in the water nearby. Around the bird's left leg was a white plastic band—certain evidence that puffins had returned to Eastern Egg Rock. "Oh, what a great day!" he says.

P The rush of excitement, however, was followed by more disappointment. "Weeks went by and nothing," Kress says. Finally the researchers checked other nearby islands. On Martinicus Rock, about 26 miles east, they found what they'd hoped to see at Eastern Egg Rock—puffins with white and multicolored bands on their legs.

Q "It's very common for puffins to wander around for two or three years before they breed," Kress explains.

R Over the next couple of years the team set out puffin decoys and mirrors on the island's rock formations in an effort to attract the real birds. They began an effort to attract terns by playing tape recordings of bird calls. Terns breed rapidly and are especially aggressive against gulls, thus they are a puffin ally.

S Between 1977 and 1980 puffins returned to the island in increasing numbers, and the despair of the first years turned to excitement.

T Their return didn't necessarily mean the puffins were breeding, however, and breeding was the key to the success of the project. Since frequent inspection of the boulders where the puffins might nest would only inhibit mating, Kress and his team depended on other evidence as proof of breeding—a puffin returning to the island with fish in its beak.

U On July 4, 1981, it happened. Kress reported in his journal: "I was amazed to see a puffin with its beak crammed full of fish walk-fly-scramble into the boulders. A moment later a bird flew off while a second stood by watching the entire show . . . it's the best proof yet that after 100 years of absence and nine years of working toward this goal, puffins are again nesting at Eastern Egg Rock—a Fourth of July celebration I'll never forget."

ⓔ COMPREHENSION CHECK

Choose the correct answer.

COMPARISON

16. Steve Kress compares the puffin to
    a. a seagull.
    b. a block of sod.
    c. a little clown.
    d. a small fish.

SCANNING

17. After two or three years, puffins usually
    a. fly away from the nest for the first time.
    b. fly to Maine.
    c. return home to breed.
    d. begin to eat fish.

SCANNING

18. How did Steve Kress get puffin chicks to Eastern Egg Rock?
    a. He brought them in a boat.
    b. He brought them in a plane.
    c. He planted decoys there to lure them.
    d. He brought fish there to lure them.

FACT / OPINION

19. Which of these sentences from the story is an opinion?
    a. The puffin looks like a little clown.
    b. It took a couple of years to clear the island of most of the gulls.
    c. Terns breed rapidly and are especially aggressive against gulls.
    d. The puffin in Maine make its nest in rock crevices.

SCANNING

20. How many years did Steve work on his project before he had proof that the puffins were breeding?
    a. Two years
    b. Three years
    c. Five years
    d. Nine years

INFERENCE

△ 21. How did Steve's team identify the puffin chicks they brought to Eastern Egg Rock?
    a. By looking for fish in their beaks
    b. By attaching plastic bands to their legs
    c. By recording their bird calls
    d. By painting decoys to match the chicks

PROBLEM / SOLUTION

22. How did the research team solve the problem of making nests for the puffins?
    a. They built rock burrows from cement blocks.
    b. They dug burrows in the soil.
    c. They made nests out of old gull nests.
    d. They built burrows in blocks of sod.

SCANNING

23. How did the puffin chicks show that they were almost ready to leave their nests?
    a. They refused to eat.
    b. They began to eat fish.
    c. They scratched at their burrows.
    d. They refused to swim.

INFERENCE

△ 24. Why is a puffin carrying fish a sign that a puffin is nesting nearby?
    a. The puffin is probably going to feed its young.
    b. The puffin is probably building a nest from fish bones.
    c. The puffin is probably trying to attract terns that help protect it from enemies.
    d. The puffin is probably making sure that the area has enough food.

MAIN IDEA

○ 25. This story is mainly about
    a. why the number of seabirds in Maine is diminishing.
    b. why some seabirds adapt to Maine better than others.
    c. how a research team restored puffins to the Maine coast.
    d. how a research team prevented puffins from becoming extinct.

Check your answers with the key.

HA-9

SKILL PRACTICE
CAUSE AND EFFECT

A **cause** makes something happen. An **effect** is what happens as a result. Find the causes and effects in these examples:

> The brakes on Pepe's car failed; as a result, he crashed into a tree.
>
> Selma got a job as a mechanic because she likes working on cars.

To find the cause, think of which event happens first. To find the effect, think of what results.

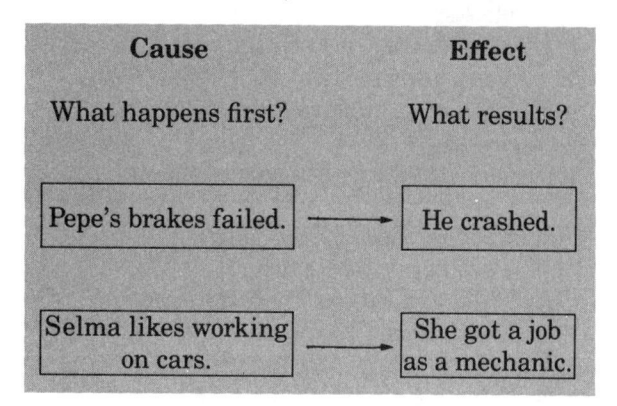

Cause	Effect
What happens first?	What results?
Pepe's brakes failed. →	He crashed.
Selma likes working on cars. →	She got a job as a mechanic.

Sometimes one cause has several effects, or several causes have one effect. Here's an example of several causes leading to a single effect:

> Ms. Conklin won the election for several reasons. She promised not to raise taxes. She promised to open up new government jobs to women. She had a well-organized campaign.

Causes	Effect
She promised not to raise taxes.	
She promised to open up new government jobs to women. →	Ms. Conklin won the election.
She had a well-organized campaign.	

Reread each paragraph listed below. Write the causes and effects as indicated. You do not have to use the exact words from the story, but what you write should make sense on its own.

26. Paragraph A

    Cause:

    Effect:

27. Paragraph B

    Cause:

    Effect:

28. Paragraph D

    Causes: 1.

    2.

    Effect:

29. Paragraph G

    Cause:

    Effect:

30. Paragraph K

    Cause:

    Effect:

31. Paragraph R

    Cause:

    Effect:

Check your answers with the key.

ⓖ VOCABULARY REVIEW

Choose the best answer.

32. Which of these are **predators**?
    a. Trees that are very old.
    b. Birds that fly south for the winter.
    c. Sharks that eat other fish.
    d. Research teams that study animals.

33. If a restaurant offers a **diversity** of fish, it serves
    a. many kinds of fish.
    b. a special recipe for fish.
    c. fresh fish every day.
    d. fish dishes at a low price.

34. If you **transplant** your family, you
    a. phone them.
    b. write them.
    c. move them.
    d. leave them.

35. An **excessive** price for something means the price is
    a. very cheap.
    b. very expensive.
    c. very likely to change.
    d. very different in different countries.

36. Dinosaurs are **extinct.** This means they are
    a. able to be studied by scientists.
    b. bigger than other animals.
    c. dangerous to other animals.
    d. no longer in existence.

37. The lion is very **aggressive.** This means it
    a. is not afraid to attack.
    b. is very tired.
    c. lives by itself.
    d. walks on four legs.

38. If sounds **inhibit** your sleep, they
    a. soothe you to sleep.
    b. keep you awake.
    c. make you laugh.
    d. make you dream.

39. The man reported the **plight** of the children. He told about the
    a. children riding in planes.
    b. party he gave for the children.
    c. problems of the children.
    d. pictures the children drew.

40. Which of these is a **hindrance** to a dog that wants to get out of the yard?
    a. A hole in the ground.
    b. A bone that he buried.
    c. A tall fence.
    d. A cloud in the sky.

41. If you eat eggs **avidly,** that means you probably
    a. don't like eggs.
    b. like eggs.
    c. leave some on your plate.
    d. are in a restaurant.

Check your answers with the key.

HA-10 PROBLEM AND SOLUTION

JOB OPPORTUNITIES IN HEALTH CARE

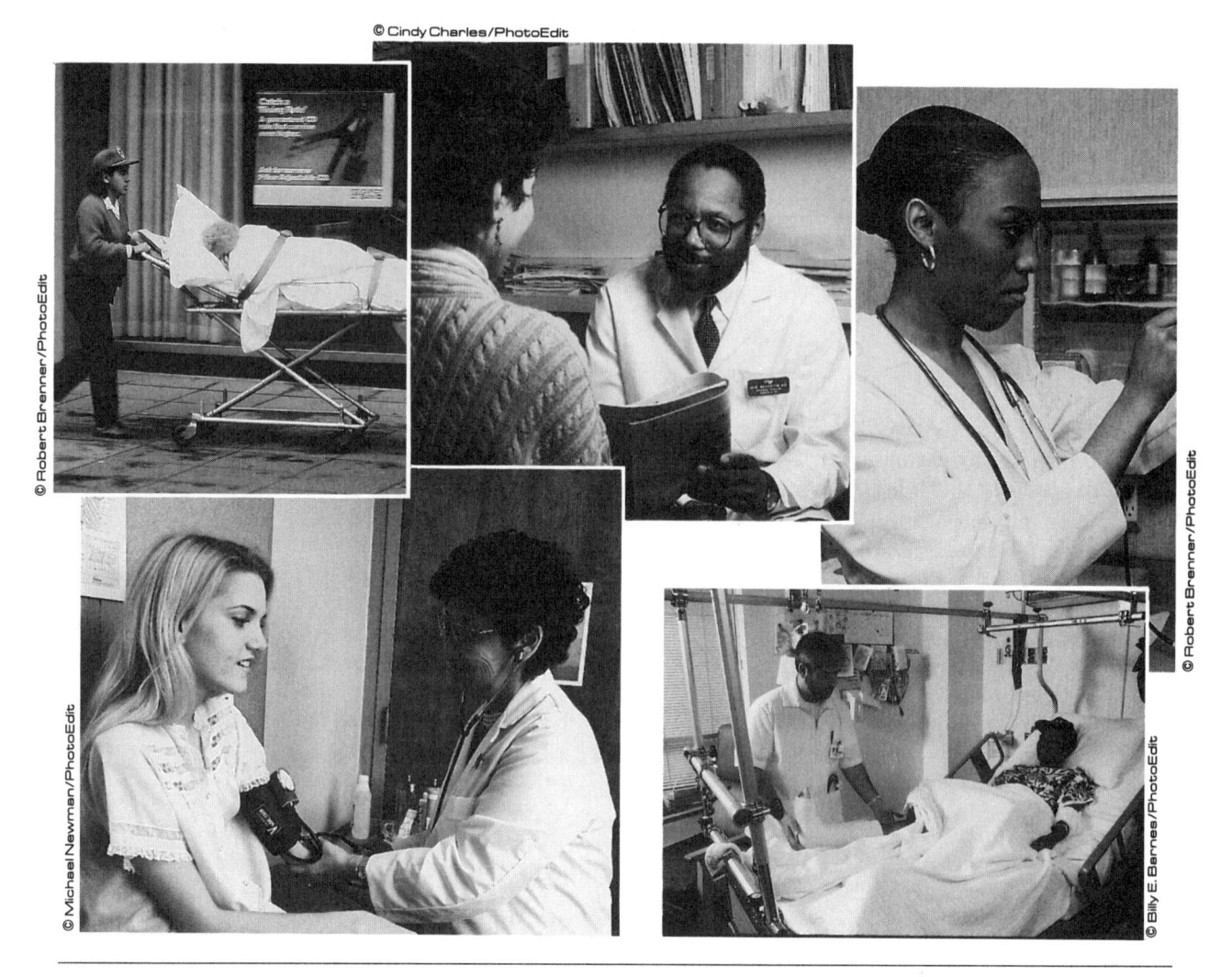

ⓐ GETTING READY

The picture above shows different health care professionals at work. Try to identify each of the pictured jobs. Which of these, if any, do you think you might be interested in doing? Explain your choices. How would you go about finding more about different health care careers?

Today many job opportunities have opened up in the health care professions. Why do you think this is true? Do you think that the need for health care professionals will continue to increase? Why or why not? If you wanted to pursue a job in health care, how would you proceed?

When you read "Job Opportunities in Health Care," you will learn about the health care job explosion and what you can do to pursue a job in one of these fields.

VOCABULARY BUILDING

Study each key word to make sure you know its pronunciation and definition. Then study the way the word is used in the sentence based on the story.

applicants (ap′ lə kənts) People who apply for a job or position. *In order to attract applicants for key jobs, recruiters often pay full expenses for on-site interviews.*

attentive (ə ten′ tiv) Considerate. *Supervisors are looking for enthusiastic employees who can work independently, have the basic skills and training, can get along with other workers, and are attentive to the patients.*

clinics (klin′ iks) Places for medical treatment. *Health care professionals are needed at hospitals, clinics, and other health care institutions.*

economic (ē′ kə nom′ ik) Of or having to do with the science of the production, distribution, and use of goods and services. *The results of the economic slowdown of the 1990s have been dramatic: the number of available jobs has diminished, while unemployment has soared.*

extensive (ek sten′ siv) Thorough; lengthy. *As with any other job search, finding a suitable position requires extensive research, time, and effort.*

guidance (gīd′ ns) Direction; advice. *One good way to network is to obtain an informational interview, during which you gather facts about a particular occupation and seek guidance on how to locate a suitable position.*

rehabilitation (rē′ hə bil′ ə tā′ shən) The process of restoring to a condition of usefulness or good health. *People of all ages are now more concerned with their health and taking care of their bodies. This leads to additional sources of new jobs in such areas as rehabilitation.*

tendency (ten′ dən sē) A leaning; bent. *Many promising candidates have the tendency to give up before giving their efforts a chance to work.*

therapists (ther′ ə pists) People who treat diseases or disorders. *According to the Bureau of Labor Statistics, more than 155,000 additional physical therapists and 20,000 occupational therapists will be needed.*

vacancies (vā′ kən sēz) Unfilled jobs, positions, or places. *Job vacancies for health care professionals are actually on the rise.*

Now choose a word that fits in each of the following sentences. Write the best word for each sentence.

1. With rising unemployment and slow industrial growth, the _____ forecast is not good.

2. I need some _____ on how to go about finding a job.

3. There were twenty _____ for the ten jobs that needed to be filled.

4. The detective will conduct an _____ examination of the crime scene.

5. Many people have a _____ to gain weight during the holidays.

6. Good hosts are _____ to their guests.

7. I thought that there were three jobs available, but it seems there are only two _____ .

HA-10

8. The _____ used heat to treat the patient's injured back.

9. The _____ of the accident victim took many months of hard work.

10. Our city has five free _____ for emergency medical care.

Check your answers with the key.

SPECIAL WORDS

aides (ādz) Helpers; assistants. *According to the Bureau of Labor Statistics, more than 263,000 home health aides will be needed.*

nutrition (nü trish′ ən) The science or study of proper, balanced diet to promote health. *People of all ages are now more concerned with their health and taking care of their bodies. This leads to additional sources of new jobs in such areas as nutrition.*

resumé (rez′ ə mā′) A statement of a job applicant's previous employment experience, education, etc. *If an informational interview is granted, take along a copy of your resumé and a cover letter describing your desires and qualifications.*

c PREVIEW

Read the first sentence of each paragraph to discover what you will learn from the story. Do this now.

Did you notice that the story gives you certain information about jobs in health care? You will soon be reading some topics that may or may not be discussed in the story.

Based on what you learned from previewing, the story, write *yes* if you think the topic might be discussed. Write *no* if you think the topic will not be discussed.

11. _____ Why there is an increase in the need for health care

12. _____ Salary ranges for various health care jobs

13. _____ How to find out about available health care jobs

14. _____ Which colleges and universities train health care workers

15. _____ What goes on at an informational interview

Check your answers with the key.

d READING

Now read the story to find out how you might take advantage of the job opportunities in the health care professions.

JOB OPPORTUNITIES IN HEALTH CARE
by Estelle Kleinman

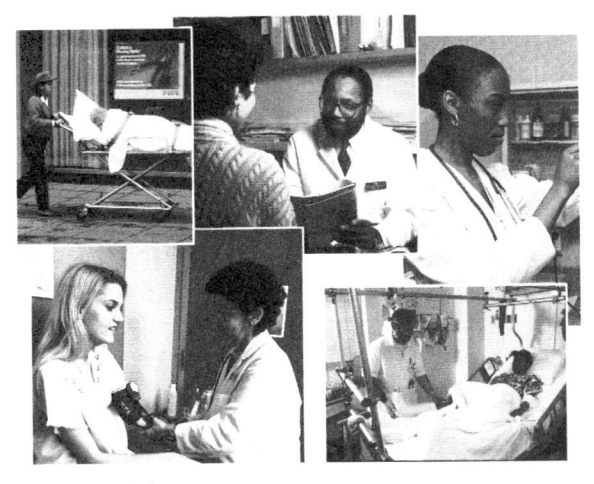

A The results of the economic slowdown of the 1990s have been dramatic: the number of available jobs has diminished, while unemployment has soared. Where can you find a good job these days? The answer may lie in the health care professions.

B Job vacancies for health care professionals are actually on the rise at hospitals, clinics, and other health care institutions. By the early twenty-first century, health services employment is projected to provide 3,900,000 new jobs. According to the Bureau of Labor Statistics, more than 155,000 additional physical therapists; 20,000 occupational therapists; 263,000 home health aides; 122,000 medical assistants; and 757,000 registered nurses will be needed. And opportunities will not be limited to traditional health care professionals. Health care institutions will need thousands of additional employees including lawyers, chemists, word processors, secretaries, clerks, and food service helpers.

C Why is there such an increase in the need for health care? First of all, the number of aged Americans, those most in need of health care, is increasing rapidly. There are now about five million more people 75 or older than there were five years ago. As medical science finds new cures and treatments, the older population will continue to swell. Even Americans not in their golden years are using more medical services than ever before. People of all ages are now more concerned with their health and taking care of their bodies. This leads to additional sources of new jobs in such areas as rehabilitation, health and fitness, wellness, nutrition, and prevention.

D The lack of health care employees is a continuing problem, with many health care providers requiring months to locate qualified staff. In a recent survey, 70% of the hospitals questioned reported a lack of qualified candidates. In order to attract applicants for key jobs such as physical therapists, recruiters often pay full expenses for on-site interviews and offer well-paying packages to new employees willing to move. Sign-on bonuses are also becoming common and can be as high as several thousand dollars.

E Does all this mean that finding a job in the health field will be a snap? Unfortunately, the answer is no. As with any other job search, finding a suitable position requires extensive research, time, and effort.

F Job seekers who only check the newspaper want ads may be disappointed. Only a small percent of all jobs, less than 25%, actually appear in the want ads. To locate the remaining 75%, serious job hunters must try to identify possible employment opportunities through alternative means such as newsletters, directories, job fairs, job hotlines, and personal contacts.

G Networking is the process of opening employment opportunities by developing relationships that are jointly helpful to both parties. The essential elements of a practical networking plan are personal commitment, the ability to identify organizations and people who can help you, and following through. In addition to having the necessary qualifications and training, the key to successful networking is personal contact.

H One good way to network is to obtain an informational interview, during which you gather facts about a particular occupation and seek guidance on how to locate a suitable position. Call or write likely employees and ask to talk with a supervisor in a field that interests you. Briefly explain that you only desire information and ask if they would be willing to talk with you in person about career opportunities. Stress that you will only take 15 minutes of their time. The informational interview will help you examine familiar and diverse employment opportunities. The outcome of these interviews will help you make an objective career decision and hopefully develop a contact inside the company who may help you secure a job.

If an informational interview is granted, take along a copy of your resumé and a cover letter describing your desires and qualifications. Also be sure to dress appropriately for the position you seek. If an interview is not granted, ask permission to send a cover letter and resumé for their files. You can expect numerous rejections while pursuing these methods. Don't get discouraged. Persistence pays off when networking. Many promising candidates have the tendency to give up before giving their efforts a chance to work.

What should you ask at an informational interview? Your questions will probably cover the following areas: training and skills needed for the type of work, the most important qualifications, ways to find out about available jobs, career advancement opportunities, and additional training that would be helpful. Come up with a written list of questions to bring to the interview, and don't hesitate to take notes as you hear the answers. End the interview by asking if there are other people you should talk with and if you can use the interviewer's name as a referral. Within a short period after the interview, you should prepare and mail a thank-you letter to the interviewer.

Through networking, job seekers make a positive impression on a likely employer long before an actual job interview. Supervisors are looking for enthusiastic employees who can work independently, have the basic skills and training, can get along with other workers, and are attentive to the patients. If you have the basics, don't be overly concerned that other candidates may have more training or experience. Selections are often based more on positive attitude, personality, and drive than on other considerations. Institutions would prefer to spend money on training an employee than to hire someone who may disturb the work environment.

Very often job seekers are too narrow in their approach. They apply for one job or make a few contacts and then do nothing until they receive a reply. The result may be disappointing. Although health career jobs are plentiful, they still attract qualified candidates who will be your rivals. You must make numerous contacts to increase your chances of securing the job you want.

There is a job waiting for you in the health care field if you want it. If you decide to pursue such a position, do your homework. Gather information on jobs you think would interest you. Once you have your sights set on a particular job, go after it. Locate available positions not only in the want ads but also through alternative sources such as newsletters, directories, job fairs, and networking. Be positive and persistent, and you will land the job of your dreams.

COMPREHENSION CHECK

Choose the best answer.

SCANNING

16. How many new jobs will be provided by health services employment by the early twenty-first century?
    a. 155,000
    b. 263,000
    c. 3,900,000
    d. 757,000

CAUSE/EFFECT

17. Which of the following cause an increase in the need for health care? (Choose all the correct answers.)
    a. The number of aged Americans is increasing rapidly.
    b. Medical science has found new cures and treatments.
    c. People of all ages are more concerned with their health and taking care of their bodies.
    d. There is a lack of health care professionals.

SCANNING

18. Approximately what percent of jobs appear in want ads?
    a. more than 75%
    b. 100%
    c. about 50%
    d. less than 25%

RECOGNIZING BIAS/AUTHOR'S VIEWPOINT

19. The author believes that a job seeker should
    a. check the want ads as well as identify possible employment opportunities through alternative means.
    b. only check the want ads.
    c. go after one job at a time.
    d. wait for health care institutions to contact them.

CONTEXT CLUES

20. Networking is
    a. doing research to find out about job openings in various books, directories, and newsletters.
    b. watching television to identify likely employers.
    c. the process of opening job opportunities by developing relationships through personal contact.
    d. subscribing to as many newspapers as possible so that you can check on job opportunities in various locations.

INFERENCE

21. Which of the following would be a good question to ask at an informational interview?
    a. How long does it take you to get to work?
    b. How many years have you been working for this organization?
    c. What is the company policy on sick days?
    d. What experience and training is absolutely essential for this job?

TYPES OF SUPPORTING DETAILS

22. What paragraph pattern is used in Paragraph J?
    a. Enumeration
    b. Generalization
    c. Opinion/Reason
    d. Question/Answer

SEQUENCE

23. Which of the following should happen last?
    a. Call or write likely employers and ask to talk with a supervisor in a field that interests you.
    b. Prepare and mail a thank-you letter to the interviewer.
    c. Ask the interviewer questions that will help you gather facts about a particular occupation and find out how to locate a position.
    d. Stress that you will only take 15 minutes of the interviewer's time.

INFERENCE

24. Who would have the most difficult time landing a job?
    a. Someone who gets into conflicts with other workers.
    b. Someone who does not have a great deal of experience.
    c. Someone who needs a small amount of training.
    d. Someone who is very enthusiastic.

MAIN IDEA

25. This story is mainly about
    a. the results of the economic slowdown of the 1990s.
    b. how hospitals go about attracting qualified applicants to fill their vacancies.
    c. the rise in job vacancies for health care professionals and how to go about finding a job.
    d. what to ask at an informational interview.

Check your answers with the key.

HA-10

SKILL PRACTICE
PROBLEM AND SOLUTION

In some kinds of writing, the author discusses **problems** and their **solutions**. The discussion may take up a paragraph, may be part of a paragraph, or may take up several paragraphs. More than one problem or more than one solution may be given. The solutions the author presents may or may not solve the problem.

Read the paragraph below, looking for the problem and any possible solutions:

> The employees at the bus company have gone on strike, and Carmen doesn't know how she will get to work. She thought about taking a taxi, but decided that this would be too expensive. She asked her friend Rani for a ride, but Rani leaves too late for Carmen to get to work on time. Finally, Carmen decided to ride her bike to work.

We can list the problem and possible solutions like this:

> **Problem:** How Carmen will get to work during the strike
> **Solutions:** 1. Take a taxi
> 2. Ask her friend Rani for a ride
> 3. Ride her bike

Reread the parts of the story indicated by the paragraph letters. Then write the missing problem and solution(s).

26. Paragraphs A, B

    Problem:

    Solution:

27. Paragraph D

    Problem:

    Solutions: 1.
    2.
    3.

28. Paragraph F

    Problem:

    Solution:

29. Paragraph L

    Problem:

    Solution:

Check your answers with the key.

VOCABULARY REVIEW

Choose the best answer.

30. Who would most likely be in need of **guidance**?
    a. A doctor who is examining a patient
    b. A singer who is about to give a concert
    c. A farmer who is harvesting his crop
    d. A student who wants to find out about careers in health care

31. Which of the following is an **economic** consideration?
    a. A trade agreement
    b. World peace
    c. Saving wildlife
    d. A Presidential election

32. Which of the following would **therapists** do?
    a. Perform operations
    b. Make sure that the patients' beds are made
    c. Teach stroke victims how to walk better
    d. Prepare healthy food for sick people

33. Which of the following is an example of someone being **attentive**?
    a. A salesman goes out of his way to help a customer.
    b. A teacher scolds a student for not paying attention.
    c. A police officer arrests a thief.
    d. An author completes a novel.

34. If I have a **tendency** to do something, then I
    a. have a fear of doing it.
    b. am likely to do it.
    c. never do it.
    d. only do it now and then.

35. If there are **vacancies** in our company, then we need
    a. to fire people.
    b. to hire people.
    c. to work faster.
    d. more office furniture.

36. People go to **clinics** when they are
    a. learning a trade.
    b. looking for a job.
    c. arrested by the police.
    d. sick or injured.

37. Juan and Barbara are job **applicants**. This means they
    a. are quitting their jobs.
    b. are hiring someone.
    c. want a job.
    d. don't want to work.

38. If you have done an **extensive** study of a subject, then you
    a. should know that subject very well.
    b. know only a little bit about the subject.
    c. don't like the subject.
    d. think the subject is of little importance.

39. After his automobile accident, Frank had a long period of **rehabilitation**. This means that he spent a long time
    a. in bed.
    b. working to get well.
    c. getting his car repaired.
    d. at the doctor's office.

Check your answers with the key.

HA-11 SUMMARIZING

A WOMAN'S ICY STRUGGLE

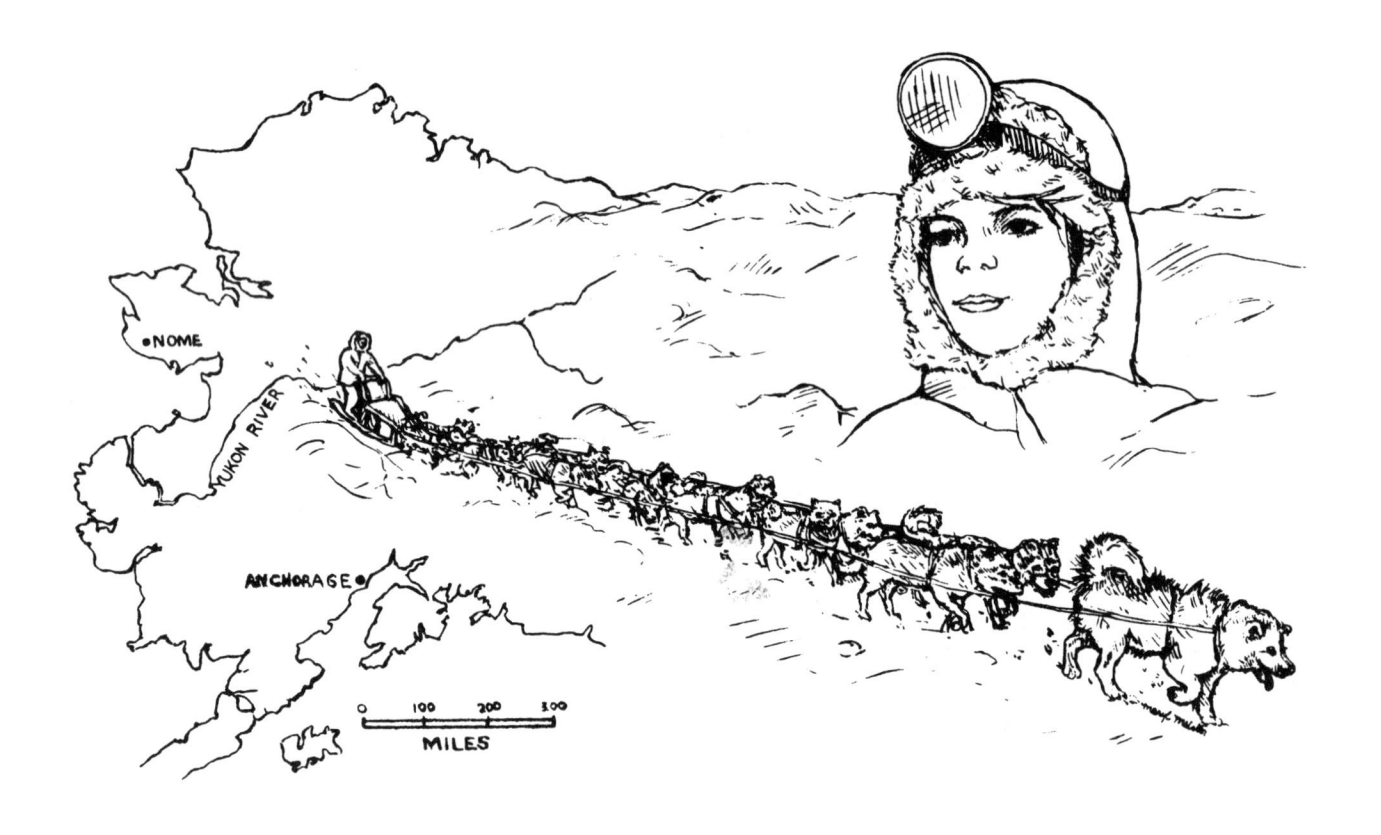

ⓐ GETTING READY

Have you ever seen runners, drivers, or skiers compete in a race that lasted longer than one day? If you have, you know that in a long race anything can happen. Contestants in that kind of race must have great endurance. If you were competing in such a race, how would you train in order to build up your endurance?

The woman in the picture above is Susan Butcher, a famous sled-dog racer. By 1995, Butcher had won the Iditarod Trail International Sled-Dog Race four times; however, in 1982 when this story takes place, she had yet to win her first race. During the Iditarod, the participants race a team of dogs many hundreds of miles through the snow from Anchorage to Nome, Alaska. The race lasts many days, during which the drivers must battle nature as well as other teams. Can you think of some problems that the racers must face? How do you think they might solve these problems?

When you read "A Woman's Icy Struggle," you will discover what happened to Susan Butcher and her dogs during the course of the 1982 race.

b VOCABULARY BUILDING

Study each key word to make sure you know its pronunciation and definition. Then study the way the word is used in the sentence based on the story.

amorphous (ə môr′ fəs) Without a definite form or shape. *The trail runs across miles of flat, amorphous country.*

compulsory (kəm pul′ sər ē) Required; ordered by a rule or law. *I think only of reaching the next checkpoint, where I will spend a compulsory 24-hour layover.*

energetic (en′ ər jet′ ik) Lively; full of pep. *I let go of the sled, and the energetic dogs are soon out of sight.*

massage (mə säzh′) Rub and knead the muscles. *I massage the dogs' shoulders and legs.*

resume (ri züm′) Continue again after stopping. *All the racers resume the race with new strength and spirit.*

straggle (strag′ əl) To wander. *At 6:55 a.m. we straggle into the first checkpoint, a full four hours behind my schedule.*

tripods (trī′ podz) Three-legged stands. *I cannot see the driftwood tripods that mark the trail.*

ultimate (ul′ tə mit) Supreme. *The wilderness is my life now, and the sled-dog race its ultimate experience.*

unencumbered (un′ en kum′ bərd) Not held back; unhindered. *I let go of the sled so the dog team can clamber up a steep bank unencumbered by my weight.*

yearned (yernd) Longed for; desired. *As I grew older, I yearned for a life that would combine dogs and the outdoors.*

Now choose a word that fits in each of the following sentences. Write the best word for each sentence.

1. The lonely girl _____ for her old friends back home.

2. The hikers _____ down the mountain as though they are exhausted.

3. It is _____ for children to attend school.

4. This modern painting is made up of _____ shapes rather than realistic figures.

5. Ever since I started exercising regularly, I feel more _____.

6. The big cameras were mounted on _____.

7. Jennifer does not carry a purse because she likes to be _____ when she walks.

8. The meeting will _____ after the lunch break.

9. My _____ dream is to climb Mt. Everest.

10. When I get home, I'll ask my husband to _____ my tired feet.

Check your answers with the key.

HA-11

SPECIAL WORDS

frôstbitten (frôst' bit' tən) Severely injured by cold. *I finally reach the next village with a frostbitten face.*

Iditarod (ī di' tä rod) The world's longest sled-dog race, which crosses Alaska from Anchorage to Nome. *For three years I trained a team for my first Iditarod.*

mushers (mush' ərz) People who drive dog sleds through the snow. *The dogs and I join a field of 54 mushers and 796 dogs.*

c PREVIEW

Read the first sentence of each paragraph to discover what the story is about. Do this now.

Did you notice that the story tells you certain things about the sled-dog race? Below are some events that may or may not occur in the story.

Based on what you learned from previewing the story, write *yes* if you think the event occurs. Write *no* if you think the event does not occur.

11. ____ Some of Susan Butcher's dogs go lame.

12. ____ Susan Butcher has to stop and rest.

13. ____ Susan Butcher passes some of the other racers.

14. ____ Susan Butcher refuses to help another racer who is hurt.

15. ____ Susan Butcher finishes last in the race.

Check your answers with the key.

d READING

Now read the story to find out just what happened in the race.

A WOMAN'S ICY STRUGGLE
by Susan Butcher

A   I was born into a comfortable family life in Cambridge, Massachusetts. During childhood summers at the Maine seashore, I spent every waking hour learning about the outdoors. Of many pets, my favorite was my dog.

B   As I grew older, I yearned for a life that would combine dogs and the outdoors. Deep inside I also had a feeling that there was a place where I could breathe more freely, where my own hard work would be the measure of my success and the source of my existence.

C   I came to Alaska in 1975, hoping to find my dream. Today, from my cabin door 140 miles northwest of Fairbanks and 4 miles from my nearest neighbor, I look at my sled-dog team and know my dream is as real as Mount McKinley far beyond. And as challenging as the Iditarod.

D   For three years I lived in the wilderness, building and training a team for my first Iditarod, the world's longest sled-dog race. I finished 19th, barely in the money. (Only the first 20 into Nome share in some $100,000 in cash prizes.) I came in ninth the next year, fifth the following two years. This is 1982 and this year I am determined to win.

E   The dogs and I arrive in Anchorage to join an eventual field of 54 mushers and 796 dogs. We hear talk of an icy trail with dangerous turns. This only adds to my nervousness.

F   Each one of my 50 dogs has a distinct personality. I race only 15, but more are always being trained so as to keep this number at full strength.

G   My dogs are so eager to get going that it takes ten people to restrain them as earlier starters move out. My countdown begins, and then we're off! On an icy hill a mile out, we go into a slide; we hit a downed tree and roll over. Three of the team, clearly shaken, are running off pace. Even so, we're making good time. "Gee, Tekla!" I cry. My lead dog pulls to the right, and we pass two teams.

H   Miles peel away, and snow begins as darkness falls. One by one, I overtake 22 teams; only three are ahead of me now.

I   Cracker, Ruff, and Screamer quit pulling and begin to limp. As much as it will slow me, I load them onto the sled to prevent further injury.

J   Mile after mile I ride behind them on the runners; I should have seen the first checkpoint by now. I sense something is wrong. At dawn a musher approaches from the opposite direction and hails me: "We're at least ten miles off course!"

K   I turn my team around. My misery cannot be expressed.

L   Tekla starts to limp. The strain of those extra miles without rest has been too much. I take her out of the lead.

M   At 6:55 a.m. we straggle into the first checkpoint, a full four hours behind my schedule. Cracker, Ruff, and Screamer are flown home. Forty-five miles farther and my limping Tekla has also reached her limit. Sorrowfully, she is left behind.

N   With only eleven weary dogs left, I strike out again for Nome, still 938 miles away. After just ten miles, I know we have to stop. I lie in the snow next to Ali and Copilot. They cuddle up against me, and I massage their shoulders and legs. Other teams flash past. My resolve is shaken, but I'm not ready to give up.

O   On the move again, I think only of reaching the Rohn checkpoint, where I will spend a compulsory 24-hour layover. In these first two days on the trail, I have had only four hours' sleep.

P   I let go of the sled so the team can clamber up a steep bank unencumbered by my weight. But the energetic dogs are soon out of sight.

Q   I find them six miles later. The sled is intact. They bark as if to say, "Where have *you* been?" We arrive at Rohn at 5:01 p.m.

R   After the 24-hour rest and four hot meals,

my team is yowling and barking to be off, and my determination to stay in the race is firmer than ever. The falling snow grows heavier, wiping out the trail, but I keep going. I catch up with the leaders, who have lost their way and are waiting for daylight. Now we must work together, taking turns at trailbreaking through the deep snow.

S. We travel in this tedious and time-consuming manner for 4½ days and 353 miles. Skies are clear, but temperatures drop to 45 degrees below zero as I start out alone down the frozen Yukon River.

T. Another day's travel brings us to the next checkpoint. It is midnight. Even with my headlamp I cannot see the driftwood tripods that mark the trail across these miles of flat, amorphous country. Groping from tripod to tripod, I reach the next village with a frostbitten face.

U. By morning, winds are gusting up to 80 miles per hour, piling up 30-foot drifts. I wait 52 hours in the village before the storm lets up. All the mushers there resume the race with new strength and spirit. Only 231 miles to go, but all of them tough. My team picks up its pace.

V. Soon I am in fifth place, only a short distance behind Rick, Jerry, Emmitt, and Ernie. The final push is on: 30 miles to go. My heart is pounding.

W. I pass Ernie and pull away. I pass Emmitt, but he stays right on my tail. Through the last checkpoint we dash; only 22 miles now. Someone yells out that Rick and Jerry are just two minutes ahead of me. Emmitt remains close behind. I chase hard and pass Jerry. But there's still Rick, barely visible in the distance.

X. My dogs and I try with all our might to overtake him, but he still beats us into Nome by 3 minutes and 43 seconds. The race has lasted 16 days. Cheers ring out around me. I gratefully accept a second-place prize of $16,000.

Y. The wilderness is my life now, and the Iditarod its ultimate experience. I love Alaska and the opportunity it has given me to realize my dreams. I have only one dream to go: to be No. 1.

ⓔ COMPREHENSION CHECK

Choose the best answer.

CAUSE / EFFECT
16. Why did Susan reach the first checkpoint late?
    a. She started the race late.
    b. She had stopped to eat.
    c. She had fallen asleep.
    d. She had gotten lost.

INFERENCE
△ 17. Why did Susan stop her team shortly after Tekla was left behind?
    a. Susan felt like giving up.
    b. They were off course.
    c. The dogs were worn out.
    d. The dogs got cold.

INFERENCE
△ 18. Which is the hardest position for a dog to take in a sled-dog team?
    a. The lead
    b. The second place
    c. The middle position
    d. The rear

COMPARISON
19. In what way does Susan say her dream is similar to Mount McKinley?
    a. They are both big.
    b. They are both real.
    c. They are both in Alaska.
    d. They are both frightening.

SCANNING
20. Which sled-dog leads the team during the first part of the race?
    a. Cracker   c. Tekla
    b. Copilot   d. Ruff

SEQUENCE
21. Which of these events happens last?
    a. Susan lets go of the sled and the dogs run off without her.
    b. Susan puts three injured dogs on the sled.
    c. Susan has to turn around because she is off course.
    d. Susan reaches the first checkpoint.

SCANNING
22. How many days did the race take?
    a. 11 days   c. 24 days
    b. 16 days   d. 52 days

PROBLEM / SOLUTION
23. What did the mushers do when snow covered the trail?
    a. They made their own trail.
    b. They waited for help to arrive.
    c. They turned back.
    d. They set out in different directions.

CAUSE / EFFECT
24. Which of these caused Susan to stop?
    a. Darkness   c. A storm
    b. Snow   d. Getting lost

MAIN IDEA
○ 25. This story is mainly about
    a. a woman who successfully trained a team of sled-dogs.
    b. a woman who realized her dream by finishing the race.
    c. a woman's determined efforts to win a sled-dog race.
    d. a woman who overcame fear and danger in a sled-dog race.

Check your answers with the key.

HA-11

SKILL PRACTICE: SUMMARIZING

When you **summarize**, you restate in shorter form the important ideas and essential details of a piece of writing. So look for the main ideas and essential details when you want to summarize. And, to avoid confusion, make sure that the events in the summary are in the correct sequence. Read this example paragraph and its summary:

> Did you know that if it hadn't been for a man named William Seward, Alaska would not be part of the United States? In the 1860s, the Russian government wanted to sell Alaska. However, most members of the United States government didn't think Alaska was worth buying. Nothing of value had been found there except for furs. Also, the weather was so severe that few people wanted to live there. Still, Secretary of State Seward bought Alaska in 1867 for $7,200,000. It was called "Seward's Folly" and "Seward's Icebox." Later, however, gold and oil were discovered there, and people realized that Seward had made a good buy after all.
>
> **Summary:** Alaska is part of the United States because of the efforts of Secretary of State Seward. He bought Alaska from Russia in 1867 when no one else believed Alaska was of any value. Later, people realized he had made a good decision when gold and oil were discovered there.

Notice that the summary contains the main idea, "William Seward is responsible for the purchase of Alaska," and the most important details. It is also written so that it is clear and easy to understand.

Read the list of sentences below from Paragraphs A through M of the story. Write *no* beside the sentences that should be left out of the summary. Then number the sentences that should be included in the summary in the order in which they occurred in the story. Reread Paragraphs A through M if you need additional help.

26. ____ Her cabin is four miles from the nearest neighbor.

27. ____ In 1982 Susan Butcher and her dogs arrived in Anchorage, Alaska, to compete in the Iditarod sled-dog race.

28. ____ In the first two days on the trail, Susan had only four hours' sleep.

29. ____ At one point, she learned that she was ten miles off course and had to backtrack to get back in the race.

30. ____ During the race, Susan overtook 22 teams, which left only three teams ahead of her.

31. ____ It took ten people to restrain her eager dogs.

Check your answers with the key.

Read the list of sentences below from Paragraphs N through Y of the story. Write *no* beside the sentences that should be left out of the summary. Then number the sentences that should be included in the summary in the order in which they occurred in the story. Reread Paragraphs N through Y if you need additional help.

32. ____ The falling snow grew heavier.

33. ____ Despite her efforts to win the Iditarod, Susan came in second.

34. ____ Then, when her energetic dogs ran off without her, she had to chase after them for an additional six miles.

35. ____ Susan arrived at the village with a frostbitten face.

36. ____ A snowstorm with 80-mile-an-hour winds and 30-foot drifts forced Susan and other mushers to wait for 52 hours until the weather cleared.

37. ____ With only 22 miles to go in the race, Susan was in third place.

Check your answers with the key.

38. Now write the summary sentences in the correct order, starting with those from Paragraphs A through M and then adding those from Paragraphs N through Y.

When you have finished, you will have a complete summary of the story.

Check your answer with the key.

g) VOCABULARY REVIEW

Choose the best answer.

39. A person who feels **energetic** might
  a. take a nap.
  b. sit in the sun.
  c. ride a bike.
  d. make a phone call.

40. If Clara **yearned** for a car, she
  a. needed it.
  b. wanted it.
  c. refused to work for it.
  d. had no use for it.

41. A written test is **compulsory** for everyone who wants to get a driver's license. That means
  a. you may take the test if you want to.
  b. you may take the test only once.
  c. you must take the test.
  d. you must qualify to take the test.

42. If you feel **unencumbered**, you feel
  a. burdened.   c. free.
  b. sad.   d. embarrassed.

43. Carl left the porch light on because he thought Fred might **straggle** in. Carl thought Fred might
  a. be out of breath from running.
  b. be early.
  c. wander in later.
  d. come in on time.

44. My sand castle became an **amorphous** pile of sand when
  a. I put the final touches on it.
  b. a wave ruined its shape.
  c. another person helped me build it.
  d. the sun dried it out.

45. You need a **massage** if
  a. your back is sore.
  b. you are hungry.
  c. you missed a phone call.
  d. you lost your way.

46. The lights resting on **tripods** are on
  a. wire screens.
  b. stands with three legs.
  c. cables hung from the ceiling.
  d. mirrors on the floor.

47. If the movie will **resume** in five minutes, the movie will
  a. be shown for the first time.
  b. continue in five minutes.
  c. end in five minutes.
  d. be rewound in five minutes.

48. According to Sandra, the **ultimate** experience is parachuting out of an airplane. That means that Sandra thinks parachuting is
  a. foolish.   c. wonderful.
  b. frightening. d. dangerous.

Check your answers with the key.

HA-12 FACT AND OPINION
THE GREATEST ADVENTURE

ⓐ GETTING READY

Have you ever watched a space launch on television? What do you think it's like to walk on the moon? Do you think that someday we may have colonies of people living in space on artificial satellites circling the earth? Explain.

This story relates some of the important events in the space program from its beginning in 1957 to the recent past. From the title of the selection, how do you think the author feels about the space program?

When you read "The Greatest Adventure," try to find those statements which are only the author's opinions, and keep in mind that the author mixes facts and opinions to try to influence you into accepting her viewpoint.

VOCABULARY BUILDING

Study each key word to make sure you know its pronunciation and definition. Then study the way the word is used in the sentence based on the story.

brink (bringk) Edge. *We now stand at the brink of the future in space, beginning what President John F. Kennedy called "one of the greatest adventures of all time."*

economical (ē′ kə nom′ ə kəl) Not wasteful; cost-efficient. *With reusable craft, space travel could be economical as well as exhilarating.*

enthralled (en thrôld′) Fascinated. *Millions of people watched the moon landing on television, enthralled by the sight.*

magnitude (mag′ nə tüd) Great importance or effect. *When the Soviet Union launched Sputnik I, people everywhere were stunned by the magnitude of this accomplishment.*

maiden (mād′ n) First. *The first shuttle, Columbia, made its maiden flight in 1981.*

probed (prōbd) Examined; investigated. *Special spacecraft have even probed neighboring planets, traveling to the edges of our solar system and beyond.*

prolonged (prə lôngd′) Extended in time. *Scientists could study the effects of prolonged weightlessness because crews lived for months in space.*

saga (sä′ gə) A long story. *And in 1961, a new chapter in the saga of space exploration began. Yuri Gagarin of the Soviet Union orbited the earth in a spacecraft.*

surpassed (sər pasd′) Was greater than. *The bravery of the first astronauts equaled or surpassed that of great explorers of the past.*

valor (val′ ər) Courage. *The valor of the first astronauts surpassed that of the great explorers of the past.*

Now choose a word that fits in each of the following sentences. Write the best word for each sentence.

1. The soldier was given a medal for his _____ in combat.

2. The _____ of the flood damage forced the store to close.

3. Grandma told us the _____ of her family and their journey to America.

4. The new ship will sail from Boston to France on its _____ voyage.

5. By winning the championship, he showed that he _____ his big brother at sports.

6. It is usually more _____ to buy the large package of soap rather than the small one.

7. Your dog will recognize you even after a _____ absence.

8. The audience was _____ by the magician's brilliant performance.

9. Some people think that we are on the _____ of discovering a cure for cancer.

10. The scientists _____ the volcano so that they could tell if it was likely to erupt soon.

Check your answers with the key.

HA-12

SPECIAL WORDS

extraterrestrial (ek′ strə tə res′ trē əl) Outside the Earth. *They landed on the rocky surface of the moon. Then they stepped out—the first human beings ever to set foot on extraterrestrial soil.*

lunar module (lü′ nər moj′ ůl) A lightweight manned spacecraft carried by a larger spacecraft, detached while in lunar orbit so it can land on the moon and then rejoin the larger craft. *Astronauts entered the craft's lunar module. They guided the module to a landing on the moon.*

ⓒ PREVIEW

Read the first sentence of each paragraph to get an idea of what the story is about. Do this now.

Did you notice that the author talks about certain aspects of space travel? Below are some topics that may or may not be discussed in the story.

Based on what you learned from previewing the story, write *yes* if you think the topic might be discussed. Write *no* if you think the topic will not be discussed.

11. _____ Life on other planets

12. _____ The first moon landing

13. _____ The benefits of space exploration

14. _____ Different kinds of spacesuits

15. _____ Cost of the individual space programs

Check your answers with the key.

ⓓ READING

Now read the story to discover how the author says space travel has opened up opportunities for the human race.

THE GREATEST ADVENTURE
by Elaine Sedito

The exploration of space has brought the human race to the start of a new era. We now stand at the brink of the future in space, beginning what President John F. Kennedy called "one of the greatest adventures of all time." Indeed, the story of space exploration is one of the most inspiring stories of our time.

For centuries, people have dreamed of traveling among the stars. But the Space Age did not dawn until 1957. In that year, the former Soviet Union launched *Sputnik I*, the earth's first artificial satellite. People everywhere were stunned by the magnitude of this accomplishment.

Soon the United States was also sending satellites into space. People thrilled to the sight of powerful rockets lifting the satellites from earth on columns of orange flame. And in 1961, a new chapter in the saga of space exploration began. Yuri Gagarin of the Soviet Union orbited the earth in a spacecraft. Less than a year later, John Glenn of the United States completed three orbits.

Lifted into space on top of huge rockets, these pioneers of space were guided by their faith in the future. Alone, miles from earth, they faced the unknown. Their valor equaled or surpassed that of Columbus and the other great explorers of the past.

In the years that followed, many manned flights took other courageous astronauts into orbit around the earth. And in the United States, all attention turned to a challenging new project: the exploration of the moon.

Scientists worked feverishly to develop equipment that would permit people to walk on the hostile, airless surface of the moon. In 1968 three astronauts from the United States orbited the moon in their *Apollo 8* spacecraft. And just one year later the U.S. *Apollo 11* spacecraft set out on what was to be one of the most historic journeys of all time.

While the main craft slowly orbited the moon, two of the three *Apollo 11* astronauts entered the craft's lunar module. They guided the module to a landing on the rocky surface of the moon. Then they stepped out —the first human beings ever to set foot on extraterrestrial soil.

Millions of people watched the event on television, enthralled by the sight of history unfolding. Neil Armstrong, the first person to step onto the moon, immortalized the moment with the words, "That's one small step for man, one giant leap for mankind." The *Apollo 11* astronauts strolled about the moon's surface for several hours, collecting samples of soil and rocks. In addition, they set up several scientific experiments before they returned to the main craft for the trip back to earth. The *Apollo 11* mission filled people around the world with awe, and other moon missions followed.

But exciting moments like the first moon landing would be meaningless if humanity were not to benefit. Indeed, space exploration has opened up new worlds for science and industry. Satellites now provide us with precise information about the weather. Communications satellites speed information around the globe, bringing us news from anywhere on earth in an instant. Special spacecraft have even probed neighboring planets, traveling to the edges of our solar system and beyond to unlock the secrets of space.

Orbiting laboratories have put scientists

right in space, where they can study the stars without interference from the earth's atmosphere. The Soviet space station *Salyut 1*, which was sent into orbit in 1971, was the first of these remarkable craft. It was followed by *Skylab*, a U.S. space station, and by other Salyut stations. The space stations allowed crews to live for months at a time in space. Thus, scientists could study the effects of prolonged weightlessness and gain valuable information about the sun and the stars.

No less extraordinary are the U.S. space shuttles, the first reusable spacecraft. Rocketed into space, these amazing craft orbit the earth and then return, making an airplanelike landing on a runway. The first shuttle, *Columbia*, made its maiden flight in 1981, heralding a new era for space travel: With reusable spacecraft, space travel could be economical as well as exhilarating.

The history of the shuttle is not without its tragic side. In 1986, the shuttle *Challenger* exploded, killing all seven crew members including schoolteacher Christa McAuliffe. The next shuttle, *Discovery*, was not launched until 1988. After that, shuttle launchings became familiar sights, rewriting history with each flight. The 1990s saw the first African-American woman to travel in space, aboard the shuttle *Endeavour*. Another *Endeavour* crew serviced and repaired the Hubble Space Telescope. The first two-week shuttle mission took place aboard *Columbia*.

What lies ahead? Scientists expect that the shuttle will become a workhorse for industry, carrying satellites into orbit and bringing them back for repairs. It may help build huge space stations, so large that they could serve as space factories. Then the shuttle would transport people to and from the stations.

The possible benefits of space exploration are staggering. In years to come, we may mine precious minerals from the asteroids that circle our sun. We may travel to the edge of our solar system, there to explore new worlds. And we may journey beyond our solar system to distant stars. The future is limited only by our imagination.

ⓔ COMPREHENSION CHECK

Choose the best answer.

COMPARISON
16. The author compares the first astronauts to
    a. John F. Kennedy.
    b. Yuri Gagarin.
    c. Neil Armstrong.
    d. Christopher Columbus.

SEQUENCE
17. According to the story, which happened last?
    a. *Salyut 1* was launched.
    b. The United States launched *Skylab*.
    c. Neil Armstrong walked on the moon.
    d. Yuri Gagarin orbited the earth.

INFERENCE
△ 18. Why did the *Apollo 8* spacecraft orbit the moon?
    a. To study the moon at close range
    b. To drop supplies for the moon landing
    c. To prepare a landing place
    d. To collect rock samples

SEQUENCE
19. Which of these did the United States do before the Soviet Union?
    a. Sent a man into space
    b. Orbited the earth
    c. Launched a space station
    d. Landed on the moon

INFERENCE
△ 20. What did Neil Armstrong mean when he said that landing on the moon was "one giant leap for mankind"?
    a. People could jump more easily on the moon.
    b. He had to jump out of the landing module.
    c. Humanity had reached a new level of achievement.
    d. People had learned how to overcome gravity.

SCANNING
21. According to the story, what can be studied in space stations? (Choose all the correct answers.)
    a. The weather
    b. The stars
    c. The effects of weightlessness
    d. The effects of moon landings

SCANNING
22. In what year did the first moon landing take place?
    a. 1957
    b. 1969
    c. 1971
    d. 1981

INFERENCE
△ 23. Why do scientists want to study the effects of prolonged weightlessness? (Choose all the correct answers.)
    a. They feel it might help people who are overweight.
    b. They want to find out if we are weightless in outer space.
    c. They expect that people someday will be living on space stations in outer space.
    d. They want to be certain that prolonged weightlessness is not harmful.

COMPARISON
24. How are space shuttles different from other spacecraft?
    a. They can stay in space for months.
    b. They can serve as scientific laboratories.
    c. They can land and take off again and again.
    d. They can send information anywhere on earth.

MAIN IDEA
○ 25. This story is mainly about
    a. the race between the United States and the Soviet Union to be first in space.
    b. how the space program has benefited industry.
    c. the history of the space program and how it has given us new information about the moon, the planets, and the stars.
    d. how people dreamed of traveling to the stars.

Check your answers with the key.

HA-12

SKILL PRACTICE
FACT AND OPINION

A **fact** is a statement of truth that can be checked or verified. Some facts can be checked easily, as in this example:

> On April 11, 1970, an attempt to land on the moon failed because of trouble with the spacecraft.

You can find out if this statement is true by looking in an almanac or an encyclopedia.

Other facts may be harder to check, as in this example:

> Sometimes serious problems developed when the astronauts performed tasks outside the space vehicle.

To check this fact, you would have to find out what were considered serious problems by the space scientists. This is a **fact needing further explanation**.

Opinions are statements that a person believes to be true. Opinions cannot be checked because they express feelings or beliefs, as in this example:

> The unmanned satellite landing on Mars was the most important accomplishment of space exploration so far.

In the story "The Greatest Adventure," there are many facts as well as many opinions. Below are some sentences based on the story.

For each sentence, write *F* if it is a fact and *O* if it is an opinion.

26. ____ It's expected that the shuttle will become a workhorse for industry.

27. ____ The Soviet Union launched *Sputnik I*, the earth's first artificial satellite.

28. ____ The *Apollo 11* astronauts strolled about on the moon's surface for several hours.

29. ____ The first astronauts' valor equaled or surpassed that of Columbus and other explorers of the past.

Check your answers with the key.

Below are some sentences adapted from the story. For each sentence, write *FC* if it is a fact easily checked or *FE* if it is a fact needing further explanation.

30. ____ Yuri Gagarin of the Soviet Union orbited the earth in a spacecraft.

31. ____ In the United States, all attention turned to a challenging new project: the exploration of the moon.

32. ____ With reusable spacecraft, space travel could be economical as well as exhilarating.

33. ____ Many manned flights took other astronauts into orbit around the earth.

Check your answers with the key.

VOCABULARY REVIEW

Choose the best answer.

34. Fire fighters act with **valor** when they
    a. polish their fire engines.
    b. go away from the fire.
    c. hang up their uniforms.
    d. save people from burning buildings.

35. A **prolonged** telephone call might last for
    a. ten seconds.
    b. one minute.
    c. three minutes.
    d. an hour.

36. If you wrote the **saga** of how Americans settled the West, you wrote
    a. the whole story from beginning to end.
    b. about how one pioneer family farmed.
    c. your opinions about the way the West was settled.
    d. about how the West was different from the East.

37. A spacecraft that **probed** Jupiter
    a. avoided Jupiter.
    b. crashed on Jupiter.
    c. took pictures of Jupiter.
    d. took men to Jupiter.

38. Martha was on the **brink** of a scientific discovery. Martha
    a. was ready to give up.
    b. was close to succeeding.
    c. was a long way from succeeding.
    d. was ready for a vacation.

39. An airplane that goes on its **maiden** flight
    a. is on its last trip.
    b. is on its first trip.
    c. has no people aboard.
    d. does not make round trips.

40. The **magnitude** of the election caused a large number of people to vote. In this sentence, magnitude means
    a. necessity.   c. importance.
    b. cost.   d. publicity.

41. If you are **economical**, you
    a. spend your money wisely.
    b. buy the most expensive items.
    c. always buy on credit.
    d. buy many luxuries.

42. If your new car's performance **surpassed** that of your old car, your new car was
    a. not as good as your old car.
    b. about the same as your old car.
    c. better than your old car.
    d. not working at all.

43. If you were **enthralled** by the performance, you
    a. were bored.
    b. fell asleep.
    c. left early.
    d. were impressed.

Check your answers with the key.

13 RECOGNIZING BIAS/AUTHOR'S VIEWPOINT

WHEN WILL COMPANIES BECOME FAMILY-FRIENDLY?

ⓐ GETTING READY

Today the demands of job and home compete for the attention of many Americans. What conflicts do you see occurring for parents holding full-time jobs? What might be some problems faced by a full-time employee who must care for an elderly parent? What are some possible solutions to these problems?

The author of this story believes that employers must provide family-friendly programs to help employees deal with work-family conflicts. Do you agree that this is the employer's responsibility? Why or why not? What might be some benefits the employer can reap by providing these programs?

When you read this story, keep in mind that the author is trying to make you believe as she does. Keep your eyes open for ways that she tries to accomplish this.

VOCABULARY BUILDING

Study each key word to make sure you know its pronunciation and definition. Then study the way the word is used in the sentence based on the story.

accommodate (ə kom′ ə dāt) Adjust to; make suitable for. *Workers have asked employers to accommodate their needs in the form of "work-family" programs.*

authorize (ô′ thə rīz′) Allow; consent to. *Even when companies do authorize work-family programs, use of these programs is not widespread.*

callous (kal′ əs) Unfeeling. *Employers' callous response to employee needs is shortsighted as well as miserly.*

compassion (kəm pash′ ən) Sympathy; pity. *Showing compassion to employees with work-family conflicts is the right thing to do.*

comprehend (kom′ pri hend′) Understand fully and perfectly. *Employers don't seem to comprehend that helping employees with work-family conflicts is good business.*

decades (dek′ āds) Ten-year periods. *In a matter of decades, society has gone through notable changes in the American family and workplace.*

expertise (ek′ spər tēz′) Expert knowledge. *"Corporate cops" are executives with expertise both in addressing work-family conflicts and in enforcing company rules.*

intricate (in′ trə kit) Complicated. *Instead of timidly running away from intricate issues, employers must face them head-on and investigate practical solutions.*

materialize (mə tir′ ē ə līz) Come into being; become a fact. *Opponents of work-family programs fear that new problems might materialize, such as additional employer obligations, protection of confidentiality, and charges of unfair practices in providing such programs.*

penalized (pē′ nl īzd) Punished. *Employees are penalized for using work-family programs by facing loss of seniority, decreased benefits, and resentment from co-workers.*

Now choose a word that fits in each of the following sentences. Write the best word for each sentence.

1. I can't apply for that job because it requires _____ and skills that I don't possess.

2. Finding it difficult to _____ the reading passage, the student had to read it many times.

3. The 1980s and 1990s are the last two _____ in the twentieth century.

4. The figure skater was _____ for missing an important jump.

5. The _____ landlord turned off the heat during the freezing temperatures.

6. The rabbit did not _____ until the magician said the magic words.

7. This bus has been altered to _____ passengers in wheelchairs.

8. The woman had _____ for the hungry cat and gave it some food.

HA-13

9. The President will _____ special funds for the flood victims.

10. The problem was so _____ that it took me many hours to solve it.

Check your answers with the key.

SPECIAL WORDS

absenteeism (ab′ sən tē′ iz′ əm) Absence from work when willful or constant. *A survey taken at Johnson & Johnson revealed that absenteeism among employees who used flexible time and family-leave policies was, on average, 50 percent less than that for the workforce as a whole.*

downsized (doun′ sīzd′) Made smaller by decreasing the number of employees. *At downsized companies, fewer people must do the same amount of work.*

productive (prə duk′ tiv) Marked by abundant production or effective results. *Firms failing to take steps to adapt to the needs of their employees will be unable to attract and retain a productive workforce.* **Productivity** is the power to produce.

c PREVIEW

Read the first sentence of each paragraph to discover what the author's point of view is. Do this now.

Did you notice how the author feels about work-family programs? A list of statements that may or may not support the author's viewpoint follows.

Based on what you learned from previewing the story, write *yes* if you think the statement supports the author's viewpoint. Write *no* if you think the statement does not support her point of view.

11. _____ Companies do not supply enough work-family programs.

12. _____ Money has nothing to do with employers' reluctance to start such programs.

13. _____ Employers don't want to be more involved in their employees' lives.

14. _____ Employers should be looking for ways to decrease the hours their employees put in on the job.

15. _____ Companies with work-family programs whole-heartedly support them.

Check your answers with the key.

d READING

Now read the story to find out more about the author's view on work-family programs.

WHEN WILL COMPANIES BECOME FAMILY-FRIENDLY?

by Estelle Kleinman

In a matter of decades, society has gone through notable changes in the American family and workplace. More married mothers have entered the workforce, up from about 40 percent from the 1960s; and the number of minor children living with one parent has risen about 20 percent. In addition, caring for elderly parents is also fast becoming a major concern for workers. By 2020 an estimated one in three employees will have elder-care responsibilities. For those with full-time jobs, these changes have made managing job and family a very difficult task. As a result, workers have asked employers to accommodate their needs in the form of "work-family" programs, such as flexible work schedules, family leave, and child- and adult-care assistance. Unfortunately, the response has been less than enthusiastic.

According to the *Wall Street Journal,* a recent nationwide survey of firms with more than 50 employees showed that only 7.2 percent had provided child-care programs, and two-thirds said they would never offer employees even such minimum child- or elder-care help as referrals and workshops. It is painfully obvious that companies care nothing for their devoted employees. What is at the root of such an unsympathetic response?

As with most things, money is at the root of this evil. Greedy company heads want to achieve a "lean and mean" organization that will appeal to shareholders and the financial markets. In a recent survey by the Society for Human Resource Management of Alexandria, Virginia, more than 70 percent of the companies surveyed believed that most work-family programs were too costly. This callous response to employee needs is shortsighted as well as miserly. Employers don't seem to comprehend that showing compassion to employees with work-family conflicts is not only the right thing to do, but it's good business. Recent studies show that helping employees in this way boosts morale and increases productivity. A survey taken at Johnson & Johnson revealed that absenteeism among employees who used flexible time and family-leave policies was, on average, 50 percent less than that for the workforce as a whole. It also showed that 58 percent of the employees questioned said such policies were very important in their decision to stay at the company.

Another reason why companies are reluctant to initiate work-family programs is their feeling that employers should not involve themselves more deeply in workers' lives. They fear that new problems might materialize, such as additional employer obligations, protection of confidentiality, and charges of unfair practices in providing such programs. It's time for companies to stop acting like scared rabbits. Instead of timidly running away from these intricate issues, employers must face them head-on and investigate practical solutions. Failure to do so will not only cause their employees to suffer, but will come back to haunt them. Firms failing to take steps to adapt to the needs of their employees will be unable to attract and retain a productive workforce that will assure their success now and in the future.

With all that companies have to gain in being sympathetic to their workers' need for more family time, you would think that they would be looking for ways to decrease the hours employees put in on the job. Instead, companies are now demanding extra time of their workers. This is particularly true at downsized companies, where fewer people must do the same amount of work. When *Fortune* polled over 200 companies, close to 80 percent said they will have to push their people harder than ever before to be competitive. To the unfeeling heads of these companies, family life means nothing when compared with workplace responsibilities.

Even if companies don't verbally demand more time of their workers, they might send the same message in other ways. For example, bosses who regularly work 65 to 70 hours a week set an example employees find hard to ignore. How can a worker with family responsibilities feel comfortable leaving early when the boss will be staying well into the evening? The result of this pressure is striking. People today work more than they did 25 years ago, an amount equal to an extra month each year. One survey found that working mothers average 44 hours a week on the job and 31 on family-related tasks; fathers put in 3 more hours at work, but spend half as much time as their wives on child and household responsibilities. Any way you look at this, the family comes out a loser.

Even when companies do authorize work-family programs, use of these programs is not widespread. A survey of employees at 80 major companies showed that fewer than 2 percent of qualified employees take advantage of job sharing, telecommuting (working off-site or from home), and part-time work options. The reason for this is simple: Employees are penalized for using such programs. They may face loss of seniority, decreased benefits, and resentment from co-workers. It's no wonder that most workers would rather struggle to put in regular hours than pay the price for using work-family programs.

Another problem is that many companies with work-family programs are more interested in the public-relations boost these programs provide than in properly putting them to use. Even when top management authorizes such programs, supervisors down the line may not feel obligated to carry them out. This is because managers tend to mimic dinosaurs, fighting every new idea. Few companies have had the will or the knowledge to compel managers to allow these programs to work. As a result, chief executives make pronouncements, companies issue new rules—and the dinosaurs on the front line ignore them. If companies were really serious about getting rid of this problem, they would hire what is known as "corporate cops." These are executives with expertise both in addressing work-family conflicts and in enforcing company rules by removing management's rigid resistance to flexible schedules, work-at-home arrangements, job sharing, and family leaves.

If companies don't begin to accommodate the needs of their employees by whole-heartedly supporting work-family programs, everyone will suffer. Employees will have to make the difficult choice between work and family. Employers will sacrifice worker productivity, and might even lose valuable employees. The time for work-family programs has arrived. Only one question remains: When will companies realize this?

ⓔ COMPREHENSION CHECK

Choose the best answer.

CAUSE/EFFECT

16. What changes in the American family in the last few decades have caused conflict in managing job and family? (Choose all the correct answers.)
    a. More married mothers have entered the workforce.
    b. Many couples are deciding not to have children.
    c. The number of minor children living with one parent has increased.
    d. Caring for elderly parents is becoming a major concern for workers.

SCANNING

17. In the survey by the Society for Human Resource Management, what percent of the companies surveyed believed that work-family programs were too costly?
    a. 70 percent
    b. 58 percent
    c. 90 percent
    d. 7.2 percent

CAUSE/EFFECT

18. What are the effects of providing work-family programs? (Choose all the correct answers.)
    a. Morale is boosted.
    b. Absenteeism increases.
    c. Productivity increases.
    d. Employees look for other jobs.

PROBLEM/SOLUTION

19. What new problems might occur from initiating work-family programs? (Choose all the correct answers.)
    a. A decrease of productivity
    b. Additional employer obligations
    c. Protection of confidentiality
    d. Charges of unfair practices

COMPARISONS

20. Compared with workers 25 years ago, today's employees work
    a. about one month less.
    b. farther from the home.
    c. closer to the home.
    d. an amount equal to an extra month each year.

COMPARISONS

21. One survey found that working fathers
    a. put in 3 less hours each week at work and spend twice as much time on child and household responsibilities as their wives.
    b. average 44 hours a week on the job compared with 31 on family-related tasks.
    c. put in 3 more hours each week at work but spend half as much time as their wives on child and household responsibilities.
    d. put in 65 to 70 hours each week at work and spend the same time as their wives on family-related tasks.

CONTEXT CLUES

22. The word *telecommuting* means
    a. traveling to get to work.
    b. communicating by telephone.
    c. working off-site or from home.
    d. taking a television course.

INFERENCE

23. The fact that employees do not make widespread use of work-family programs suggests that
    a. the programs are not set up and managed properly.
    b. the programs are not helpful to employees.
    c. employees don't know what's good for them.
    d. employees want to spite their employers.

PROBLEM/SOLUTION

24. What is a solution to getting managers to allow work-family programs to work?
    a. Fire the managers.
    b. Allow managers to take advantage of these programs.
    c. Hire "corporate cops" to enforce company rules.
    d. Issue new company rules.

MAIN IDEA

○ 25. This story is mainly about
    a. how society has changed in the last few decades.
    b. why companies are reluctant to initiate work-family programs.
    c. why employees must put in more time at work.
    d. how employers are not doing enough to initiate and support work-family programs for their employees.

Check your answers with the key.

HA-13

SKILL PRACTICE
RECOGNIZING BIAS/AUTHOR'S VIEWPOINT

Many times in their writing, authors try to relate a specific **viewpoint**—that is, an attitude or belief about what they write. Some authors try to present only the bare facts when they write. Others present a **bias**; in other words, their writing is slanted to try to convince you that their opinion is correct.

In this story, the author presents a strong bias for the use of work-family programs. She mixes facts with opinions to try to get you to accept her viewpoint. In order to form your own opinion, you must recognize the author's bias so that you don't confuse her opinion with the facts.

The author of this story uses several methods to try to make you believe her opinion. An explanation of these methods follows.

The author uses **emotionally-loaded words**—words that make you feel a certain way. Look for emotionally-loaded words in these sentences:

> A. The clever lawyers worked tirelessly to convince the jury of the poor man's innocence.
> B. The contemptible lawyers used every dirty trick in the book to confuse the jury into freeing the crook.

In Sentence A, the words *clever, tirelessly,* and *poor* are meant to make you admire the lawyers. Sentence A is biased in favor of the lawyers. In Sentence B, the words *contemptible, dirty trick,* and *crook* are meant to make you have a bad opinion of the lawyers. Sentence B is biased against lawyers.

Besides emotionally-loaded words, the author also uses **half-truths** to present her viewpoint. Half-truths mix fact and opinion, as in this example:

> One lawyer was fined $500 by the judge, and he got what he deserved.
>
> Fact: One lawyer was fined $500 by the judge.
>
> Opinion: He got what he deserved.

The author also uses **guilt by association** to try to get the reader to adopt her view. When authors use guilt by association, they describe something negative and then say their subjects are similar to that. Here is an example:

> Snakes can eat their prey alive. In the same way, lawyers can devour a witness on the stand.

By comparing lawyers with snakes, the author is hoping that you will see the former in a negative light.

Now you will be identifying the ways in which the author of the story uses emotionally-loaded words, half-truths, and guilt by association.

First read lines 32-42 of the story. Then answer questions 26 and 27.

26. The author's viewpoint is that company heads care
    a. about workers.
    b. only about keeping expenses down.
    c. about work-family programs.
    d. only about absenteeism.

27. What five emotionally-loaded words show the author's bias?

Check your answers with the key.

Read the part of the story indicated by the line numbers below. Then write the fact part and the opinion part for each of the half-truths in questions 28-30.

28. Lines 21-29

    Fact:

    Opinion:

29. Lines 85-91

    Fact:

    Opinion:

30. Lines 113-120

    Fact:

    Opinion

    Check your answers with the key.

Read the part of the story indicated by the line numbers below. Then write the two things that are being compared in order to achieve guilt by association. In other words, write the negative description and the subject the author wants to put under suspicion by using the comparison.

31. Lines 61-69

    Negative description:

    Subject under suspicion:

32. Lines 130-140

    Negative description:

    Subject under suspicion:

    Check your answers with the key.

⑨ VOCABULARY REVIEW

Choose the best answer.

33. How might a basketball player be **penalized**?
    a. He might get more money.
    b. He might be forced to leave the game.
    c. He might make a basket.
    d. He might take a foul shot.

34. If Wilma doesn't **comprehend** what you are saying, she will most likely
    a. take offense at your comments.
    b. laugh at you.
    c. ignore you.
    d. ask you to explain what you mean.

35. If you have **expertise** in writing, you
    a. are learning how to write.
    b. never write.
    c. write well.
    d. always write.

36. An **intricate** puzzle
    a. has many colors.   c. is difficult to do.
    b. is very big.   d. is very small.

37. To **accommodate** very tall people, the airline
    a. refused to sell tickets to them.
    b. put more space between the rows of seats.
    c. didn't allow them to take any luggage to their seats.
    d. served dinner on larger trays.

38. If the members of Congress **authorize** troops to be sent to another country, then
    a. the troops will be able to go.
    b. the troops will not be able to go.
    c. it was Congress's idea to send the troops.
    d. it was not Congress's idea to send the troops.

39. Which of these is a **callous** statement?
    a. May I help you?
    b. Which way is the center of town?
    c. Don't bother me with your problems.
    d. The boat is sinking and I can't swim!

40. Two **decades** is
    a. 10 years.   c. 50 years.
    b. 20 years.   d. 200 years.

41. Alberto is waiting for his salary increase to **materialize**. He is waiting for his salary increase to
    a. be taken away.   c. be promised.
    b. take place.   d. be doubled.

42. If you have **compassion** for people, then you
    a. tease them.   c. help them.
    b. follow them.   d. ignore them.

Check your answers with the key.

HA-14 PERSUASION

WAR PROPAGANDA

ⓐ GETTING READY

What do you think of when you hear the word *propaganda*? Perhaps you think of the television commercials that interrupt your favorite shows. Or you might think of the political ads that bombard the newspapers and airways at election time. You probably know that Adolf Hitler launched a major propaganda campaign that was frighteningly effective in World War II. But do you ever think of George Washington as being propagandist? Probably not, but he was.

Propaganda is a means of spreading opinions, and it is used by all of us. Think of some ways that you yourself have used propaganda and the reasons why you used it. Do you think that your reasons warranted the methods used? Why or why not?

In this story, you will be learning about war propaganda that has been used as far back as the American Revolution. As you read, decide if you think the goals of the propagandists warranted the methods used. Also, think about what the consequences might have been if these people had not used propaganda.

106

VOCABULARY BUILDING

Study each key word to make sure you know its pronunciation and definition. Then study the way the word is used in the sentence based on the story.

accelerated (ak sel′ ə rāt′ əd) Caused to develop more quickly. *Saddam Hussein's accelerated build-up of arms was compared to that of Adolf Hitler.*

catastrophe (kə tas′ trə fē) A sudden disaster. *One leaflet warned of a catastrophe if Germans didn't surrender.*

competent (kom′ pə tənt) Well qualified; capable. *Thomas Paine was a competent propagandist.*

disparaging (dis par′ ij ing) Belittling; condemning. *Samuel Adams used disparaging language when referring to the British soldiers.*

impelling (im pel′ ling) Driving forward. *William Randolph Hearst was partly responsible for impelling Americans to go to war with Spain.*

indifferent (in dif′ ər ənt) Having or showing no interest. *Samuel Adams wanted to unite indifferent Americans against the British.*

massacre (mas′ ə kər) The brutal killing of a large number of people or animals. *Adams said that the British soldiers had committed a "bloody massacre."*

occurrence (ə kėr′ əns) Event; incident. *This occurrence might have passed into obscurity.*

propaganda (prop′ ə gan′ də) Any plan or method for spreading opinions or beliefs. *Some people mistakenly believe that propaganda is a modern device used only by the enemy during wartime.*

reinforced (rē′ in fôrst′) Added support to; made more powerful or effective. *Hearst reinforced the image of the Spanish governor as a butcher with horror stories of tortured Cuban women and children.*

Now choose a word that fits in each of the following sentences. Write the best word for each sentence.

1. Tyrone's moving speech was responsible for _____ me to get involved in helping the homeless.

2. Kim's kind acts _____ my good opinion of her.

3. The increased need for durable goods accounts for the _____ production seen in the last few months.

4. The candidate sued the newspaper after reading the _____ remarks made about her by the editor.

5. The cruel queen was _____ to the suffering of her subjects.

6. The San Francisco earthquake of 1906 was a major _____.

7. Rather than having students merely memorize information, a _____ teacher will instruct them to ask questions about the world around them.

HA-14

8. General Custer led the brutal _____ of the Southern Cheyenne village.

9. Adolf Hitler was able to exercise great control over the German people because he was skillful in spreading _____ .

10. Going to work is an everyday _____ .

Check your answers with the key.

SPECIAL WORDS

leaflets (lēf′ lits) Small, flat or folded sheets of printed matter. *In the American Civil War, leaflets were widely used to try to persuade the enemy to surrender.*
loudspeakers (loud′ spē′ kərs) Devices for converting electrical impulses into sounds and for increasing this sound to the desired volume as in public address systems. *Now voices over loudspeakers urged the enemy to surrender.*

c PREVIEW

Read the first paragraph and the first sentence of each of the other paragraphs to discover what the story is about. Do this now.

Did you notice how the author organized the information in the selection? Below are some statements about the way the story is organized.

Based on what you learned from previewing the story, write *true* for each true statement and write *false* for each false statement.

11. _____ The story begins discussing propaganda in war and then moves on to peacetime uses.

12. _____ The story makes a general statement that propaganda is used by all sides in war and then supports this statement by using particular wars as examples.

13. _____ The story discusses war propaganda in sequence from the American Revolution through the Persian Gulf War.

14. _____ The story begins discussing propaganda in recent wars and then traces its use back to previous wars.

Check your answers with the key.

d READING

Now read the story to find out how propaganda has been used in war.

WAR PROPAGANDA
by Estelle Kleinman

Some people mistakenly believe that propaganda is a modern device used only by the enemy during wartime. The truth is that all sides use this effective "weapon" in war and that we use the same propaganda methods today as were used well over two hundred years ago.

In 1770, less than a dozen British soldiers were provoked by a Boston crowd of about sixty armed with clubs, stones, and bottles. Outnumbered and afraid, some of the soldiers fired on the crowd. This occurrence might have passed into obscurity except for an American patriot named Samuel Adams, who was a master of propaganda. Believing in American independence, Adams wanted to unite indifferent Americans against the British. To do this, he used disparaging language when referring to the British soldiers, labeling them "cold-blooded murderers" who had committed a "bloody massacre." In fact, the incident is known to this day as the Boston Massacre.

When the American Revolution began, Adams was joined by another competent American propagandist named Thomas Paine. Paine used stirring and simple language to appeal to the common person. To inspire his troops, George Washington had words from Paine's *The Crisis* read to them. In this pamphlet, Paine talks about the high value of "freedom" and states that "the coal" fueling "the flame of liberty" cannot be destroyed.

Washington himself was not bad at spreading propaganda. Knowing the reputation his frontiersmen had for their deadly accuracy with a rifle, Washington placed a story in a colonial newspaper with the following warning to the British: "The worst of them [frontiersmen] will put a ball into a man's head at a distance of 150 or 200 yards; therefore advise your officers who shall hereafter come out to America to settle their affairs in England before their departure."

In the American Civil War of 1861-1865, leaflets were widely used to try to persuade the enemy to surrender. Newspapers also played an important role in the propaganda war. The Richmond, Virginia, *Examiner* described Union soldiers as "brutal" men "drunken with wine, blood, and fury." Union newspapers used similar devices.

Newspapers played even a greater role in the Spanish-American War. In fact, publisher William Randolph Hearst was partly responsible for impelling Americans to go to war. In his newspaper, the *New York Journal*, Hearst used common propaganda methods to turn Americans against Spain while encouraging their support of Cuba's bid for independence. He compared Spain's rule of Cuba to England's harsh rule of America, thus stirring Americans' hatred of Spain and sympathy for Cuba. Referring to the Spanish governor of Cuba as a "butcher," Hearst reinforced this image with horror stories of tortured Cuban women and children. But most importantly, he credited Spain with the sinking of the American battleship *Maine*, even though there was strong evidence that the Cubans had actually been responsible. All these devices worked well: the United States went to war with Spain in 1898.

World War I was the first war in which all the governments concerned launched a full-scale propaganda campaign. Two weeks after the United States declared war against Germany in 1917, President Wilson set up the Committee of Public Information (CPI) to be run by George Creel, whose job it was to oversee the government's propaganda efforts. Soon, American propaganda leaflets aimed at unnerving enemy troops began appearing in German trenches. At home, Creel released books, articles, and posters aimed at getting Americans to rally behind the war effort. Particularly effective were slogans with strong emotional appeal and little real meaning like "The war to make the world safe for democracy."

By the beginning of World War II, propaganda was an essential part of government. The head of the propaganda organization in Great Britain held a cabinet rank. The Minister of Propaganda in Germany, Paul Joseph Goebbels, was second in power only to Adolf Hitler himself. In the United States, the propaganda department was called the Office of War Information (OWI).

To combat Hitler's powerful Nazi propaganda machine, the OWI used tried-and-true methods such as the dropping of leaflets. One such leaflet, warning of a catastrophe if Germans didn't surrender, stated, "German blood will sink into the German earth." Besides leaflets, now voices over loudspeakers urged the enemy to surrender. Radio was another new weapon in the propaganda war. The goal of the Voice of America was to unnerve the enemy and feed them deceptive information.

The propaganda effort in the Korean and Vietnam Wars was no less zealous. Once again, use was made of leaflets, loudspeakers, and the radio. American propaganda efforts included offering money and vocational training to enemy soldiers who would desert. One leaflet urging the enemy to surrender stated, "Thousands have done it; why not you? Come over, and join your buddies in the safety of the rear."

In the Persian Gulf War of 1991, support for the war in the United States was encouraged in a number of ways. Before and during the war, Iraq's leader Saddam Hussein was described as the new Hitler. Parallels were made between Hussein's gassing of the Kurds and Hitler's gassing of the Jews, between Iraq's aggression against Kuwait and Germany's aggression against Poland and Czechoslovakia, and between Hussein and Hitler's accelerated build-up of arms. The people of Iraq were described as the unfortunate followers of Hussein, "the butcher of Baghdad."

Next time you hear the word *propaganda*, don't dismiss it as a "dirty" trick used by evil individuals. To reject propaganda devices because people like Hitler used them is to reject devices that people like George Washington have also used. The goals are different, but the methods are the same.

COMPREHENSION CHECK

Choose the best answer.

CAUSE/EFFECT

15. Samuel Adams used disparaging language when referring to the British soldiers because he
    a. wanted to unite indifferent Americans against the British.
    b. needed to convince Thomas Paine to join his cause.
    c. knew the soldiers were very cruel.
    d. wanted the British to surrender.

CAUSE/EFFECT

16. What was at least partly responsible for causing Americans to go to war with Spain in 1898?
    a. Leaflets dropped by Cuba
    b. Propaganda in the *New York Journal*
    c. Propaganda in the *Examiner*
    d. Propaganda on the radio

INFERENCE

17. The fact that Hearst's propaganda worked so well indicates that
    a. people don't trust foreigners.
    b. the truth is the best method of persuasion.
    c. not many people read the *New York Journal*.
    d. people believe what they read in the newspapers.

SCANNING

18. The first war in which all the governments concerned launched a full-scale propaganda campaign was
    a. World War I.
    b. World War II.
    c. the Spanish-American War.
    d. the Korean War.

COMPARISONS

19. Which devices used in World War II were not used in World War I?
    a. Leaflets and slogans
    b. Newspapers and posters
    c. Loudspeakers and the radio
    d. Slogans and posters

INFERENCE

20. Why did propaganda become an essential part of government by the beginning of World War II?
    a. The common people strongly supported the use of propaganda.
    b. The heads of propaganda organizations forced the governments to use propaganda.
    c. The governments recognized the effectiveness of propaganda in the war effort.
    d. The government made a great deal of money by spreading propaganda.

SCANNING

21. In the Korean and Vietnam Wars, what did Americans offer enemy soldiers who deserted?
    a. Money and vocational training
    b. Shelter in the United States
    c. A position in the United States Armed Forces
    d. Protection from their officers

COMPARISON

22. Support for the Persian Gulf War was encouraged by comparing Saddam Hussein to
    a. Samuel Adams.
    b. George Creel.
    c. Paul Joseph Goebbels.
    d. Adolf Hitler.

AUTHOR'S VIEWPOINT

23. How does the author feel about propaganda?
    a. It is always wrong to use propaganda.
    b. It is always right to use propaganda.
    c. The use of propaganda can be right or wrong depending on the reasons for its use.
    d. Propaganda is not very effective.

MAIN IDEA

24. This story is mainly about
    a. the role newspapers play in war.
    b. the use of propaganda in various wars.
    c. how people in colonial times used propaganda.
    d. the evils of war propaganda.

Check your answers with the key.

SKILL PRACTICE
PERSUASION

The story discusses a number of **persuasion techniques** used during wartime to spread propaganda. Here are the names and definitions of some of these techniques and an example of each one. Notice that these techniques can be used by anyone trying to persuade you to do something.

A. **Name Calling** is used to persuade you that certain people or groups are bad.

Example: "My opponent in this election is a crooked, thieving, corrupt politician."

B. **Glittering Generalities** are terms that everyone agrees with or admires, but the general terms don't really give you any solid information.

Example: "We believe in peace for all nations."

C. **Negative Transfer** is used when a persuader associates some person or group with something that is bad so that you transfer your negative feelings to that person or group.

Example: "My opponent has been seen in photographs with known gangsters."

D. **The Bandwagon** method is used to get you to follow the crowd. The persuader wants to make you believe that everyone else is doing something—so you should do it too.

Example: "Everyone is running out to buy the latest best-seller by Marian Miller. Shouldn't you?"

E. **Fear** is used to persuade you that something unpleasant will happen if you don't do what the persuader wishes.

Example: "If you don't use a Swifty Smoke Detector, everything you own may go up in flames."

Reread the parts of the selection indicated by the line numbers below. Choose the persuasion technique that is used in each part you read.

25. Lines 18–21
    a. Name Calling
    b. Glittering Generalities
    c. Bandwagon
    d. Negative Transfer

26. Lines 31–34
    a. Name Calling
    b. Glittering Generalities
    c. Bandwagon
    d. Negative Transfer

27. Lines 40–45
    a. Glittering Generalities
    b. Bandwagon
    c. Negative Transfer
    d. Fear

28. Lines 50–53
    a. Name Calling
    b. Glittering Generalities
    c. Bandwagon
    d. Negative Transfer

29. Lines 65–69
    a. Glittering Generalities
    b. Bandwagon
    c. Negative Transfer
    d. Fear

30. Lines 69–73
    a. Name Calling
    b. Glittering Generalities
    c. Bandwagon
    d. Negative Transfer

31. Lines 91–92
    a. Name Calling
    b. Glittering Generalities
    c. Bandwagon
    d. Negative Transfer

32. Lines 107–108
    a. Glittering Generalities
    b. Bandwagon
    c. Negative Transfer
    d. Fear

33. Lines 121–123
    a. Name Calling
    b. Glittering Generalities
    c. Bandwagon
    d. Negative Transfer

34. Lines 135–137
    a. Glittering Generalities
    b. Bandwagon
    c. Negative Transfer
    d. Fear

35. Lines 138–140
    a. Name Calling
    b. Glittering Generalities
    c. Bandwagon
    d. Negative Transfer

Check your answers with the key.

ⓖ VOCABULARY REVIEW

Choose the best answer.

36. Which of these is a **catastrophe**?
    a. The explosion of a chemical factory
    b. A very big crop of corn
    c. A sneeze
    d. An election

37. Which of these is a **disparaging** statement?
    a. You're my best friend.
    b. You're a fine soldier.
    c. You're a sneaky coward.
    d. You're the tallest person here.

38. After the **massacre** of the villagers, the fighting ended. This means the fighting ended after many villagers
    a. ran away.
    b. surrendered.
    c. were captured.
    d. were killed.

39. A speech that **reinforced** my opinion
    a. made me change my mind.
    b. backed up my opinion.
    c. was based on my opinion.
    d. denied that my opinion was right.

40. Anna thinks campaign speeches are **propaganda**. She thinks they are
    a. too long.
    b. too short.
    c. fair.
    d. biased.

41. Which of these might lead to an **accelerated** production of building materials?
    a. A great number of people buying new homes
    b. Very high interest rates
    c. A small number of people buying new homes
    d. A Presidential election

42. Which of these is most likely to be an example of a **competent** doctor?
    a. A doctor who charges a high fee
    b. A doctor who fails to show up for an operation
    c. A doctor who cures patients
    d. A doctor who dresses well

43. If you are **indifferent** to the feelings of others, then you are
    a. thoughtful.
    b. uncaring.
    c. intelligent.
    d. unhappy.

44. Which of these is an **occurrence**?
    a. A bright red automobile
    b. The War of 1812
    c. Steak and potatoes
    d. A low-flying helicopter

45. If an advertisement on television was **impelling** a little boy to buy a toy, the child would most likely
    a. not want to buy the toy.
    b. turn the television off.
    c. ask his parents to buy the toy.
    d. ask his parents to buy a different toy.

Check your answers with the key.

HA-15 JUDGING RELEVANCE / FINDING PROOF

LETTERS FROM THE PAST

ⓐ GETTING READY

Have you ever written an informal letter like the one shown above? Through the ages, many, many people have written informal letters to relatives and friends.

This story tells about some ancient letters found in Egypt. They included letters similar to the one shown above.

Are you surprised that a letter such as this was written nearly two thousand years ago? Why or why not? What other kinds of problems similar to yours could people have written about in those ancient times?

When you read "Letters from the Past," you will find out how these letters lasted for more than a thousand years, who wrote them, what they wrote about, and how they were delivered.

VOCABULARY BUILDING

Study each key word to make sure you know its pronunciation and definition. Then study the way the word is used in the sentence based on the story.

agitating (aj′ ə tāt ing) Urging a matter vigorously. *One father had to deal with a son in the army who was agitating for a transfer to Coptos.*

entreats (en trēts′) Asks sincerely; pleads. *Some wives wrote lovingly, as this one, who entreats: "Send for me."*

harassed (har′ əsd) Bothered by annoying cares. *One harassed father had to deal with a son in the army who wanted a transfer.*

impromptu (im promp′ tü) Without preparation. *The letter writer asked the traveler to become an impromptu mail carrier.*

inevitably (in ev′ ə tə blē) Surely; certainly. *Most letters that we send inevitably end up in the trash.*

infantry (in′ fən trē) Army troops that fight on foot. *A son who was attached to the infantry at Alexandria wanted a transfer to Coptos.*

inscribed (in skrībd′) Written. *Many an ancient document has been uncovered just as legible as it was on the day when it was inscribed.*

ordeals (ôr dēlz′) Very unpleasant experiences. *All too frequently the journey was extended by traditional travelers' ordeals.*

profusion (prə fyü′ zhən) Great abundance. *The paper was made of strips sliced from the stalks of reeds that once grew in profusion along the Nile.*

ravages (rav′ ij iz) Severe damages. *In Egypt, rain is so scarce that even the most fragile substance, spared the ravages of dampness, can last forever.*

Now choose a word that fits in each of the following sentences. Write the best word for each sentence.

1. The field was covered with wheat growing in _____ .

2. The movie star's name was _____ in the cement.

3. Jack will join the _____ after he finishes basic training at Fort Benning.

4. If I water the garden today, it will _____ rain tomorrow.

5. When Carlos won first prize, he gave an _____ speech.

6. Fran had no idea of the _____ she would endure when she decided to travel across the desert.

7. These trees have been bent into weird shapes by the _____ of time and weather.

8. When his father goes on a trip, Tito always _____ him to bring home a surprise.

9. Is it any wonder that I felt _____ when the phone kept ringing, the refrigerator broke, and the children began to fight?

10. The residents of this neighborhood are _____ for necessary repairs to the streets.

Check your answers with the key.

HA-15

SPECIAL WORDS

drachmas (drak′ məz) Ancient Greek units of money. *Please give the bearers of this letter two talents and 300 drachmas to pay for transportation.*

talents (tal ənts) Ancient units of money, used in parts of the Middle East. (See **drachmas** for sample sentence.)

c PREVIEW

Read the first two paragraphs and the first sentence of the other paragraphs to discover what the story is about. Do this now.

The author compares letter-writing today with that of ancient Egypt. Did you notice some things that were similar and some that were different?

Based on what you learned from previewing the story, answer these questions.

11. Name two ways in which ancient letter-writing was different from letter-writing today.

12. Name one way in which ancient letter-writing was the same as letter-writing today.

Check your answers with the key.

d READING

Now read the story to learn about the letters people wrote in ancient Egypt.

LETTERS FROM THE PAST
by Lionel Casson

"You did a fine thing! You didn't take me with you to the city! If you don't want to take me to Alexandria, I won't write you a letter, I won't talk to you. You did a fine thing: you sent me presents! Chicken feed! Send for me, please! If you don't send, I won't eat, I won't drink! That's what will happen."

This letter, in a child's clumsy hand, was sent sometime in the 3rd century A.D. by Theon Jr. from his hometown up the Nile to Theon Sr. at Alexandria.

Many letters from the past have been collected and published because of the fame or writing ability of the authors. But there are few collections of letters written by the likes of Theon Jr., letters of the kind we ourselves are constantly sending and which inevitably end up in the trash. That was the fate of such letters in the ancient world as well—with one important exception. In Egypt, where Theon lived, rain is so scarce that even the most fragile substance, spared the ravages of dampness and protected from wind and sun under a blanket of dry sand, can last forever.

The language in these letters was simple, everyday Greek. The letters were written on paper made of strips sliced from the stalks of reeds that once grew in profusion along the Nile. The paper is thicker and heavier than what we use today, but it is of good quality. Pens were pointed reeds and the ink a mix of fine soot, gum, and water. Both paper and ink were tough: many an ancient document has been uncovered just as legible as it was on the day when it was inscribed.

If writing a letter in those times was not much different from now, actually sending it was as different as can be. There was no public post for private letters. A writer had to track down a traveler who happened to be headed toward the desired destination.

After correspondents had found someone going in the right direction, they had to give careful instructions about delivery, since only main streets bore names. Anyone who has tried to find the way to a remote dinner party, following directions given on the phone by a rattled host, will sympathize.

Apart from the address, and an impromptu mailman, the letters people wrote to each other in that remote world could have been written today. Well-to-do travelers of the time often wrote back to report a safe arrival. All too frequently the journey was extended by traditional travelers' ordeals. A distracted daughter writes to her mother:

"I want you to know that on January 8 I went to Tyrannis but I found no way I could get to you, since the camel-drivers didn't want to go to Oxyrhynchus. So now I've thought it best to forward the baggage to Antinoe and wait there till I can find a boat and can sail. Please give the bearers of this letter two talents and 300 drachmas to pay for transportation."

The situation is still familiar: no connections available and funds running short. Only today it is drivers of taxis, not camels, who refuse to take you where you want to go. And, when you run out of money, you telephone and receive a check or money order instead of having to depend upon impatient messengers to pick up a sack of coins.

Boys left home for military service but not for just a year or so. They signed on for a full hitch, and in the Roman armed forces that meant 20 to 25 years for the army, 26 for the navy—in effect, a lifetime commitment. To many, the sacrifice was well worth it—a respected profession, fair enough pay, and, for a native Egyptian, Roman citizenship when he left the service (if he managed to last that long).

"I want you to know, Mother," writes one young naval recruit, "that I arrived safely at

Rome on May 20, and that I was assigned to Misenum. Please, Mother, take good care of yourself. And don't worry about me—I've come to a good place!"

That letter is full of hope and enthusiasm, but one from another youngster who joined the army has nothing but complaints:

"On receiving this letter it would be very nice of you if you sent me 200 drachmas because I bought a mule carriage and spent all my change on it. Send me a heavy cape, a rain-cape with hood, a pair of leather wraps, oil, and the washbasin as you promised. For the rest, then Mother, send me my monthly allowance right away. You sent me nothing. You left me this way without a thing. You just left me this way, like a dog. So, please, Mother, send me, don't neglect me this way."

The mother might well have been dismayed on receiving such an outburst: if her beloved was able to buy himself a mule carriage, she must have sent him off with plenty of money; in 300 B.C. that was the equivalent of buying a car today.

Parents had other problems with their spoiled children. One harassed father had to deal with a son who, attached to the infantry at Alexandria, was agitating for transfer to Coptos, where his family lived. The father explains it all in a letter to his brother:

"I have written you before about my boy taking service in a legion. However, since he no longer wanted to serve in a legion but in a division, I had to go and see him, even though I didn't want to. So, after much pleading on the part of his mother and sister, I went to Alexandria and used ways and means till he was transferred to the division at Coptos."

How familiar it sounds! The son expresses a wish; the adoring mother and sister badger the father to pull strings. In those days, the distance from Coptos to Alexandria and back again was 1200 miles by boat, a trip of better than two weeks even if the vessel traveled night and day. Small wonder Father "didn't want to."

We have lingered over letters from children to parents. There are as many preserved between the parents themselves since husbands were often away on business. Some wives wrote lovingly, as this one who entreats: "Send for me—if you don't I'll die without seeing you daily. How I wish I could fly and come to you."

Good children and spoiled children, harassed parents and loving wives—they speak from the correspondence of that bygone age just as they do today.

COMPREHENSION CHECK

Choose the best answer.

INFERENCE
△ 13. The boy who wrote the first letter was probably
   a. shy.   c. tall.
   b. spoiled.   d. grown up.

CAUSE / EFFECT
14. How did the letters quoted in the story happen to be preserved?
   a. They were buried in dry sand.
   b. People in ancient Egypt saved everything.
   c. The Romans put them in museums.
   d. The armed forces saved them.

COMPARISON
15. The author compares the search for a hard-to-find address in ancient Egypt with
   a. joining the army.
   b. taking a boat trip down the Nile.
   c. taking a camel ride in the desert.
   d. getting to a dinner party in a remote area.

PROBLEM / SOLUTION
16. Because there was no mail delivery, a letter writer had
   a. to take the letter himself or herself.
   b. to ask the Roman army to deliver it.
   c. to ask a traveler to deliver it.
   d. to hire a camel driver to deliver it.

SCANNING
17. The boat trip from Coptos to Alexandria took about
   a. one day.   c. one week.
   b. five days.   d. two weeks.

CAUSE / EFFECT
18. Why are many of the ancient documents that have been found still legible today? (Choose all the correct answers.)
   a. Because good quality paper was used.
   b. Because the sun dried out the documents.
   c. Because the people had nice handwriting.
   d. Because durable ink was used.

INFERENCE
△ 19. At the time when the letters were written, Egypt was
   a. building up a huge army.
   b. developing a public mail-delivery system.
   c. part of the Roman Empire.
   d. at war with Rome.

INFERENCE
△ 20. The father of the soldier who wanted to be transferred was probably
   a. very poor.
   b. wealthy.
   c. a captain in the Roman army.
   d. missing his son very much.

FACT / OPINION
21. Which of these sentences from the story are opinions?
   a. The language in these letters was simple, everyday Greek.
   b. You just left me this way, like a dog.
   c. I've come to a good place.
   d. I went to Tyrannis, but I found no way I could get to you.

MAIN IDEA
○ 22. This story tells mainly about
   a. how studying objects from ancient Egypt tells about how people lived then.
   b. how ancient Egypt was similar to the United States in many ways.
   c. how problems of day-to-day life have not changed much in 2,000 years.
   d. how ancient everyday Egyptian letters resemble those we might write today.

Check your answers with the key.

SKILL PRACTICE
JUDGING RELEVANCE / FINDING PROOF

Suppose you have been told some things about ancient Egypt for the period around 300 A.D., and you want to find out whether these things are true.

You would go to the library and look in the card catalog for books that have **relevant** information—that is, information about ancient Egypt. You can tell from the book titles that some books have relevant information, that other books do not, and you can only guess about others.

For example, *A History of Ancient Egypt,* by P. R. Jackson, probably has relevant information. *Egypt's Role in the United Nations,* by C. T. Simone, probably does not have relevant information. *Life Along the Nile,* by L. M. White, may or may not have relevant information.

If you saw the following book titles in the card catalog under "Egypt," which ones do you think would have information about ancient Egypt?

Write *R* for each title that would have relevant information. Write *N* for each title that would not have relevant information. Write *?* for titles that might or might not have relevant information.

23. ____ *Modern Egypt,* by Tom Little

24. ____ *Art and Architecture of Ancient Egypt,* by W. S. Smith

25. ____ *Egyptian Customs,* by K. C. Steele

26. ____ *Egypt and the Roman Empire,* by A. C. Johnson

Check your answers with the key.

Once you find several books with relevant information you can look for proof. That is, you can discover whether the things you were told are true or not.

To find proof, scan each book until you find the information you need. If the books support what you were told, then what you were told is **valid**—that is, true. If not, then what you were told is **not valid** and, therefore, untrue.

Suppose someone told you that the statements below are about ancient Egypt around the third century A.D. You want to check these statements to see if they are valid or not valid. Use the story as your source of true information.

Scan the story until you find proof that a statement is either true or not true. Write *valid* for each true statement. Write *not valid* for each untrue statement. Write the line numbers from the story where you find the proof.

	Valid or Not Valid	Line Number	
27.	_____	_____	Paper was made from reed stalks.
28.	_____	_____	Alexandria was a city.
29.	_____	_____	Everyday letters were written in Greek.
30.	_____	_____	The Roman army had trouble recruiting Egyptian men.
31.	_____	_____	A normal tour of duty in the Roman army was about five years.

Check your answers with the key.

VOCABULARY REVIEW

Choose the best answer.

32. If Angie sang an **impromptu** song, she
    a. practiced it for a long time.
    b. sang very loudly.
    c. made it up on the spot.
    d. had a very high voice.

33. If weeds grow in **profusion** in my garden,
    a. there are a few young weeds.
    b. there are lots of weeds.
    c. there are no weeds.
    d. there are weeds in one corner.

34. Who is in the **infantry**?
    a. A baby sitter   c. A soldier
    b. A baby   d. A letter carrier

35. Ruby had many **ordeals** getting her car repaired. This means she
    a. had no problems getting it fixed.
    b. had many problems getting it fixed.
    c. got it painted.
    d. had many offers to sell it.

36. Which of these **inevitably** happens daily?
    a. The sun rises.
    b. Your letter gets lost in the mail.
    c. A taxi driver gets lost.
    d. A soldier gets transferred.

37. You would most likely be **harassed** by
    a. a whining child.
    b. a long letter from a friend.
    c. a trip that lasts several hours.
    d. a caring mother.

38. Someone who **entreats** you
    a. orders you to go away.
    b. refuses to lend you money.
    c. pays for your dinner.
    d. wants something badly.

39. If you are **agitating** for a raise, you are
    a. dreaming about getting a raise.
    b. trying to convince your boss to pay you more.
    c. worried because you need more money.
    d. upset because others are getting paid more than you.

40. The **ravages** of rain might cause
    a. flowers to bloom.
    b. birds to sing.
    c. river banks to crumble.
    d. puddles to form.

41. Mojo **inscribed** his name on a book. This means he
    a. wrote his name.
    b. admired his name.
    c. read his name.
    d. erased his name.

Check your answers with the key.

HA-16 SETTING / TONE / THEME

THE MAN WHO PUT UP AT GADSBY'S

ⓐ GETTING READY

Has anyone ever given you advice that you didn't take, but later wished you had? What happened? Do you think you learn better by someone telling you what to do or by experience? Why?

The man shown on the left above is new in town. He is trying to conduct business in the way he is used to doing. But he is in Washington, D.C., which has its own way of doing things.

"The Man Who Put Up at Gadsby's" is not in the picture. When you read the story, you will find out why the man who stayed at Gadsby's has an important lesson for the new man in town.

VOCABULARY BUILDING

Study each key word to make sure you know its pronunciation and definition. Then study the way the word is used in the sentence based on the story.

blandly (bland′ lē) In a smoothly agreeable or polite manner. *Riley blandly turned on his heel and left the astonished schoolteacher.*

confirmed (kən fėrmd′) Formally approved. *After I get appointed to the job, I'll go to the executive session of the Senate—got to get the appointment confirmed.*

delegation (del′ ə gā′ shən) Group of representatives. *Now I want you to go around with me to the Pacific delegation.*

gawk (gôk) Stare stupidly. *He just wanted to see those green Tennesseans stare and gawk when they saw him riding along.*

hale (hāl) Healthy. *I'm just fifty-seven, hale and hearty—there ain't anything in the world so splendid as a tramp on foot through the fresh spring woods.*

hearty (här′ tē) Full of energy; vigorous. (See **hale** for sample sentence.)

meditatively (med′ ə tā′ tiv lē) Thoughtfully; with reflection. *"Yes," said Riley meditatively. "You are right again."*

musing (myü′ zing) Pondering; absorbed in thought. *He left the astonished schoolteacher, a musing and motionless snow image.*

patriarch (pā′ trē ärk) A respected elderly man. *I'm great friends with that old patriarch.*

reverie (rev′ ər ē) Condition of being lost in dreamy thoughts or imaginings. *Riley stood silent, apparently deep in reverie, during a minute or more.*

Now choose a word that fits in each of the following sentences. Write the best word for each sentence.

1. I like to listen when the town _____ tells his stories about the old days.

2. Ten people in the Ohio _____ voted for the amendment.

3. Ted _____ helped Doris on with her coat.

4. Barry stared into space, unseeing and unhearing, deep in _____ .

5. Carla responded _____ to her daughter's questions about death.

6. The crowd turned to _____ at the strange vehicle rumbling up the street.

7. The Senate _____ the President's choice for Secretary of State.

8. Arnold joined in the loud _____ singing around the fire.

9. In the art gallery, the _____ art critic carefully considered each entry.

10. Grandmother was still _____ at the age of ninety.

Check your answers with the key.

HA-16

SPECIAL WORDS

postmastership (pōst' mas' tər ship) The job of being in charge of a post office. *As soon as I heard the San Francisco postmastership was vacant, I made up my mind to get it.*

saddle-girth (sad' l gėrth) A band of leather or other material that circles the body of a horse to fasten the saddle to its back. *He sold the saddle—said he wasn't going to risk his life with any perishable saddle-girth while he could ride bareback.*

sulky (sul' kē) A light one-horse open carriage. *He sold the buggy and bought the remains of an old sulky.*

---

c PREVIEW

Read the first five paragraphs to discover how the story begins. Do this now.

So far you have been introduced to three characters in the story—the narrator, Mr. Riley, and Mr. Lykins. Just from what you've read, you've learned something about these characters.

Below are some statements about the characters.

Based on what you learned from previewing the story, write *true* if the statement gives correct information about the character. Write *false* if the information is not correct.

11. _____ Mr. Lykins is in a great hurry.

12. _____ The narrator does not like Mr. Riley.

13. _____ Mr. Lykins seems to be a man of action.

14. _____ Mr. Riley is not polite to Mr. Lykins.

15. _____ Mr. Lykins has come to Washington from San Francisco to get a postmastership.

Check your answers with the key.

---

d READING

Now read the story to find out how Mr. Riley tries to help Mr. Lykins.

THE MAN WHO PUT UP AT GADSBY'S
by Mark Twain

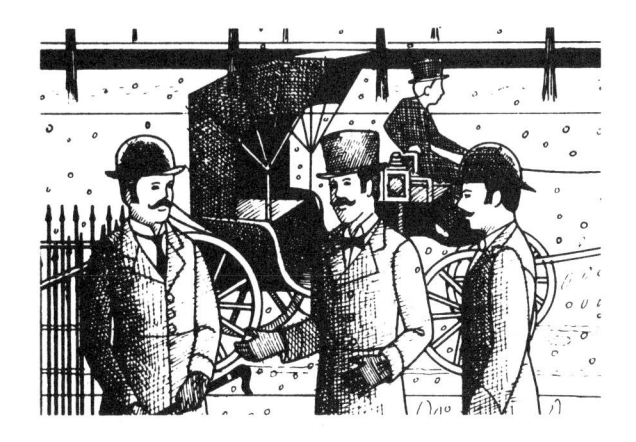

When my friend Riley and I were in Washington, in the winter of '67, we were coming down Pennsylvania Avenue one night, in a driving storm of snow, when the flash of a street lamp fell upon a man who was tearing along in the opposite direction. This man instantly stopped and exclaimed, "You are Mr. Riley, ain't you?"

Riley stopped and said, "I am Mr. Riley. Did you happen to be looking for me?"

"That's just what I was doing," said the man joyously. "My name is Lykins. I'm one of the teachers of the high school in San Francisco. As soon as I heard the San Francisco postmastership was vacant, I made up my mind to get it—and here I am."

"Yes," said Riley, slowly. "Here you are. And have you got it?"

"Well, not exactly got it, but I've brought a petition signed by more than two hundred people. Now I want you to go around with me to the Pacific delegation. I want to rush this thing through and get along home."

"If the matter is so pressing, you will prefer that we visit the delegation tonight," said Riley, in a voice which had nothing mocking in it—to an unaccustomed ear.

"By all means! I haven't got any time to fool around."

"Yes . . . When did you arrive?"

"An hour ago."

"When are you intending to leave?"

"For New York, tomorrow evening—for San Francisco, next morning."

"Just so . . . What are you going to do tomorrow?"

"Do! Why, I've got to go to the President and the delegation, and get the appointment haven't I?"

"Yes . . . And then what?"

"Executive session of the Senate—got to get the appointment confirmed."

"Yes," said Riley meditatively. "You are right again. Then you take the train for New York in the evening and the boat for San Francisco next morning?"

"That's the way I map it out!"

Riley considered a while and then said:

"You couldn't stay . . . well, say two days longer?"

"Bless your soul, no!"

Riley stood silent, apparently deep in reverie, during a minute or more. Then he looked up and said, "Have you ever heard about that man who put up at Gadsby's?" He backed Mr. Lykins against an iron fence and proceeded to unfold his narrative. "I will tell you about that man. Gadsby's was once the principal hotel around these parts. Well, this man arrived from Tennessee about nine o'clock one morning, with a splendid four-horse carriage and an elegant dog, which he was evidently fond and proud of. He drove up before Gadsby's, and everybody rushed out to take charge of him, but he said, 'Never mind,' and jumped out. He told his coachman to wait—said he only had a little claim against the government to collect, would run across the way to the Treasury and fetch the money, and then get right along back to Tennessee, for he was in a hurry.

"Well, about eleven o'clock that night he came back and told them to put the horses up—said he would collect the claim in the morning. This was in January, 1834—the 3rd of January.

"Well, on the 5th of February he sold the fine carriage, and bought a second-hand one—said it would answer just as well, and he didn't care for style.

"On the 11th of August he sold a pair of the fine horses—said he'd often thought a pair was better than four, to go over the rough mountain roads with, where a body had to be careful about his driving.

"On the 13th of December he sold another

horse—said one could drag his old light vehicle along faster than was absolutely necessary, now that it was good solid winter weather and the roads were in splendid condition.

"On the 17th of February, 1835, he sold the old carriage and bought a cheap second-hand buggy—said a buggy was just the trick to skim along mushy, slushy early spring roads.

"On the 1st of August he sold the buggy and bought the remains of an old sulky—said he just wanted to see those green Tennesseans stare and gawk when they saw him riding along in a sulky.

"On the 15th of February, 1837, he sold the sulky and bought a saddle—said he wasn't about to risk his neck going over those mountain roads on wheels in the dead of winter, not if he knew himself.

"On the 9th of April he sold the saddle—said he wasn't going to risk his life with any perishable saddle-girth while he could ride bareback—always had despised to ride on a saddle, anyway.

"On the 24th of April he sold his horse—said 'I'm just fifty-seven today, hale and hearty—it would be a pretty howdy-do for me to be wasting such a trip as that and such weather as this on a horse, when there ain't anything in the world so splendid as a tramp on foot through the fresh spring woods. And I can make my dog carry my claim in a little bundle anyway.'

"On the 22nd of June he sold his dog—said 'A dog is a perfect nuisance—chases the squirrels, barks at everything—a man can't get any chance to reflect and enjoy nature.' "

There was a pause and a silence—except the noise of wind and the pelting snow. Mr. Lykins said, impatiently, "Well?"

Riley said, "Well—that was thirty years ago."

"Very well, very well—what of it?"

"I'm great friends with that old patriarch. He comes every evening to tell me good-bye. I saw him an hour ago—he's off for Tennessee early tomorrow morning—as usual."

Another silent pause. The stranger broke it, "Is that all?"

"That is all."

"Well for the time of night, and the kind of night, it seems to me the story was full long enough. But what's it all for?"

"Oh, nothing in particular."

"Well, where's the point of it?"

"Oh, there isn't any particular point to it. Only, if you are not in too much of a hurry to rush off to San Francisco with that post-office appointment, Mr. Lykins, I'd advise you to 'put up at Gadsby's' for a spell."

So saying, Riley blandly turned on his heel and left the astonished school teacher, a musing and motionless snow image shining in the glow of the street lamp.

He never got that postmastership.

COMPREHENSION CHECK

Choose the best answer.

SCANNING

16. Why was Mr. Lykins looking for Mr. Riley?
    a. He wanted Mr. Riley to help get him appointed postmaster.
    b. He wanted Mr. Riley to tell him who to see to get the job of postmaster.
    c. He wanted Mr. Riley to go to San Francisco with him.
    d. He wanted Mr. Riley to explain how people did things in Washington.

CHARACTER / FEELINGS

17. Mr. Riley thought that Mr. Lykins was
    a. brave.   c. tired.
    b. foolish.   d. callous.

CHARACTER / FEELINGS

18. Mr. Riley was
    a. annoyed and frightened.
    b. angry but helpful.
    c. thoughtful and considerate.
    d. polite but mocking.

INFERENCE

△ 19. What did Mr. Riley mean when he told Mr. Lykins to " 'put up at Gadsby's' for a spell"?
    a. Mr. Lykins should check into the hotel to get out of the snow.
    b. Mr. Lykins could wait forever for the postmastership.
    c. Mr. Lykins could get the postmastership if he checked into the hotel.
    d. Mr. Lykins could get the postmastership if he bribed the hotel owner.

PROBLEM / SOLUTION

20. Why did the man who stayed at Gadsby's keep on selling his possessions?
    a. To fit in with the style of other people in Washington
    b. To make his life simpler and easier
    c. To raise money so he could stay in Washington
    d. To give to the men in the Treasury Department

SEQUENCE

21. According to the story, which happened last?
    a. The man sold his dog.
    b. The man sold his sulky.
    c. The man sold his saddle.
    d. The man sold his buggy.

INFERENCE

△ 22. Why did the man who put up at Gadsby's give false reasons for selling his possessions?
    a. He didn't want to admit that it was taking so long to finish his business.
    b. He didn't want to leave Washington and go back to Tennessee.
    c. He didn't want anyone to know that he didn't like horses and dogs.
    d. He didn't want anyone to know that he had lost his job.

INFERENCE

△ 23. When did the man who put up at Gadsby's collect his claim from the Treasury?
    a. The first day
    b. Three years later
    c. Thirty years later
    d. Never

INFERENCE

△ 24. Why didn't Mr. Lykins ever become a postmaster?
    a. Because he didn't stay at Gadsby's.
    b. Because he didn't have enough signatures on his petition.
    c. Because there is no way to rush getting things done in Washington.
    d. Because he didn't work quickly enough, and Mr. Riley became the postmaster.

MAIN IDEA

○ 25. This story is mainly about a man who
    a. learns the hard way how to act in Washington in order to be appointed postmaster.
    b. wants to become a postmaster but doesn't understand that there is no way to make things happen quickly in Washington.
    c. is in too much of a hurry to listen to a story about a man who tried to collect money from the government.
    d. learns that he is better off having nothing to do with Washington politicians.

Check your answers with the key.

SKILL PRACTICE
SETTING / TONE / THEME

The **setting** of a story is the time and place in which the story takes place. The setting may change during the story, or the narrator might be telling about an event that happened in another time and place.

The **tone** is the mood of a story. For example, the tone could be happy, sad, funny, exciting, or any combination of these feelings. The author may use descriptive words, such as *cold* and *lonely*, to set a tone of despair. The events of a story do more to set the tone, as in this example:

> Lucia wandered through the woods for hours, trying vainly to find her way back to the campsite. When darkness descended, she was still hopelessly lost.

The event of being lost in the woods at night sets a tone of fear and helplessness.

The **theme** of a story is the lesson or message the author wants to tell the reader. Most often, the author does not state the theme. The reader must add up the clues to find the point the author is trying to make.

Below are some questions about the setting, tone, and theme of "The Man Who Put Up at Gadsby's." Refer back to the story if you need help answering the questions.

Answer the following questions.

26. Name the city and year in which the main story takes place.

27. Name the city and the years in which the story that Mr. Riley tells takes place.

28. What is the tone of "The Man Who Put Up at Gadsby's"?
    a. Funny
    b. Sad
    c. Suspenseful
    d. Violent

29. Which of the following helps set the tone of the story?
    a. Mr. Lykins does not really know how to run a post office.
    b. The exaggerations in the story about the man who put up at Gadsby's
    c. Mr. Riley talks too fast.
    d. Mr. Riley does not really know how to help Mr. Lykins.

30. What is the theme of "The Man Who Put Up at Gadsby's"?
    a. People have to adapt to the situations in which they find themselves.
    b. People should learn to slow down.
    c. People should learn to accept people who are different.
    d. People shouldn't expect results without a lot of effort.

Check your answers with the key.

VOCABULARY REVIEW

Choose the best answer.

31. When Barbara's vacation was **confirmed**, it was
    a. cancelled.
    b. finished.
    c. approved.
    d. paid for.

32. If Sandra disturbed the **musing** student, she bothered someone who was
    a. lost in thought.
    b. taking a music lesson.
    c. telling a funny story.
    d. dialing the telephone.

33. If you read **meditatively**, you
    a. read quickly.
    b. read religious books.
    c. read for long periods of time.
    d. carefully thought over what you read.

34. Which of these might be a **patriarch**?
    a. A boy starting college
    b. The oldest man in town
    c. A young man just arriving in town
    d. A man celebrating his 30th birthday

35. If you **gawk** at people, you might be told to stop
    a. calling them names.
    b. pointing at them.
    c. staring at them.
    d. ignoring them.

36. Marna saw the **delegation**. She saw
    a. an auto accident.
    b. a crime.
    c. a group of people.
    d. a long move.

37. The audience gave Shana **hearty** applause. They clapped
    a. softly.
    b. loudly.
    c. politely.
    d. not at all.

38. If you feel **hale**, you might want to
    a. see a doctor.
    b. sleep all day.
    c. go on a hike.
    d. tell your problems to a friend.

39. Someone who is deep in **reverie** is
    a. not paying attention to you.
    b. shivering from the cold.
    c. too angry to speak.
    d. in debt to everyone.

40. Jack **blandly** ordered the most expensive watch in the store. Jack ordered the watch
    a. nervously.
    b. angrily.
    c. happily.
    d. smoothly.

Check your answers with the key.

HA-17 CHARACTER AND FEELINGS

THE NECKLACE — PART ONE

a GETTING READY

Most people long for things they know they can never have. What are some of the things you dream of having, but feel are out of your reach? How would you feel if someone told you your dreams could come true for just one day? How would you feel at the end of that day when everything was taken away from you?

The woman shown in the picture above constantly wishes she was rich. She wants an elegant home, beautiful gowns, and expensive jewelry. But she and her husband are just getting by on his salary as a clerk, and they do not have money for luxuries.

The woman and her husband are living in Paris in the late 1800s, a time when the rich loved to display their wealth in a spectacular and showy manner. This made it particularly difficult for the woman in the story because she wants to be a part of that lifestyle.

When you read "The Necklace — Part One," you will find out how the woman realizes part of her dream.

b VOCABULARY BUILDING

Study each key word to make sure you know its pronunciation and definition. Then study the way the word is used in the sentence based on the story.

adornments (ə dôrn′ mənts) Ornaments; decorations. *She tried on a pearl necklace and many other adornments in front of the mirror.*

adulation (aj′ ə lā′ shən) Excessive praise. *At the party, she was in the triumph of her beauty, the pride of her success, in a kind of happy cloud composed of all the adulation.*

dinginess (din′ jē nes) The state of being dull or dirty-looking. *She grieved over the shabbiness of her apartment, the dinginess of the walls.*

dowry (dou′ rē) Money or property that a woman in some societies brings to her husband when she marries. *With no dowry, no way of any kind of being met, loved, and married by a man both rich and famous, she finally married a petty clerk.*

ecstasy (ek′ stə sē) Great delight; overwhelming happiness. *Clasping the necklace around her throat, she stood in ecstasy looking at her reflection.*

incessantly (in ses′ nt lē) Continually, without stopping. *Because she was poor, she grieved incessantly, feeling that she had been born for all the luxuries of living.*

irritated (ir′ ə tāt id) Angry; annoyed. *When her husband showed her the invitation, she gave him an irritated glance and spoke to him impatiently.*

pauper (pô′ pər) Someone who is very poor. *"It is embarrassing not to have a jewel or a gem—nothing to wear on my dress. I'll look like a pauper."*

predicament (pri dik′ ə mənt) A difficult or unpleasant situation. *Thinking that Mme. Forestier might lend her a jewel, she told her friend of her predicament.*

prosperous (pros′ pər əs) Well-off; successful. *Because she was poor, she had no way of being married by a man both prosperous and famous.*

Now choose a word that fits in each of the following sentences. Write the best word for each sentence.

1. Ralph can afford luxuries because he runs a _____ business.

2. "Stop it!" he said in an _____ voice.

3. After Saul lost all his money in a bad business deal, he was a

   _____ .

4. Kit was falsely accused of stealing, and she told a lawyer about her

   _____ .

5. Jane hoped to get rid of the _____ of the room by repainting it.

6. In rural areas a hundred years ago, a woman's _____ might include some cattle.

7. The baby cried _____ all night long.

8. Luis admired the _____ on Donna's hat.

HA-17

9. The popular singer received the _____ of his fans.

10. Georgina was in _____ when she found out that she had won the trip to Hawaii.

Check your answers with the key.

SPECIAL WORDS

francs (frangks) Unit of money in France. *For ten francs you can get two or three magnificent roses.*

M. (mə syèr′) Mr.; short for the French word *Monsieur*.

Mme. (mə dəm′) Mrs.; short for the French word *Madame*. *The Minister of Education begs M. and Mme. Loisel to do him the honor of attending an evening reception on Friday, January 18.*

c PREVIEW

Read the first three paragraphs to discover how the story begins. Do this now.

The woman you just read about is the main character of the story. Did you notice that the author has already told you many things about this woman? Below are some descriptions of the woman in the story.

Based on what you learned from previewing the story, write *yes* for each word that describes the woman. Write *no* for each word that does not.

The woman in the story is

11. _____ pretty.

12. _____ unhappy.

13. _____ content.

14. _____ poor.

15. _____ divorced.

Check your answers with the key.

d READING

Now read the story to find out what happens to help make some of the woman's dreams come true.

THE NECKLACE — PART ONE
by Guy de Maupassant

She was one of those pretty and charming girls, born, as if by an accident of fate, into a family of clerks. With no dowry, no way of any kind of being met, loved, and married by a man both prosperous and famous, she finally married a minor clerk in the Ministry of Education.

She dressed plainly because she could not afford fine clothes, but was as unhappy as a woman who has come down in the world.

She grieved incessantly, feeling that she had been born for all the luxuries of living. She grieved over the shabbiness of her apartment, the dinginess of the walls, the worn-out appearance of the chairs. All these things, which another woman of her class would not even have noticed, gnawed at her and made her furious. She would dream of silent chambers, draped with tapestries and lighted by tall bronze floor lamps.

She would dream of great reception halls hung with old silks of fine furniture, and of small, stylish sitting rooms just right for the four o'clock chat with distinguished and sought-after men.

When dining at the table, which was covered for the third day with the same cloth, her husband would declare delightedly, "Ah! A good stew! There's nothing I like better." But she would dream of fashionable dinner parties, of gleaming silverware; she would dream of delicious dishes served on wonderful china, of gallant compliments whispered and listened to with a secret smile.

She had no evening clothes, no jewels, nothing. But those were the things she wanted. She so much longed to be envied, fascinating, and sought after.

She had a well-to-do friend whom she would no longer go to see, simply because she would feel so distressed on returning home. And she would weep for days on end from vexation and despair.

Then one evening, her husband came home proudly holding out a large envelope.

"Look," he said, "I've got something for you."

She excitedly tore open the envelope and pulled out a printed card bearing these words:

"The Minister of Education begs M. and Mme. Loisel to do him the honor of attending an evening reception on Friday, January 18."

Instead of being delighted, she scornfully tossed the invitation on the table, murmuring, "What good is that to me?"

"But, my dear, I thought you'd be thrilled. You never get a chance to go out, and this is a real affair! I had an awful time getting a card. Not many clerks have a chance at one. You'll see all the most important people there."

She gave him an irritated glance and burst out impatiently, "What do you think I have to go in?"

He hadn't given that a thought. He stammered, "Why, the dress you wear when we go to the theater. That looks quite nice, I think."

He stopped talking, dazed and distracted to see his wife burst out weeping. He gasped, "Why, what's the matter? What's the trouble?"

By sheer will power she answered in a calm voice while wiping the tears from her cheeks: "I don't have an evening dress and therefore I can't go to that affair. Give the card to some friend at the office whose wife can dress better than I can."

He was stunned. He said, "Let's see, Mathilde. How much would a suitable outfit cost—something very simple?"

She thought it over, going over her allowance and thinking of the amount she could ask for without bringing an immediate refusal.

Finally, she answered hesitatingly, "I think with four hundred francs I could manage it."

He turned a bit pale, for he had set aside just that amount to buy a rifle. However, he said, "All right. I'll give you four hundred francs. But try to get a nice dress."

As the day of the party approached, Mme. Loisel seemed moody. Her outfit was ready, however. Her husband said to her one evening, "What's the matter? You've been all out of sorts for three days."

And she answered, "It's embarrassing not to have a jewel or a gem—nothing to wear on my dress. I'll look like a pauper: I'd almost rather not go to that party."

He answered, "Why not wear some flowers? For ten francs you can get two gorgeous roses."

She wasn't at all convinced. "No. There's nothing more humiliating than to look poor among a lot of rich women."

But her husband exclaimed, "My, but you're silly! Go see your friend Mme. Forestier and ask her to lend you some jewelry. You and she know each other well enough for you to do that."

She gave a cry of joy, "Why that's so! I hadn't thought of it."

The next day she paid her friend a visit and told her of her predicament.

Mme. Forestier went toward a closet with mirrored doors, took out a large jewel box, opened it, and said to Mme. Loisel: "Pick something out, my dear."

At first her eyes noted some bracelets, then a pearl necklace. She tried on many adornments in front of the mirror, but hesitated, unable to decide which to part with and put back. She kept on asking, "Haven't you something else?"

"Oh, yes, keep on looking."

All at once she found, in a satin box, a magnificent diamond necklace; and her pulse beat faster with longing. Her hands trembled as she took it up. Clasping it around her throat, she stood in ecstasy looking at her reflection.

Then she asked, hesitatingly, pleading, "Could I borrow that, just that and nothing else?"

"Why, of course."

She threw her arms around her friend, kissed her warmly, and fled with her treasure.

The day of the party arrived. Mme. Loisel was a sensation. She was the prettiest one there, fashionable, gracious, smiling, and wild with joy. All the men turned to look at her, asked who she was, begged to be introduced.

She danced wildly, drunk with pleasure, giving no thought to anything. She was in the triumph of her beauty, the pride of her success, in a kind of happy cloud composed of all the adulation, of all the awakened longings, of a sense of complete victory.

End of Part One

ⓔ COMPREHENSION CHECK

Choose the best answer.

CAUSE / EFFECT
16. Why did Mme. Loisel marry a minor clerk?
   a. When she was younger, she didn't think having money was important.
   b. She had no dowry and wasn't able to meet anyone more prosperous.
   c. Her parents forced her to marry a clerk.
   d. She married a clerk to spite her parents.

CAUSE / EFFECT
17. Why did Mme. Loisel dress plainly?
   a. She couldn't afford fine clothes.
   b. She didn't like to waste money on clothes.
   c. Her husband didn't have a job.
   d. She spent her money on jewelry instead.

CAUSE / EFFECT
18. Why did Mme. Loisel dislike visiting her rich friend?
   a. Because her friend teased her about her poverty
   b. Because her friend was unkind
   c. Because she was upset by her friend's riches
   d. Because she wanted to spend more time with her husband

SCANNING
19. How much money did Mme. Loisel need to buy the dress?
   a. About 200 francs
   b. About 400 francs
   c. About 1000 francs
   d. About 4000 francs

SCANNING
20. What was M. Loisel originally planning to do with the money he gave his wife?
   a. Buy a necklace for his wife
   b. Use it to pay bills
   c. Buy flowers for his wife
   d. Buy a rifle for himself

PROBLEM / SOLUTION
21. How did Mme. Loisel solve the problem of not having any jewels to wear with her evening dress?
   a. She wore roses pinned to her dress.
   b. She wore a cape over her shoulders.
   c. She borrowed a necklace from a friend.
   d. She wore a cheap necklace of her own.

INFERENCE
△ 22. Why did Mme. Forestier agree to lend jewelry to Mme. Loisel?
   a. She did not care about her jewelry.
   b. She wanted to impress M. Loisel.
   c. She wanted to become Mme. Loisel's friend.
   d. She liked and trusted Mme. Loisel.

SCANNING
23. How did Mme. Loisel look when she was dressed for the party?
   a. Ridiculous
   b. Gaudy
   c. Beautiful
   d. Poor

INFERENCE
△ 24. At the party, M. Loisel probably
   a. was jealous of his wife.
   b. enjoyed watching his wife enjoy herself.
   c. was distressed seeing his wife dancing.
   d. tried to ignore his wife.

MAIN IDEA
○ 25. This part of the story is mainly about
   a. a woman who realizes how foolish she is to waste her life constantly dreaming of becoming rich.
   b. a greedy and selfish woman who causes her kind and generous husband to go broke.
   c. a poor, resentful woman whose dreams of the good life come true when she's able to borrow an expensive necklace and dress up to go to a fancy party.
   d. a woman who has a wonderful time at a fancy party and can't wait to give her own party.

Check your answers with the key.

SKILL PRACTICE
CHARACTER AND FEELINGS

Your **feelings** are your emotions—sorrow, anger, hatred, happiness, and so on. Sometimes an author tells you how a character feels, and sometimes you must figure out a character's feelings from the actions in a story.

The reason a person does something is called a **motive**. Sometimes feelings are the motives that cause a character to act in a certain way. At other times, events can be motives for actions.

A person's **character** is a combination of that person's personality, disposition, and abilities. When you read, you get to know about the characters from the way they act, feel, think, and speak.

In "The Necklace – Part One," the author gives us a very clear picture of the feelings and motives of M. and Mme. Loisel. The questions below deal with these feelings and motives.

Choose the best answer for each question.

26. What kind of person is Mme. Loisel? (Choose all the correct answers.)
    a. Selfish about what she wants
    b. Considerate of her husband
    c. Lively and charming with the rich and famous
    d. Helpless and shy

27. How did Mme. Loisel feel when her husband showed her the invitation to the party?
    a. Thrilled   c. Scornful
    b. Embarrassed   d. Delighted

28. Why did Mme. Loisel insist that she needed to wear jewelry to the party?
    a. She wanted to make her husband unhappy.
    b. She wanted to make up for her lack of beauty.
    c. She wanted to cover up her ugly dress.
    d. She wanted to impress the other people there.

29. How did Mme. Loisel feel when she saw the diamond necklace?
    a. Thrilled   c. Scornful
    b. Embarrassed   d. Unhappy

30. Why did Mme. Loisel have a wonderful time at the party?
    a. She was where she wanted to be.
    b. She got to show off her husband.
    c. Her dress was nicer than Mme. Forestier's.
    d. She saw all her friends.

31. What kind of person is M. Loisel?
    a. Old and uncaring
    b. Thoughtless and mean
    c. Loving and generous
    d. Nasty and untrustworthy

32. How does M. Loisel feel about his wife?
    a. He hates her.
    b. He loves her.
    c. He feels sorry for her.
    d. He is afraid of her.

33. How did M. Loisel feel when he showed his wife the invitation?
    a. Impatient   c. Proud
    b. Afraid   d. Disgusted

34. How did M. Loisel feel when his wife said she couldn't go to the party?
    a. Disgusted   c. Ashamed
    b. Angry   d. Bewildered

35. Why did M. Loisel give his wife 400 francs for a new dress?
    a. He wanted to prove to her that he had money.
    b. He wanted her to have whatever she wanted.
    c. He wanted to get a promotion by impressing his boss.
    d. He wanted to show off his wife.

Check your answers with the key.

VOCABULARY REVIEW

Choose the best answer.

36. Which of these is a **predicament**?
  a. Talking with an old friend
  b. Getting a flat tire
  c. Eating dinner
  d. Visiting Paris

37. Clothing that is in a state of **dinginess** needs to be
  a. sewn.
  b. ironed.
  c. cleaned.
  d. altered.

38. Someone who is **prosperous** might
  a. have soup for lunch.
  b. look for a second job.
  c. try hard to make new friends.
  d. buy a mink coat.

39. If Walter chewed gum **incessantly**, he
  a. didn't like gum.
  b. always had gum in his mouth.
  c. always chewed gum after meals.
  d. chewed gum in a strange rhythm.

40. Fillippo was in **ecstasy** when he heard he
  a. got a promotion.
  b. had to work late.
  c. broke his arm.
  d. got over his cold.

41. Which of these are **adornments** for a car?
  a. Windshield wipers and bumpers
  b. A large trunk
  c. Special wheel covers and racing stripes
  d. A powerful engine

42. Who once needed a **dowry**?
  a. A woman about to go to a fancy party
  b. A man about to give a party
  c. A man looking for a good job
  d. A woman about to get married

43. Enrico feared becoming a **pauper**. This means he was afraid of becoming
  a. ill.
  b. poor.
  c. lost.
  d. weak.

44. Antonia sounded **irritated** when she answered the phone, so we thought she was
  a. bothered by the call.
  b. expecting the call.
  c. happy about the call.
  d. frightened by the call.

45. Who probably received **adulation** at the baseball game?
  a. The umpire
  b. A player who struck out
  c. A player who hit a home run
  d. The last player up

Check your answers with the key.

HA-18 PLOT

THE NECKLACE – PART TWO

ⓐ GETTING READY

The story so far: Beautiful Mme. Loisel is married to a minor clerk who does not earn much money. She hates living in a modest apartment and constantly dreams of being wealthy. Her husband does not mind their lifestyle, but he wants to make his wife happy. So, he manages to get an invitation to a fancy party, hoping his wife will enjoy it.

Mme. Loisel buys an evening dress with their savings and borrows a beautiful **diamond necklace** from her friend, Mme. Forestier. Mme. Loisel has a wonderful time at the party. Do you think her happiness will last? Why or why not? What do you think will happen next in the story?

When you read "The Necklace – Part Two," you will discover what happens to M. and Mme. Loisel and how it changes their lives **forever**.

VOCABULARY BUILDING

Study each key word to make sure you know its pronunciation and definition. Then study the way the word is used in the sentence based on the story.

aghast (ə gast′) Horrified; filled with shocked amazement. *When they discovered that the necklace was missing, they looked at each other, aghast.*

askew (ə skyü′) Twisted; out of position. *Her skirts were askew.*

clashed (klashd) Did not belong together; failed to fit together agreeably. *Her husband threw over her shoulders the wraps he had brought for going home, modest garments that clashed with her evening clothes.*

disconsolate (dis kon′ sə lit) Forlorn; sad; without hope. *When they were on the street, they didn't find a carriage. They walked on, disconsolate and shivering.*

drabness (drab′ nes) Dullness; plainness. *They found one of those carriages that one sees in Paris only after nightfall, as if they were ashamed to show their drabness during the day.*

exorbitant (eg zôr′ bə tənt) Excessive; more than what is fair. *Finally, all was paid back, everything including the exorbitant rates of the moneylenders and accumulated interest.*

gamut (gam′ ət) The whole range; the whole series. *He went about raising money. He ran the gamut of moneylenders.*

heroism (her′ ō iz′ əm) Great courage. *Mme. Loisel experienced the horrible life the needy live. She played her part, however, with sudden heroism.*

privations (prī vā′ shənz) Lack of the necessities and comforts of life. *He was terrified by the prospect of all the privations of the body and tortures of the spirit that go with being poor.*

untended (un tend′ id) Not taken care of. *Her hair was untended.*

Now choose a word that fits in each of the following sentences. Write the best word for each sentence.

1. Let's paint this room a bright color to get rid of its _____ .

2. Mitzi's purple hat _____ with her green scarf.

3. The food in that restaurant is good, but they charge _____ prices for it.

4. A pauper must endure many _____ .

5. The garden was _____ and full of weeds.

6. When Alan's friends learned that he had been arrested, they were

   _____ .

7. The soldier received a medal for his acts of _____ .

8. Carlotta was _____ when her dog died.

9. I had to laugh at Frank because his hat was _____ .

10. Cy ran the _____ of want ads before he found a job.

Check your answers with the key.

HA-18

SPECIAL WORDS

loan sharks (lōn shärks) People who lend money at a very high rate of interest. *Finally, all was paid back, everything including the exorbitant rates of the loan sharks.*

sous (sōōz) French coins which are no longer used. *He copied documents at five sous a page.*

© PREVIEW

Read the first five paragraphs of "The Necklace – Part Two" to see what happens to M. and Mme. Loisel when they leave the party. Do this now.

Did you notice how the two characters felt as the party ended? M. and Mme. Loisel are experiencing different emotions at this point in the story. Below are some words describing feelings.

Based on what you learned from previewing the story, write *yes* for each word that describes how each character feels. Write *no* for each word that does not.

Mme. Loisel

11. _____ ashamed

12. _____ depressed

13. _____ happy

14. _____ impatient

M. Loisel

15. _____ embarrassed

16. _____ angry

17. _____ concerned

18. _____ proud

Check your answers with the key.

ⓓ READING

Now read Part Two of the story to see how the necklace changes the lives of M. and Mme. Loisel.

THE NECKLACE – PART TWO
by Guy de Maupassant

She left around four o'clock in the morning. Her husband threw over her shoulders the wraps he had brought for going home, modest garments that clashed with her evening clothes. She longed to escape, unseen by the other women.

Loisel held her back.

"Hold on! You'll catch cold outside. I'll call a cab."

But she wouldn't listen and went rapidly down the stairs. When they were on the street, they didn't find a carriage.

They walked on, disconsolate and shivering. Finally they found one of those carriages that one sees in Paris only after nightfall, as if they were ashamed to show their drabness during the day.

It dropped them at their door, and they climbed wearily up to their apartment. For her, it was all over. For him, there was the thought that he would have to be at work at ten o'clock.

Before the mirror, she let the wraps fall from her shoulders to see herself once again in all her glory. Suddenly she gave a cry. The necklace was gone.

Her husband said, "What's the trouble?"

She turned toward him despairingly, "I . . . I . . . I don't have Mme. Forestier's necklace."

"What! You can't mean it! It's impossible!"

They hunted everywhere, through the folds of the dress, in the pockets. They found nothing.

He asked, "Are you sure you had it when leaving the dance?"

"Yes, I felt it when I was in the hall of the Ministry."

"But if you had lost it on the street we'd have heard it drop. It must be in the cab."

"Yes. Did you get its number?"

"No. Didn't you notice it either?"

"No."

They looked at each other aghast.

"I'll retrace our steps on foot," he said, "to see if I can find it."

Her husband came in about seven o'clock. He had had no luck.

He went to the police station, to the newspapers to post a reward, to the cab companies, everywhere the slightest hope drove him.

That evening Loisel returned, pale, his face lined; still he had learned nothing.

"We'll have to write your friend," he said, "to tell her you have broken the catch and are having it repaired. That will give us a little time."

At the end of the week, they had given up all hope.

And Loisel, looking five years older, declared, "We must replace that piece of jewelry."

The next day they took the case to the jeweler whose name they found inside. He consulted his records. "I didn't sell that necklace," he said. "I only supplied the case."

Then they went from one jeweler to another, hunting for a similar necklace. Finally they found a string of diamonds which seemed exactly like the one they were seeking. It was priced at forty thousand francs. They could get it for thirty-six.

Loisel had eighteen thousand francs he had inherited from his father. He would borrow the rest.

He went about raising the money, asking a thousand francs from one, four hundred from another. He ran the gamut of moneylenders. He compromised the rest of his life. Then, terrified by the prospect of all the privations of the body and tortures of the spirit, he went to claim the new necklace with the thirty-six thousand francs.

When Mme. Loisel took the necklace back, Mme. Forestier said to her frostily, "You should have brought it back sooner; I might have needed it."

She didn't open the case, an action Mme. Loisel was afraid of. If she had noticed the substitution, what would she have said? Would she have thought her a thief?

Mme. Loisel experienced the horrible life the needy live. She played her part, however, with sudden heroism.

She learned to do the heavy housework, the cooking. She washed dishes, wearing down her shell-pink nails; she scrubbed dirty linen; she took the garbage down to the street each morning and brought up water. And, clad like a peasant woman, basket on arm, she bargained with the shopkeepers and was insulted by them.

Each month notes had to be paid, and others renewed to give more time.

Her husband labored evenings to balance a merchant's accounts, and at night, he copied documents at five sous a page.

And this went on for ten years.

Finally, all was paid back, everything including the exorbitant rates of the loan sharks and accumulated interest.

Mme. Loisel appeared an old woman, now. She had become heavy, rough, harsh, like one of the poor, her hair untended, her skirts askew. But sometimes she would sit near the window and think of that long-ago evening when, at the dance, she had been so beautiful and admired.

What would have happened if she had not lost that necklace? Who knows? How strange life is! How little there is between happiness and misery!

Then one Sunday when she had gone for a walk to relax a bit, she suddenly noticed a woman strolling with a child. It was Mme. Forestier, still young-looking; still beautiful, still charming.

Mme. Loisel felt a rush of emotion. Now that everything was paid off, she would tell her the whole story. Why not?

She went toward her. "Hello, Jeanne."

Mme. Forestier, not recognizing her, stammered, "But . . . madame . . . I don't recognize . . . You must be mistaken."

"No. I'm Mathilde Loisel."

Her friend gave a cry, "Oh, my poor Mathilde, how you've changed!"

"Yes, I've had a hard time since last seeing you. And plenty of misfortunes—and all on account of you!"

"Of me . . . How do you mean?"

"Do you remember that diamond necklace you loaned me to wear to the dance at the Ministry?"

"Yes, but what about it?"

"Well, I lost it."

"You lost it! But you returned it."

"I brought you another just like it. And we've been paying for it for ten years now. You can imagine that wasn't easy for us who had nothing. Well, it's over now, and I am glad of it."

Mme. Forestier stopped short. "You mean you bought a diamond necklace to replace mine?"

"Yes. You never noticed, then? They were quite alike."

And she smiled with proud and simple joy.

Mme. Forestier, quite overcome, clasped her by the hands. "Oh, my poor Mathilde. But mine was only an imitation. Why, at most it was worth only five hundred francs!"

COMPREHENSION CHECK

Choose the best answer.

SEQUENCE

19. According to the story, what happened last?
   a. M. Loisel went to the police station.
   b. M. Loisel walked along the route they had taken home from the party.
   c. They hunted through Mme. Loisel's clothing.
   d. They took the necklace case to a jeweler.

PROBLEM / SOLUTION

20. How did the Loisels manage to delay returning the necklace to Mme. Forestier?
   a. They avoided her.
   b. They told her that Mme. Loisel needed to wear it again.
   c. They wrote to say the catch on the necklace was being repaired.
   d. They pretended to forget about it.

INFERENCE

△ 21. Why didn't Mme. Loisel tell Mme. Forestier that she lost the necklace?
   a. She was mad at Mme. Forestier for lending it to her.
   b. She was too proud to admit that she lost it.
   c. She knew it would be easy to replace it.
   d. She knew Mme. Forestier didn't really need it then.

SCANNING

22. How many jobs did M. Loisel have while he was paying off the loans?
   a. One   c. Three
   b. Two   d. Four

CAUSE / EFFECT

23. Mme. Loisel had to do heavy work because
   a. her husband was too sick to do it.
   b. she got a job as a maid.
   c. she could not afford to hire help.
   d. her husband forced her to.

INFERENCE

△ 24. What might have happened to the necklace?
   a. Someone stole it at the party.
   b. Mme. Loisel dropped it on the street.
   c. Mme. Forestier stole it back.
   d. The cab driver found it and kept it.

SCANNING

25. How long did it take the Loisels to pay back all the loans?
   a. One year   c. Ten years
   b. Five years   d. Twenty years

CAUSE / EFFECT

26. Why didn't Mme. Forestier recognize Mme. Loisel when they met after many years?
   a. Mme. Loisel looked old and poor.
   b. Mme. Loisel was afraid to speak to her.
   c. Mme. Forestier had forgotten all about Mme. Loisel and the necklace.
   d. Mme. Forestier was blind.

CHARACTER / FEELINGS

27. How did Mme. Loisel feel when she told Mme. Forestier that she had replaced the necklace and paid off the debts?
   a. Bitter and angry
   b. Proud and happy
   c. Nervous and frightened
   d. Spiteful and mean

MAIN IDEA

○ 28. This story is mainly about
   a. an evening of glory at a party that led to ten years of misery for the Loisels.
   b. how foolish and ignorant the Loisels were because they couldn't recognize imitation diamonds.
   c. how M. Loisel's life was ruined by the carelessness of his wife.
   d. a woman who selfishly makes a friend repay her for the loss of a fake necklace.

Check your answers with the key.

SKILL PRACTICE
PLOT

The events in the story make up the **plot**. An interesting plot always shows a **conflict**, which is a struggle between two forces. All plots are somewhat different, but many plots present similar kinds of conflicts.

One kind of conflict is a struggle between two people. Two candidates competing to become President is an example of a conflict between two people.

Another kind of conflict is a struggle within a person. The struggle of a person who sees a friend commit a crime, and must decide whether or not to report it to the police, shows this kind of conflict.

A third kind of conflict is a struggle between a person and society; for instance, a person who must run away because he is falsely accused of a crime.

The conflict gets the reader interested in the story. The author develops the conflict until it comes to a crisis point, called the **climax**. The climax is usually the most exciting point of the plot. It is the point where the conflict comes to a head in some dramatic way. The climax of the plot about the falsely accused person might be the moment when he is surrounded by police who will shoot if he does not give himself up.

The **conclusion** is the last feature of the plot, but it does not necessarily occur at the very end of the story. The conclusion tells how the conflict is finally resolved. The conclusion of the plot about the falsely accused man might be how the man proves he is innocent.

Sometimes an author ends a story with a surprising twist. The twist makes the reader realize that the characters have not understood their real situation.

Choose the answers that identify the conflict, the climax, and the conclusion of "The Necklace." You may want to look back at Part One.

29. The basic conflict is Mme. Loisel's
a. wish to look elegant at the party although she does not have much money.
b. wish to live in luxury, but her need to live a modest life.
c. difficulty in deciding which debts to pay back first.
d. desire to leave the party quickly even though that meant walking home.

30. The climax comes when Mme. Loisel
a. is given the invitation to the party.
b. goes to the party and is a success.
c. pays off the last debt.
d. discovers that the necklace is lost.

31. The conclusion of the story comes when
a. Mme. Forestier tells Mme. Loisel that the necklace was worth only five hundred francs.
b. Mme. Loisel replaces the necklace and resolves to live a life of poverty in order to repay her debts.
c. M. and Mme. Loisel decide to tell Mme. Forestier that the catch was broken in order to buy more time.
d. the Loisels leave the party and have a great deal of trouble finding a carriage.

32. The twist at the end of "The Necklace" is that
a. Mme. Loisel looks old and poor.
b. Mme. Forestier does not recognize Mme. Loisel.
c. Mme. Loisel finds better things to do than dream of being rich.
d. the necklace was not made of real diamonds.

Check your answers with the key.

VOCABULARY REVIEW

Choose the best answer.

33. Which of these are **privations**?
    a. Loans and debts
    b. Interfering relatives
    c. Not enough food and clothing
    d. Imitation furs and jewels

34. If you don't like the **drabness** of a room, you wish the room
    a. was larger.
    b. had more furniture.
    c. cost less to rent.
    d. was brighter and more cheerful.

35. Which of these is an instance of **heroism**?
    a. Saving someone from drowning
    b. Getting an extra job
    c. Buying a new car
    d. Being kind to an old friend

36. That actress is able to display a **gamut** of emotions. She is able to display
    a. very little emotion.
    b. some emotion.
    c. all different kinds of emotions.
    d. the emotions of a gambler.

37. Which of these might make Vicky feel **disconsolate**?
    a. Opening a bank account
    b. Eating dinner
    c. Buying a new hat
    d. Losing her job

38. Cesar would probably feel **aghast** at hearing that
    a. an old friend is on the telephone.
    b. his house has burned down.
    c. his friends are giving him a party.
    d. he has won third place in a contest.

39. If Sheila paid an **exorbitant** price for the television, she paid
    a. less than the regular price.
    b. the regular price.
    c. a little more than the regular price.
    d. a lot more than the regular price.

40. A blanket that is **askew** is probably
    a. falling off the bed.
    b. tucked in tightly.
    c. folded down neatly.
    d. under another blanket.

41. Which of these probably **clashed**?
    a. Black socks with black shoes
    b. A white blouse and blue pants
    c. A striped purple coat with a green tie that has yellow dots
    d. Red roses on a white tablecloth

42. An **untended** park will probably have
    a. clean play areas.
    b. broken sidewalks.
    c. pretty gardens.
    d. well-kept lawns.

Check your answers with the key.

HA-19 SENSORY IMAGES / FIGURATIVE LANGUAGE
A GRAY SLEEVE

ⓐ GETTING READY

Suppose you were a soldier fighting in a war. How do you think you would act toward the people of that country who were not taking part in the combat? Would you think of them as human beings first—and as the enemy second? Or would it be the other way around?

The setting of this story is a battle site in the United States Civil War which was fought between the years 1861 and 1865. In that war, the Union army of the North fought the Rebel soldiers of the Confederacy (the South). The title "A Gray Sleeve" refers to the gray uniforms worn by the Rebel soldiers; the Union army wore blue uniforms.

The Civil War was sometimes called the "War between the States." The country was divided in bitter and bloody warfare. Sometimes brother fought against brother.

How would you feel if you had to go to war against people in your own country? Would it feel the same as going to war against another country? Why or why not?

When you read "A Gray Sleeve," you will learn what happened to a Northern army captain while he was searching for a Southern soldier.

VOCABULARY BUILDING

Study each key word to make sure you know its pronunciation and definition. Then study the way the word is used in the sentence based on the story.

cavalry (kav′ əl rē) Soldiers who fought on horseback. *Along the rear of the halted infantry, a column of cavalry was sweeping at a hard gallop.*

corporal (kôr′ pər əl) A low-ranking officer in the army. *A corporal in the party said, "I saw an arm move the blinds."*

exclamation (ek′ sklə mā′ shən) A sudden, shouted statement. *A corporal gave vent to a startled exclamation: "I saw an arm move the blinds!"*

formulate (fôr′ myə lāt) State in an orderly way. *He found himself unable to formulate a sentence that applied in any way to the situation.*

implored (im plôrd′) Begged. *She sprang to her feet again, and implored him with her hands.*

intervened (in′ tər vēnd′) Came in between in order to hinder. *She intervened, desperately, between the young man in gray and the officer in blue.*

perpendicular (pėr′ pən dik′ yə lər) Vertical; upright. *She faced the men, one hand extended with perpendicular palm. "Oh, please don't go up there!"*

suppressed (sə prest′) Restrained; subdued. *The tone of his voice seemed to vibrate with suppressed fury. He said, "And is that any reason why you should insult my sister?"*

upheaval (up hē′ vəl) A sudden or violent disturbance. *Suddenly the bugle sounded, and the column halted with a jolting upheaval.*

writhed (rī th d) Twisted and turned. *There was the dry crackling of musketry, with bitter, swift flashes and smoke that writhed like stung phantoms.*

Now choose a word that fits in each of the following sentences. Write the best word for each sentence.

1. The _____ saluted the general.

2. The father _____ in the fight between his two sons.

3. As the batter was called out, the expression on his face revealed the player's _____ anger.

4. Celia _____ her brother not to drive in the storm.

5. When Rubio fell off his motorcycle, he moaned and _____ in pain.

6. The _____ galloped to the scene of the battle.

7. The scientist is finding it difficult to _____ his new theory.

8. The tall, _____ rocks looked like trees in the desert.

HA-19

9. As it rumbled through the land, the earthquake caused an

   _____ .

10. Pedro was awakened by Maria's loud _____ : "I've found the missing money!"

Check your answers with the key.

SPECIAL WORDS

Rebels (reb′ əlz) Soldiers who fought in the Confederate Army for the South in the Civil War. *We had a fight with some Rebels a little while ago.*

Yankee (yang′ kē) A soldier who fought in the Union Army for the North in the Civil War. *You—you are a Yankee!*

ⓒ PREVIEW

Read the first six paragraphs to discover how the story begins. Do this now.

Did you notice that the events in the story are presented in sequence—that is, in the order in which they occurred?

Below are some sentences that describe some of the events that happened in the beginning of the story.

Based on what you learned from previewing the story, number the events in the order in which they occurred.

11. ____ The cavalry and infantry attacked Rebel soldiers.

12. ____ A Union corporal noticed a gray sleeve at a window of a house.

13. ____ A column of cavalry came to the aid of the Union infantry.

14. ____ A Union captain kicked in the door of a house.

15. ____ Rebel sharpshooters were shooting at a Union infantry.

Check your answers with the key.

ⓓ READING

Now read the story to find out how the sighting of a gray sleeve affects one Northern soldier's life.

148

A GRAY SLEEVE
by Stephen Crane

"I wish those fellows out yonder would quit pelting us," the Union infantry captain remarked.

At the edge of a grove of maples, across wide fields, there occasionally appeared little puffs of smoke. The long wave of blue and steel in the field moved uneasily at the eternal barking of the faraway sharpshooters.

Suddenly the artillery officer said, "Look! Help's on the way!"

Along the rear of the halted infantry, a column of cavalry was sweeping at a hard gallop. Suddenly the bugle sounded, and the column halted with a jolting upheaval. "Go in hard now!" the captain roared. A moment later the men had tumbled from their horses and, firearms in hand, the troopers threw themselves upon the grove like wolves upon a great animal. Along the whole front of woods there was the dry crackling of musketry, with bitter, swift flashes and smoke that writhed like stung phantoms.

Suddenly a trooper halted and said: "There's a house!" Everyone paused. A corporal in the party gave vent to a startled exclamation: "I saw an arm move the blinds. An arm with a gray sleeve!"

The captain went softly up the front steps. Some crickets chirped in the long grass, and the nearest pine could be heard in its endless sighs. One of the privates moved uneasily, and his foot crunched the gravel. Suddenly the captain kicked the door with a loud crash. It flew open.

Directly in front of the captain was a young woman. The flying open of the door had obviously been an utter astonishment to her. The captain took a step forward and said, "I didn't mean to frighten you."

The young woman's breath came in little, quick gasps, and she looked at him as she would have looked at a serpent.

"I don't wish to disturb you, but we had a fight with some Rebels a little while ago, and I thought maybe some of them might have come in here. Are there any of them here?" the captain asked.

She looked at him and said, "No!" He wondered why extreme alarm made the eyes of some women so bright.

"Well, I'm sorry to trouble you, but I shall have my men search the house, anyhow." He turned to the corporal and said, "Jones, go through the house." The men rummaged around on the ground floor of the house. But they found no one, and at last they went trooping toward the stairs which led to the second floor.

The young woman ran to the first step and standing there, faced the men, one hand extended with perpendicular palm. "Oh, please, don't go up there! Nobody is there—indeed, there is not! P-l-e-a-s-e!" Then suddenly she sank swiftly down upon the step and, huddling forlornly, began to weep.

"Ah, don't cry like that," the captain said. "Why is it that you don't want us to search upstairs? Won't you please tell me?"

"Because," she moaned, "because—there isn't anybody up there." She sprang to her feet again, and implored him with her hands. She looked deep into his eyes with her glance, which was at this time like that of the fawn when it says to the hunter, "Have mercy upon me!"

Suddenly the corporal said in a quick, low tone: "Look out, captain!"

All turned their eyes swiftly toward the head of the stairs. A youth in a gray uniform had appeared there. He stood looking coolly down at them. No word was said by the troopers. The young woman gave vent to a little wail of desolation, "Oh, Harry!"

He began slowly to descend the stairs. His right arm was in a white sling, and there were some fresh bloodstains upon the cloth. His face was rigid and deathly pale, but his eyes flashed like lights.

Six steps from the bottom of the flight he halted and said, "I reckon it's me you're looking for."

The captain nodded his head and said, "Yes."

The youth in gray looked down at the young woman and then, in the same even tone, which now, however, seemed to vibrate with suppressed fury, he said: "And is that any reason why you should insult my sister?"

At this sentence, she intervened, desperately, between the young man in gray and the officer in blue. "Oh, don't, Harry, don't! He was good to me!"

The youth had suddenly become weak. He breathed heavily and clung to the rail. He was glaring at the captain, and summoning all his will power to combat his weakness.

The young woman pleaded with the captain. "You won't hurt him, will you? He doesn't know what he's saying. He's wounded, you know. Please don't mind him!"

"I won't touch him," said the captain, with rather extraordinary earnestness. "We will go away, leaving your house just as we found it!"

The men began to filter out into the open air.

The captain crossed the hall and stood before her. "You are not angry at me, are you?" he asked timidly.

"No," she said. She hesitated a moment, and then suddenly held out her hand. "You were good to me—and I'm much obliged."

The captain took her hand, and then he blushed, for he found himself unable to formulate a sentence that applied in any way to the situation.

"Well, good-bye!" he said.

"Good-bye!"

As the captain mounted his horse, he saw a curtain move at one of the windows. He rode from his position at the head of the column and steered his horse between two flower beds.

"Well, good-bye!"

The squadron trampled slowly past.

"Good-bye!"

The captain said hoarsely: "I don't suppose—I don't suppose—I'll ever see you again!"

The young woman said: "Why, no, I don't suppose you will."

"Never?"

"Why, no, it isn't possible. You—you are a—Yankee!"

"Well, some day, you know, when there's no more fighting, we might—" He observed that she had withdrawn suddenly into the shadow, so he said: "Well, good-bye!"

She bowed her head, and he saw a pink blush steal over the curves of her cheek and neck.

"Am I never going to see you again?"

She made no reply.

At last a low voice said, "Sometimes—when there are no troops in the neighborhood—I walk over as far as that old oak tree yonder—in the afternoons."

ⓔ COMPREHENSION CHECK

Choose the best answer.

INFERENCE

△ 16. Why did the captain kick in the door to the house?
   a. To surprise anyone inside
   b. To show he was tough
   c. To impress the other soldiers
   d. To hit anyone inside the door

CHARACTER / FEELINGS

17. What kind of person was the Union captain?
   a. Brave and kind
   b. Cruel and proud
   c. Cowardly and uncaring
   d. Angry and spiteful

SEQUENCE

18. According to the story, which happened first?
   a. The Rebel soldier accused the captain of insulting his sister.
   b. The Rebel soldier became very weak.
   c. The Rebel soldier came down the stairs.
   d. The woman came between her brother and the captain.

SCANNING

19. How did the soldiers find the wounded Rebel?
   a. They searched the upstairs of the house.
   b. They searched the roof of the house.
   c. The Rebel came out of his hiding place.
   d. The Rebel fell down the stairs.

CHARACTER / FEELINGS

20. Which of the following describe the young woman? (Choose all the correct answers.)
   a. Brave   c. Frightened
   b. Angry   d. Cowardly

INFERENCE

△ 21. Why was the woman so desperate to tell her brother that the captain had not insulted her?
   a. She didn't want her brother to anger the Union soldiers.
   b. She didn't want her brother to shoot the captain.
   c. She wanted the soldiers to believe that her brother liked Yankees.
   d. She wanted the soldiers and her brother to become friends.

CHARACTER / FEELINGS

22. What kind of person was the Rebel soldier?
   a. Weak and cowardly
   b. Brave and proud
   c. Sneaky and bold
   d. Selfish and uncaring

CAUSE / EFFECT

23. Why did the corporal suddenly warn the captain to "look out"?
   a. A Rebel soldier had appeared.
   b. The woman was pointing a gun at him.
   c. The woman had fainted.
   d. The Rebel soldier was pointing a gun at him.

INFERENCE

△ 24. Why did the woman tell the captain she sometimes walked to the oak tree?
   a. She wanted to shoot him.
   b. She wanted to convince him to free her brother.
   c. She wanted to join the Northern Army.
   d. She wanted to see him again.

MAIN IDEA

○ 25. This story is mainly about
   a. a Northern captain who captures a valuable Rebel prisoner by flattering his sister.
   b. a Northern captain who does not capture a wounded Rebel soldier because of his feelings for the soldier's sister.
   c. a Southern woman who discovers that she would rather join the Northern side of the war.
   d. a Southern woman who is willing to kill a Northern captain in order to protect her wounded brother.

Check your answers with the key.

SKILL PRACTICE
SENSORY IMAGES / FIGURATIVE LANGUAGE

When an author uses words that involve our five senses—sight, hearing, touch, taste, and smell—these **sensory images** help us get a clearer picture of the author's descriptions.

Sometimes an author uses sensory images that involve comparisons. These comparisons are called **similes** and **metaphors**.

A **simile** is a comparison that uses *like* or *as*. A **metaphor** is a comparison that does not use *like, as,* or any other special word. Here are two examples:

> **Simile:** The seal barked like a dog.
> **Metaphor:** The full moon was a sad clown face floating in the sky.

Both of these figures of speech help you understand what the author is describing. The simile above appeals to the sense of hearing. The metaphor above appeals to the sense of sight.

Another kind of figurative language is called **personification.** Personification describes an animal or object as if it were a person. An author uses personification to show a certain feeling or attitude toward the thing being described. Look for the personification in this sentence:

> The waves tried to cover the beach, but dropped back, defeated, again and again.

Of course, waves don't try to do anything and they don't feel defeated. But, by describing the waves as if they had human feelings, the author helps you see how the waves moved.

Another type of figurative language is called **onomatopoeia** (on′ ə mat′ ə pē′ ə). Onomatopoeia uses words that imitate the sounds they represent. The words *buzz* and *splash* are examples of onomatopoeia. Onomatopoeia always appeals to your sense of hearing.

The questions below deal with figures of speech found in "A Gray Sleeve." The line numbers indicate where in the story the figures of speech can be found.

Answer the following questions.

26. Write the metaphor in lines 6–8.

27. Write the simile in lines 15–18.

28. The author uses the above simile to make it clear that the troops were
    a. afraid to fight.
    b. refusing to fight.
    c. eager to fight.
    d. forced to fight.

29. Write the example of onomatopoeia in lines 19–22.

30. Write the simile in lines 19–22.

31. Write the personification in lines 29–30.

32. The author uses the above personification to make the scene seem
    a. noisy and frightening.
    b. strange and unfamiliar.
    c. confusing and disturbing.
    d. calm and quiet.

33. Write the onomatopoeia in lines 31–32.

34. Write the simile in lines 39–41.

35. Write the simile in lines 70–73.

36. The author uses the simile in lines 70–73 to make the woman seem
    a. confused and angry.
    b. cowardly and mean.
    c. brave and bold.
    d. frightened and helpless.

Check your answers with the key.

VOCABULARY REVIEW

Choose the best answer.

37. A soldier in the **cavalry** needs a
    a. place to hide.   c. saddle.
    b. warm fire.   d. doctor.

38. If you **implored** someone, you probably said,
    a. "Please."   c. "No."
    b. "Thank you."   d. "Yes."

39. If Joaquin has many **suppressed** feelings, he has
    a. feelings of anger.
    b. feelings of happiness.
    c. feelings that are hidden.
    d. feelings that are expressed.

40. Which of these is usually **perpendicular**?
    a. A floor   c. A roof
    b. A wall   d. A ceiling

41. If you try to **formulate** a sentence, you are trying
    a. to write quickly.
    b. to use difficult words.
    c. to confuse someone.
    d. to express yourself clearly.

42. If Georgia is a **corporal**, she
    a. is in the armed forces.
    b. rides a horse.
    c. looks for missing people.
    d. writes stories.

43. Mei Lee **writhed** when her sister
    a. phoned her.
    b. left her.
    c. tickled her.
    d. shook her hand.

44. You might utter an **exclamation** if you are
    a. bored.   c. sleepy.
    b. surprised.   d. sad.

45. The rock star's failure to appear caused an **upheaval** among the fans. The fans probably
    a. screamed and shouted.
    b. waited quietly.
    c. left quietly.
    d. read their programs.

46. If two baseball players argued, who probably **intervened**?
    a. The crowd
    b. The hot dog seller
    c. The umpire
    d. The ticket taker

Check your answers with the key.

HA-20 QUALITIES IN LITERATURE: SUSPENSE
TO BUILD A FIRE

ⓐ GETTING READY

Have you ever been really cold? Relate the circumstances. How did you manage to get warm? Imagine a life-threatening situation outdoors in which you are faced with extremely cold temperatures. Explain what you would do to guarantee your survival.

The man and the dog in the picture above are in the wilderness in Alaska. They are trying to get back to camp, where it is warm, and where a fire and hot food will be ready. It is brutally cold, the temperature many degrees below zero.

Whom do you think is better able to deal with the cold, the man or the dog? What can the man do that the dog can't? What advantage does the dog have?

When you read "To Build a Fire," you will find out the problems the man faces in the bitter cold, and what he tries to do about his predicament.

b VOCABULARY BUILDING

Study each key word to make sure you know its pronunciation and definition. Then study the way the word is used in the sentence based on the story.

agitation (aj′ ə tā′ shən) Violent movement; disturbance. *Each time he had pulled a twig, he had communicated a slight agitation to the tree.*

apprehension (ap′ ri hen′ shən) Fear; dread. *The dog knew that it was not good to walk abroad in such fearful cold. But the dog made no effort to communicate its apprehension to the man.*

capsized (kap′ sīzd) Upset; overturned. *Each bough capsized its load of snow on the bough beneath.*

conception (kən sep′ shən) Idea; general notion. *He sat up and entertained in his mind the conception of meeting death with dignity.*

extinguished (ek sting′ gwisht) Put out. *A piece of green moss fell on the fire and extinguished it.*

flaw (flô) Weakness; fault. *Maybe, if he ran on, his feet would thaw out and he would reach camp. His theory had one flaw—he lacked the endurance.*

intangible (in tan′ jə bəl) Vague; cannot be touched. *It was a clear day, and yet there seemed an intangible sense of gloom over the face of things.*

manipulation (mə nip′ yə lā′ shən) Skillful handling. *After some manipulation, he got one match free and dropped it on his lap.*

pall (pôl) A dark and gloomy covering. *It was a clear day, and yet there seemed to be a pall over the face of things.*

reality (rē al′ ə tē) True state of things. *In reality, it was seventy-five below zero.*

Now choose a word that fits in each of the following sentences. Write the best word for each sentence.

1. I thought it was about ten o'clock, but in _____ it was past midnight.

2. When Jeff stood up, he almost _____ the boat.

3. The forest fire raged out of control until the heavy rain _____ it.

4. When Portia noticed the man following her, she was filled with _____ .

5. There was much _____ in the water when the children jumped into the pool.

6. The news that Akmir was hurt cast a _____ over the party.

7. The architect showed us her _____ of the arts center.

8. Although the minister's salary was low, there were many _____ rewards.

HA-20

9. The thieves would have succeeded in stealing the jewels had there not been a _____ in their plan.

10. It will take a lot of _____ to untangle this yarn.

Check your answers with the key.

SPECIAL WORD

husky (hus′ kē) A strong sled dog with a thick coat of fur. *At his heels trotted a dog, a big native husky.*

Ⓒ PREVIEW

Read the first three paragraphs to discover how the story begins. Do this now.

Did you notice that the author has described the setting of this story in great detail? He has told us when and where the story takes place as well as what the weather is like. He has also already told us a little bit about the man and the dog. Below are some statements about the settings and the characters.

Based on what you learned from previewing the story, write *true* if you think the statements are true. Write *false* if you think the statements are false.

11. _____ The man did not realize how cold it was.

12. _____ The dog was not aware of how cold it was.

13. _____ The Yukon River was frozen over.

14. _____ The man was lost.

15. _____ The man was confident he would be in camp by evening.

Check your answers with the key.

ⓓ READING

Now read the story to find out how the man and the dog deal with the extreme cold.

TO BUILD A FIRE
by Jack London

Day had broken exceedingly cold and gray when the man left the main Yukon trail and climbed a bank to a smaller trail that led eastward.

It was nine o'clock. It was a clear day, and yet there seemed an intangible pall over the face of things. The man looked back. The Yukon River lay a mile wide, pure white with snow as far as his eye could see. He turned and spat. There was a sharp crackle that startled him. His spit had frozen in the air before it could fall to the snow. Undoubtedly, it was colder then fifty degrees below zero—how much colder he did not know. But the temperature did not matter. He would be in camp with his friends by six o'clock.

He plunged in among the big spruce trees. At his heels trotted a dog, a big native husky. The animal was depressed by the tremendous cold. Its instinct told it a truer tale than was told to the man by the man's judgment. In reality, it was seventy-five below zero.

At half-past twelve, the man arrived at the forks of the creek. He unbuttoned his jacket and drew forth his lunch. The action consumed no more than a quarter of a minute, yet numbness laid hold of the exposed fingers. He struck them against his leg and tried to eat, but the ice that had formed on his beard prevented him.

He had forgotten to build a fire and thaw out. He chuckled at his foolishness, and as he chuckled he noted the numbness again creeping into the exposed fingers. A bit frightened, he got out matches and proceeded to make a fire. He thawed the ice from his face and ate.

When the man had finished, he started out again. The dog was disappointed. It knew that it was not good to walk abroad in such fearful cold. But the dog made no effort to communicate its apprehension to the man.

Then it happened. At a place where the soft, unbroken snow seemed to advertise solidity, the man broke through to an underground spring beneath. The water soaked him halfway to the knees.

He would have to build a fire and dry out. He climbed the bank and found some dry firewood. He worked slowly and carefully, keenly aware of his danger. When it is seventy-five below zero, a man must not fail in his first attempt to build a fire—that is, if his feet are wet. Already all sensation had gone out of his feet, and his fingers were numb. But he was safe, for the fire was beginning to burn with strength.

Unable to untie the frozen strings of his ice-coated moccasins, he drew his knife. But before he could cut the strings, it happened. It was his own fault. He had built the fire under a spruce tree. The tree had a weight of snow on its boughs. Each time he had pulled a twig he had communicated a slight agitation to the tree. Each bough capsized its load of snow on the boughs beneath. It grew like an avalanche, and descended on the man and the fire. The fire was blotted out!

The man was shocked. It was as if he had heard his own sentence of death. It was up to him to build the fire over again, and this second time there must be no failure.

The man reached in his pocket for a piece of bark. Try as he would, he could not clutch hold of it with his numb fingers. And all the time was the knowledge that each instant his feet were freezing. This thought tended to put him in a panic, but he fought against it. He threshed and beat his arms and hands until sensation returned. He stripped the mitten from his hand and fetched the bark. The exposed fingers were quickly going numb again.

After some manipulation, he got one match free and dropped it in his lap. He picked it up in his teeth and scratched it on his leg. Twenty times he scratched before he succeeded in lighting it. As it flamed, he held it with his teeth to the bark. But the burning sulphur caused him to cough. The match fell into the snow.

Suddenly, he caught the whole bunch between bared hands and scratched them along his leg. They flared into flame—seventy sulphur matches at once. He held the blazing bunch to the bark. With the heels of his hands, he placed grasses and twigs on the flame. He grew more awkward. A piece of green moss fell on the fire and extinguished it.

His eyes chanced on the dog, and this put a wild idea into his head. He would kill the dog and bury his hands in the warm body until the numbness went. Then he could build another fire.

He called the dog, but in his voice was a strange note of fear that frightened the animal. Its restless, hunching movements and the liftings and shiftings of its forefeet became more pronounced, but it would not come to the man. It made no difference. The man realized that he could not kill the dog with his helpless hands.

In a panic, he turned and ran up the old, dim trail. Maybe, if he ran on, his feet would thaw out and he would reach camp. His theory had one flaw—he lacked the endurance. Several times he stumbled, and finally he tottered, crumpled up, and fell. The dog sat in front of him, eager and intent.

He was losing his battle. He sat up and entertained in his mind the conception of meeting death with dignity. He was bound to freeze anyway, and he might as well take it decently. With this new-found peace of mind came drowsiness. A good idea, he thought, to sleep off to death. Freezing was not so bad as people thought. There were a lot of worse ways to die.

The dog sat facing him and waiting. The brief day drew to a close in the long, slow twilight. The dog whined, but the man remained silent. It crept close to the man and caught the scent of death. This made the animal bristle and back away.

A little longer it delayed, howling under the stars. Then it turned and trotted up the trail in the direction of the camp it knew.

ⓔ COMPREHENSION CHECK

Choose the best answer.

CAUSE / EFFECT

16. Because the man had fallen through the ice,
    a. he could not eat his lunch.
    b. he immediately needed a fire in order to dry out.
    c. the dog would not come to him.
    d. he broke his leg.

PROBLEM / SOLUTION

17. How did the man try to keep from freezing? (Choose all the correct answers.)
    a. He ran along the trail.
    b. He built a fire.
    c. He buried himself in the snow.
    d. He sent the dog for help.

SEQUENCE

18. According to the story, which happened last?
    a. Snow fell from the tree and put out the fire.
    b. A lighted match fell into the snow.
    c. A piece of moss put out the fire.
    d. The man lit all his matches at once.

CHARACTER / FEELINGS

19 How did the man feel when he realized that he was going to die?
    a. Frightened and angry
    b. Calm and resigned
    c. Scared and lonely
    d. Frustrated and depressed

PLOT

20. The climax of this story occurs when
    a. the man falls into the water.
    b. the man is unable to keep the fire going.
    c. the man accepts the fact that he is going to die.
    d. the dog leaves the man.

PROBLEM / SOLUTION

21. What did the man do when he could not run anymore?
    a. He tried to kill the dog.
    b. He tried to call for help.
    c. He tried to crawl to shelter.
    d. He stopped struggling and gave up.

CAUSE / EFFECT

△ 22. Why did the dog back away from the dead man?
    a. It was afraid.
    b. It was mad.
    c. It was cold.
    d. It was in a hurry.

INFERENCE

△ 23. The man in the story probably
    a. didn't realize the importance of having a fire.
    b. wasn't dressed warmly enough for the cold weather.
    c. had never been out in extremely cold weather before.
    d. had spent some time outdoors in extremely cold weather.

INFERENCE

△ 24. What probably happened to the dog?
    a. It found its way to the camp.
    b. It froze to death in the woods.
    c. It got lost trying to get back to camp.
    d. It tried to find another man's campfire in the woods.

MAIN IDEA

○ 25. This story is mainly about a man who
    a. dies because he gets lost in the woods.
    b. discovers that his dog is useless in the cold.
    c. underestimates the force of nature and pays a high price for his mistake.
    d. decided he would rather die than live.

Check your answers with the key.

SKILL PRACTICE
QUALITIES IN LITERATURE: SUSPENSE

An author uses **suspense** to make the reader feel anxious and uncertain about the welfare of one or more of the characters. The reader's feelings go back and forth between fear and hope.

All suspense stories are based on conflict. The conflict must be sufficiently serious or even life-threatening so that the reader becomes concerned.

Built around the conflict are a series of events to make the reader uncertain of the outcome. The author does this by having the hope for success offset by reversals that mean failure. Fear and hope are alternated and combined so the reader is unsure of the outcome and is anxious to find out.

Reread lines 24–35 of the story. Look for the conflict and solution as you read. Do this now.

In lines 24–29 of the story, the man finds he cannot eat because ice has formed on his beard. This is the **conflict**. In lines 30–35, the man laughs at his problem, builds a fire, and eats. This is the **solution**.

Reread the parts of the story indicated by the line numbers below. Identify the conflict or the solution for each one.

26. Lines 41–45

    Conflict:

27. Lines 46–54

    Solution:

28. Lines 55–65

    Conflict:

29. Lines 80–85

    Solution:

30. Lines 85–86

    Conflict:

31. Lines 87–90

    Solution:

32. Lines 93–94

    Conflict:

33. Lines 96–98

    Solution:

34. Lines 100–104

    Conflict:

35. Lines 108–109

    Solution:

36. Lines 109–112

    Conflict:

Check your answers with the key.

VOCABULARY REVIEW

Choose the best answer.

37. If Waithara **extinguished** the light, she
    a. fixed the lampshade.
    b. turned off the lamp.
    c. watched the sun set.
    d. changed the light bulb.

38. Which of the following is **intangible**?
    a. A sandwich   c. A husky
    b. A small fire   d. Trust

39. Which of the following is an example of **agitation**?
    a. Waves pounding the rocks
    b. Extreme cold
    c. A heavy snowfall
    d. Clouds in the sky

40. You would feel **apprehension** if you saw
    a. a friend coming to meet you.
    b. smoke billowing from your window.
    c. the moon rising.
    d. a wedding invitation.

41. Jenni hoped the **flaw** in her argument would go unnoticed. In this sentence **flaw** means
    a. exaggeration.   c. weakness.
    b. lie.   d. fear.

42. If there is a **pall** over the meeting, the people feel
    a. excited.   c. happy.
    b. angry.   d. depressed.

43. Which of the following would require **manipulation**?
    a. Tying a bow
    b. Talking on the phone
    c. Deciding what to wear
    d. Taking a nap

44. When Tony **capsized** the shelving,
    a. he put it together.
    b. he measured the boards.
    c. everything fell on the floor.
    d. everything was cleaned.

45. If Vicky has a **conception** about how to fix the broken car, she
    a. pays to have it repaired.
    b. thinks she knows how to fix it.
    c. blames herself for breaking it.
    d. denies that the car is broken down.

46. Pedro's mother told him to face **reality**. She meant that he should
    a. stand facing north.
    b. see things as they really are.
    c. get in a fight.
    d. stay home today.

Check your answers with the key.

EXTENSION ACTIVITIES

HA-1

1. View one of the films mentioned in the selection. Then write a movie review. What did you like most about the film? What did you like least? Did it scare you? Why or why not? How accurate was the science?

2. Would you like to attend the Insect Fear Film Festival? Why or why not? What film would you suggest that the festival show? What science lesson do you think that this film could be used to teach?

HA-2

1. Would you have enjoyed having Jake as a pet? Why or why not? How might you want your pet to be different?

2. Pretend that you are Jake and write a few paragraphs about the author. From Jake's point of view, discuss the author's personality and actions and your opinions of them.

3. Research various hunting dogs, including bird dogs. Find out how they work, how they differ in appearance, and what type of wild game they hunt.

HA-3

1. Research two or three musicians who showed phenomenal talent as young children. Did their families encourage their talent? Give a brief history of their lives.

2. Mental retardation is often caused by physical conditions that exist before birth. Some of these factors are beyond our control—others are not. Write a short report on some of the physical causes of mental retardation. Indicate whether they can be prevented or not.

HA-4

1. Manny Airola performed in rodeos. Research the history of rodeos. Where and why did they start? Where did the word *rodeo* come from? What other events besides bronc busting are parts of a rodeo? Are rodeos popular today?

2. Manny Airola was born in the Mother Lode country of California. Find out what the Mother Lode country is, where it is, and why it was important. Include in your report a description of what the Mother Lode country is like today and how it has changed.

HA-5

1. Research the history of pesticides such as DDT. Try to find out what good they do, in what ways they are harmful, when they were invented, and whether or not they are still used.

2. What do you think should be done about paraquat? Should it be banned completely? Controlled more strictly? Do you think the help that paraquat gives farmers is worth the lives that paraquat takes? Why or why not?

3. Find out more about the Environmental Protection Agency (EPA). When was it organized? Who is the current director? What are some important decisions made by the EPA in the last few years involving herbicides or pesticides?

EXTENSION ACTIVITIES

HA-6

1. Research the facts about cocaine. Find out how it can damage the body and the brain, why it becomes addictive, and why it is against the law to sell or buy cocaine.

2. Find out about a local drug treatment program such as Alcoholics Anonymous. Find out how it works, what kinds of addicts it helps, how it began, and how many people it served during the last year.

HA-7

1. Choose one of the trials described in the story to role play with others who have read the selection. Assign the various parts and actually carry out the trial.

2. Pretend that you are a reporter. Write an article about a recent trial. In the article, describe the events leading up to the trial, the trial itself, and the people involved. Then give your opinion of the proceedings including the verdict.

HA-8

1. Find the closest Small Business Administration office in your area. (Look under the phone listing of "United States Government—Small Business Administration.") Write or call that office. Ask how many requests for help were received there during the last month and what kinds of businesses people seeking help were involved in.

2. What do you think Jane Thorpe is like? Do you think she is a good manager? Why or why not? Do you think she will continue to take control of her life? In what ways might she do this?

HA-9

1. Find out about some other kinds of birds that are in danger of becoming extinct. These may include the whooping crane, bald eagle, California Condor, or the osprey. Determine from your research if the danger to the birds comes directly from humans, as in hunting; or indirectly, as through pollution or the destruction of breeding areas.

2. Pretend that you are applying for a job to help Steve Kress with his puffin project. Write a letter introducing yourself. Tell what job you want to do in the project and why you are qualified for that job.

3. Find out about birds that are now extinct, such as the dodo, passenger pigeon, great auk, or moa. From your research, determine when and where the birds were last seen and why they are now extinct.

HA-10

1. Find out more about the different jobs available in the health field. Decide which one you would like to pursue. What are the qualifications and training necessary for that job? What is the salary range? Look in the want ads to determine if there are many job opportunities for your chosen position.

2. Write a list of questions that you would ask at an informational interview in order to find out more about the job you chose above.

EXTENSION ACTIVITIES

HA-11

1. Find out more about the Iditarod Trail Sled-Dog Race or other long-term races such as the 24-hour auto race at Daytona Beach, Florida; the Tour de France bicycle road race; or the America's Cup sailing race. In your report tell how often the race is held, where it is held, who may compete, and how long the race has been held.

2. Write a report on either hot-air balloon races or stock-car racing. Tell where such racing occurs, who usually competes, and how long the races last. Also discuss any dangers that are associated with that type of race.

3. If you could move to any place and take up any pastime, where would you go and what would you do? Tell why you would prefer your chosen activity and how you would pursue it.

HA-12

1. Research the negative effects of the space program and write a short report on them.

2. Select *one* of the following statements as your position and defend it:
   a. The government should have used the space funds for more important programs.

   OR

   b. Space exploration is worth any sacrifice we have to make.

3. Pretend you are being transported on the space shuttle to your job on a space station. Write a diary, describing the trip and your job.

HA-13

1. The author presents the opinion that companies should be more family friendly. Do you agree? Do some more research on the topic to find information that supports your opinion. Then debate the point with others who hold a different point of view.

2. If you were the head of a company, what family-friendly programs, if any, would you introduce? Why?

3. What family obligations do you have that might conflict with your job? Which family-friendly programs would be most helpful to you? What questions might you ask a possible employer to assure that your needs would be met?

HA-14

1. Do you think that propaganda is all right to use if the cause is just? Why or why not?

2. Look for two articles on the same topic—each from a different newspaper. Try to find two different points of view. What persuasion techniques, if any, are used in the articles? Which article do you agree with more? Why?

3. Pretend that you are in charge of propaganda during wartime. What persuasion techniques would you use? Why? Create a poster, television or radio ad, or speech that uses one or more of these techniques.

EXTENSION ACTIVITIES

HA-15

1. Pretend you are the mother of the soldier who asked for 200 drachmas. Write a letter responding to his request. Explain your reasons for sending or not sending the money.

2. Find out more about Egypt in the third century A.D. How was Egypt governed? What kinds of local rulers were there? Why were the letters quoted in the story written in Greek? Why was Roman citizenship desired by native Egyptians?

HA-16

1. Research the life of Mark Twain. Find out what his real name was, when he lived, and what kind of literature he wrote. Decide if "The Man Who Put Up at Gadsby's" is like many of Mark Twain's other stories. Tell why or why not.

2. Compare Mr. Lykins and the man in Mr. Riley's story. Why do you think Mr. Lykins did not see the similarities?

HA-17

1. Write a letter to Mme. Loisel suggesting ways in which she could make her life happier.

2. Research the life and work of Guy de Maupassant. What kinds of stories did he write? Do you think his life affected the stories he wrote? In what ways?

HA-18

1. Pretend you have lost the necklace. Write a letter to your friend explaining your problem. Write how you plan to solve the problem and why. Remember that the time period is the late 1800s, and it happened in Paris.

2. Do you think this story could happen today? Do you think today's society is very different from the one described in the story? In what ways? How do you think people's needs and wants differ today?

HA-19

1. Research the life and works of Stephen Crane. What kinds of stories did he write? Do many of his stories have the same setting? In what ways do you think his life may have affected his writing?

2. What do you think will happen to the woman and the captain? What events might keep them apart? What events might enable them to get together? Why?

HA-20

1. The story takes place in Alaska around the turn of the century. Research what was happening in Alaska at that time in an area called the Klondike. Describe what life in Alaska was like for this man and the others who came to the Klondike pursuing a dream.

2. Can you think of other examples where people and nature seem to be in conflict with one another? Look in newspapers and news magazines to find out how people have dealt with floods, tornados, earthquakes, or volcanic eruptions. Write a brief report about one of these disasters. Identify the conflict and tell how the person(s) solved it.

HOW TO SCORE FOR MASTERY

To evaluate mastery efficiently, the chart below may be used. The percentage scores are then transferred to the record form on the next page.

It is suggested that the teacher use judgment in raising or lowering the mastery criteria when the items in question are more difficult or easier than the "general" level of difficulty of evaluative items in the program.

As a rule, an approximate score of 80% of correct responses is considered to be mastery. Note that the mastery percentage is underlined in the chart below. For example, mastery in a ten-item test is eight right, or 80%.

Number of Items

	3	4	5	6	7	8	9	10	11	12	13	14	15	16	17	18	19	20	21	22	23	24	25	26	27	28	29	30
1	33	25	20	17	14	13	11	10	9	8	8	7	7	6	6	5	5	5	5	5	4	4	4	4	4	4	3	3
2	<u>66</u>	50	40	33	29	25	22	20	18	17	15	14	13	13	12	11	11	10	9	9	9	8	8	8	7	7	7	7
3	100	<u>75</u>	60	50	43	38	33	30	27	25	23	21	20	19	18	17	16	15	14	14	13	13	12	12	11	11	10	10
4		100	<u>80</u>	67	57	50	44	40	36	33	31	29	27	25	24	22	21	20	19	18	17	17	16	15	15	14	14	13
5			100	<u>83</u>	72	63	56	50	45	42	38	36	33	31	29	28	26	25	24	23	22	21	20	19	19	18	17	17
6				100	86	<u>75</u>	67	60	55	50	46	43	40	38	35	33	32	30	29	27	26	25	24	23	22	21	21	20
7					100	88	<u>78</u>	70	64	58	54	50	47	44	41	39	37	35	33	32	30	29	28	27	26	25	24	23
8						100	89	<u>80</u>	73	67	62	57	53	50	47	44	42	40	38	36	35	33	32	31	30	29	28	27
9							100	90	82	<u>75</u>	69	64	60	56	53	50	47	45	43	41	39	38	36	35	33	32	31	30
10								100	91	83	<u>77</u>	71	67	63	59	56	53	50	48	45	43	42	40	39	37	36	34	33
11									100	92	85	<u>79</u>	73	69	65	61	58	55	52	50	48	46	44	42	41	39	38	37
12										100	92	86	<u>80</u>	75	71	67	63	60	57	55	52	50	48	46	44	43	41	40
13											100	93	87	<u>81</u>	76	72	68	65	62	59	57	54	52	50	48	46	44	43
14												100	93	88	<u>82</u>	78	74	70	67	64	61	58	56	54	52	50	48	47
15													100	94	87	83	<u>79</u>	75	71	68	65	63	60	58	56	54	52	50
16														100	94	89	84	<u>80</u>	76	73	70	67	64	62	59	57	55	53
17															100	94	89	85	<u>81</u>	77	74	71	68	65	63	61	59	57
18																100	95	90	86	<u>82</u>	78	75	72	69	67	64	62	60
19																	100	95	91	86	83	<u>79</u>	76	73	70	68	65	63
20																		100	95	91	87	83	<u>80</u>	77	74	72	69	67
21																			100	95	91	88	84	<u>81</u>	78	75	72	70
22																				100	96	92	88	85	81	<u>79</u>	76	73
23																					100	96	92	88	85	82	<u>79</u>	77
24																						100	96	92	89	86	83	<u>80</u>
25																							100	96	93	89	86	83
26																								100	96	93	89	87
27																									100	96	93	90
28																										100	96	93
29																											100	97
30																												100

Number of Items Right

HA READING STRATEGIES
PROGRESS CHART

Name _____

Lesson Number	Date	Vocabulary Building Score	Comprehension Check Score	Skill Practice Score	Vocabulary Review Score	Lesson Mastered
1						
2						
3						
4						
5						
6						
7						
8						
9						
10						
11						
12						
13						
14						
15						
16						
17						
18						
19						
20						

This page may be reproduced for school use.

ANSWER KEY

HA-1

1. browse
2. prestigious
3. immersed
4. accumulated
5. indifferent
6. obscure
7. intruder
8. distribution
9. emotions
10. inflict
11. yes
12. yes
13. no
14. yes
15. no
16. c
17. b
18. b, c, d
19. b
20. a
21. d
22. c
23. a
24. b
25. b
26. nearly 900,000
27. the dead of winter
28. by being wrong about it
29. *The Fly*
30. 1990
31. *The Wall Street Journal*
*32. They look alien.
*33. panic attacks and flight; believing bugs are living in the hair or burrowing under the skin
34. d
35. b
36. a
37. c
38. a
39. a
40. d
41. d
42. c
43. b

HA-2

1. verged
2. professorial
3. perfection
4. droll
5. awry
6. homily
7. fracas
8. reprimand
9. pompous
10. reminiscing
11. false
12. true
13. false
14. false
15. true
16. d
17. b
18. c
19. b
20. c
21. a, d
22. b, c
23. d
24. b
25. b
*26. Jake was a little pompous.
*27. Jake always expected no less of me than perfection.
*28. shrug his shoulders
*29. pointer puppies
*30. bring him in the house and offer him squeaky toys and bones, and roll around on the floor
*31. his house
*32. I was the hunter and he was the hunting dog.
*33. a story
*34. Jake
*35. the tree
*36. thinking about Jake a lot
37. b
38. a
39. b
40. d
41. b
42. c
43. a
44. a
45. c
46. a

HA-3

1. verbal
2. retarded
3. psychologists
4. phenomenal
5. extraordinary
6. administrator
7. perceptual
8. mentality
9. functions
10. intellectual
11. true
12. true
13. false
14. true
15. a
16. b
17. d
18. d
19. c
20. b
21. c
22. a
23. a, b
24. d
25. d
26. c
27. d
28. a
29. b
30. c
31. a
32. c
33. a
34. b
35. a
36. b
37. a
38. d
39. b
40. c

HA-4

1. evoked
2. flair
3. exploits
4. dominant
5. unassuming
6. flailing
7. contempt
8. frenzy
9. enhanced
10. annals
11. yes
12. no
13. yes
14. no
15. yes
16. b
17. a
18. b
19. a
20. a
21. b
22. d
23. c
24. a, d
25. c
26. c
27. d
28. c
29. b
30. a
31. b
32. c
33. a
34. d
35. b
36. d
37. a
38. a
39. d
40. d
41. b

*Your wording may be different.

ANSWER KEY

HA-5

1. inhaled
2. organic
3. lethal
4. versatile
5. registration
6. disregard
7. antidote
8. pervasive
9. violators
10. suffocation

*11. Farmers know paraquat as one of the most versatile tools in agriculture.
*12. Paraquat is probably the most effective herbicide on the Earth.
*13. Paraquat is one of the world's worst poisons.
*14. There is no known antidote for paraquat poisoning.
*15. The use of paraquat is out of control and the situation is getting worse.

16. c
17. b
18. a, b, d
19. b
20. c
21. a
22. a, c
23. c, d
24. b
25. c
26. c
27. b
28. a
29. d
30. b
31. b
32. d
33. d
34. c
35. b
36. d
37. b
38. a
39. d
40. c

HA-6

1. horrendous
2. stamina
3. diminish
4. addict
5. impervious
6. vulnerable
7. integrity
8. rigorously
9. financially
10. immature
11. yes
12. yes
13. no
14. yes
15. no
16. d
17. c
18. a, b
19. b
20. b
21. a
22. d
23. c
24. a, c, d
25. a
26. a
27. d
28. b
29. b
30. c
31. c
32. a
33. d
34. b
35. a
36. c
37. d
38. c
39. d
40. b

HA-7

1. dire
2. contrary
3. verdict
4. morale
5. contrast
6. spiritual
7. minimum
8. exalted
9. alternative
10. landmark
11. yes
12. yes
13. no
14. yes
15. no
16. a
17. b
18. b
19. a, c
20. d
21. d
22. a
23. c
24. c
25. b

*Your wording may be different.

*	Trial of Edith Cavell	Trial of Jomo Kenyatta
26.	October 7, 1915	November 24, 1952
27.	With others	With others
28.	German military (lieutenant colonel, two captains, two lower officers)	British magistrate
29.	5 days	Almost 5 months
30.	Guilty	Guilty
31.	Death by firing squad	Seven years hard labor, confinement for life thereafter
32.	Yes	No

33. the trial of Edith Cavell
34. the trial of Jomo Kenyatta
35. Edith Cavell
36. b, c
37. a
38. b
39. b
40. c
41. b
42. c
43. b
44. a
45. b
46. d

169

ANSWER KEY

HA-8

1. lease
2. refurbished
3. divorced
4. flexible
5. ethnic
6. investment
7. citing
8. inability
9. advisers
10. coalition
*11. She works longer hours; she's learned many other jobs; she enjoys her work now.
*12. She still wraps meat; she still works in the same store.
13. a
14. c
15. a, b, d
16. c
17. c
18. b, c
19. d
20. a
21. d
22. b
23. a. 3
    b. 4
    c. 1
    d. 5
    e. 2
24. a. 1
    b. 3
    c. 5
    d. 4
    e. 2
25. a. 2
    b. 1
    c. 4
    d. 5
    e. 3
26. d
27. c
28. a
29. b
30. c
31. c
32. b
33. a
34. d
35. b

HA-9

1. hindrance
2. predators
3. plight
4. extinct
5. diversity
6. transplant
7. aggressive
8. excessive
9. inhibit
10. avidly
11. 2
12. 4
13. 3
14. 1
15. 5
16. c
17. c
18. b
19. a
20. d
21. b
22. d
23. a
24. a
25. c
*26. **Cause:** Fishermen caught puffins
     Effect: Puffins were almost extinct
*27. **Cause:** Puffins scarce
     Effect: Federal and state laws passed to protect them
*28. **Causes:** 1. Story of puffins illustrates plight of seabirds
               2. Puffin unable to recover on its own from human abuse
     Effect: Kress chooses to help puffins
*29. **Cause:** Seagulls lived on islands
     Effect: Seagulls a hindrance because they are puffin predators
*30. **Cause:** Holes wouldn't drain rain water
     Effect: Many chicks nearly drowned
*31. **Cause:** Set out puffin decoys and mirrors
     Effect: Attract real birds
32. c
33. a
34. c
35. b
36. d
37. a
38. b
39. c
40. c
41. b

---
*Your wording may be different.

ANSWER KEY

HA-10

1. economic
2. guidance
3. applicants
4. extensive
5. tendency
6. attentive
7. vacancies
8. therapists
9. rehabilitation
10. clinics
11. yes
12. no
13. yes
14. no
15. yes
16. c
17. a, c
18. d
19. a
20. c
21. d
22. d
23. b
24. a
25. c

*26. **Problem:** The number of available jobs has diminished; unemployment has soared.
Solution: Look for a job as a health care professional.

*27. **Problem:** The lack of health care employees
Solutions:
1. Recruiters pay full expenses for on-site interviews.
2. Recruiters offer well-paying packages to new employees willing to move.
3. Recruiters pay sign-on bonuses.

*28. **Problem:** Job seekers miss 75% of jobs by only checking the want ads.
Solution: They must try to identify likely employment opportunities through alternative means such as newsletters, directories, job fairs, job hotlines, and personal contacts.

*29. **Problem:** Job seekers are too narrow in their approach.
Solution: They must make numerous contacts to increase the chances of finding a job.

30. d
31. a
32. c
33. a
34. b
35. b
36. d
37. c
38. a
39. b

HA-11

1. yearned
2. straggle
3. compulsory
4. amorphous
5. energetic
6. tripods
7. unencumbered
8. resume
9. ultimate
10. massage
11. yes
12. yes
13. yes
14. no
15. no
16. d
17. c
18. a

19. b
20. c
21. a
22. b
23. a
24. c
25. c
26. no
27. 1
28. no
29. 3
30. 2
31. no
32. no
33. 4
34. 1
35. no
36. 2
37. 3

38. In 1982 Susan Butcher and her dogs arrived in Anchorage, Alaska, to compete in the Iditarod sled-dog race. During the race, Susan overtook 22 teams, which left only three teams ahead of her. At one point, she learned that she was ten miles off course and had to backtrack to get back in the race. Then, when her energetic dogs ran off without her, she had to chase after them for an additional six miles. A snowstorm with 80-mile-an-hour winds and 30-foot drifts forced Susan and other mushers to wait for 52 hours until the weather cleared. With only 22 miles to go in the race, Susan was in third place. Despite her efforts to win the Iditarod, Susan came in second.

39. c
40. b
41. c
42. c
43. c
44. b
45. a
46. b
47. b
48. c

---

*Your wording may be different.

ANSWER KEY

HA-12

1. valor
2. magnitude
3. saga
4. maiden
5. surpassed
6. economical
7. prolonged
8. enthralled
9. brink
10. probed
11. no
12. yes
13. yes
14. no
15. no
16. d
17. b
18. a
19. d
20. c
21. b, c
22. b
23. c, d
24. c
25. c
26. O
27. F
28. F
29. O
30. FC
31. FE
32. FE
33. FC
34. d
35. d
36. a
37. c
38. b
39. b
40. c
41. a
42. c
43. d

HA-13

1. expertise
2. comprehend
3. decades
4. penalized
5. callous
6. materialize
7. accommodate
8. compassion
9. authorize
10. intricate
11. yes
12. no
13. yes
14. yes
15. no
16. a, c, d
17. a
18. a, c
19. b, c, d
20. d
21. c
22. c
23. a
24. c
25. d
26. b
27. evil, greedy, callous, shortsighted, miserly
28. **Fact:** According to the *Wall Street Journal*, a recent nationwide survey of firms with more than 50 employees showed that only 7.2 percent had provided child-care programs, and two-thirds said they would never offer employees even such minimum child- or elder-care help as referrals and workshops.
    Opinion: It is painfully obvious that companies care nothing for their devoted employees.
29. **Fact:** When *Fortune* polled over 200 companies, close to 80 percent said they will have to push their people harder than ever before to be competitive.
    Opinion: To the unfeeling heads of these companies, family life means nothing when compared with workplace responsibilities.
30. **Fact:** A survey of employees at 80 major companies showed that fewer than 2 percent of qualified employees take advantage of job sharing, telecommuting (working off-site or from home), and part-time work options.
    Opinion: The reason for this is simple: Employees are penalized for using such programs.
*31. **Negative description:** scared rabbits
    Subject under suspicion: companies
*32. **Negative description:** dinosaurs
    Subject under suspicion: managers
33. b
34. d
35. c
36. c
37. b
38. a
39. c
40. b
41. b
42. c

HA-14

1. impelling
2. reinforced
3. accelerated
4. disparaging
5. indifferent
6. catastrophe
7. competent
8. massacre
9. propaganda
10. occurrence
11. false
12. true
13. true
14. false
15. a
16. b
17. d
18. a
19. c
20. c
21. a
22. d
23. c
24. b
25. a
26. b
27. d
28. a
29. c
30. a
31. b
32. d
33. c
34. c
35. a
36. a
37. c
38. d
39. b
40. d
41. a
42. c
43. b
44. b
45. c

---

*Your wording may be different.

ANSWER KEY

HA-15

1. profusion
2. inscribed
3. infantry
4. inevitably
5. impromptu
6. ordeals
7. ravages
8. entreats
9. harassed
10. agitating
*11. Thicker and heavier paper, pens were pointed reeds
*12. Topics of letters were similar.
13. b
14. a
15. d
16. c
17. d
18. a, d
19. c
20. b
21. b, c
22. d
23. N
24. R
25. ?
26. R
27. valid, lines 26–29
28. valid, lines 1–4
29. valid, lines 25–26
30. not valid, lines 77–82
31. not valid, lines 74–77
32. c
33. b
34. c
35. b
36. a
37. a
38. d
39. b
40. c
41. a

HA-16

1. patriarch
2. delegation
3. blandly
4. reverie
5. meditatively
6. gawk
7. confirmed
8. hearty
9. musing
10. hale
11. true
12. false
13. true
14. false
15. true
16. a
17. b
18. d
19. b
20. c
21. a
22. a
23. d
24. c
25. b
26. Washington; 1867
27. Washington; 1834–1867
28. a
29. b
30. a
31. c
32. a
33. d
34. b
35. c
36. c
37. b
38. c
39. a
40. d

HA-17

1. prosperous
2. irritated
3. pauper
4. predicament
5. dinginess
6. dowry
7. incessantly
8. adornments
9. adulation
10. ecstasy
11. yes
12. yes
13. no
14. yes
15. no
16. b
17. a
18. c
19. b
20. d
21. c
22. d
23. c
24. b
25. c
26. a, c
27. c
28. d
29. a
30. a
31. c
32. b
33. c
34. d
35. b
36. b
37. c
38. d
39. b
40. a
41. c
42. d
43. b
44. a
45. c

---

*Your wording may be different.

ANSWER KEY

HA-18

1. drabness
2. clashed
3. exorbitant
4. privations
5. untended
6. aghast
7. heroism
8. disconsolate
9. askew
10. gamut
11. yes
12. yes
13. no
14. yes
15. no
16. no
17. yes
18. no
19. d
20. c
21. b
22. c
23. c
24. d
25. c
26. a
27. b
28. a
29. b
30. d
31. b
32. d
33. c
34. d
35. a
36. c
37. d
38. b
39. d
40. a
41. c
42. b

HA-19

1. corporal
2. intervened
3. suppressed
4. implored
5. writhed
6. cavalry
7. formulate
8. perpendicular
9. upheaval
10. exclamation
11. 3
12. 4
13. 2
14. 5
15. 1
16. a
17. a
18. c
19. c
20. a, c
21. a
22. b
23. a
24. d
25. b
26. the long wave of blue and steel
27. The troopers threw themselves upon the grove like wolves upon a great animal.
28. c
29. crackling
30. smoke that writhed like stung phantoms
31. The nearest pine could be heard in its endless sighs.
32. d
33. crunched
34. She looked at him as she would have looked at a serpent.
35. her glance, which was at this time like that of the fawn
36. d
37. c
38. a
39. c
40. b
41. d
42. a
43. c
44. b
45. a
46. c

HA-20

1. reality
2. capsized
3. extinguished
4. apprehension
5. agitation
6. pall
7. conception
8. intangible
9. flaw
10. manipulation
11. true
12. false
13. true
14. false
15. true
16. b
17. a, b
18. c
19. b
20. c
21. d
22. a
23. d
24. a
25. c
*26. **Conflict:** The man fell through the snow into an underground spring.
*27. **Solution:** He built a fire to dry himself.
*28. **Conflict:** Snow fell on his fire and put it out.
*29. **Solution:** He succeeded in lighting the match.
*30. **Conflict:** He coughed and dropped the match in the snow.
*31. **Solution:** He lit all the matches at once.
*32. **Conflict:** Green moss fell on the fire and put it out.
*33. **Solution:** He would kill the dog and warm his hands in its body.
*34. **Conflict:** The dog would not come to him.
*35. **Solution:** He ran so his feet would thaw out.
*36. **Conflict:** He lacked endurance and fell.
37. b
38. d
39. a
40. b
41. c
42. d
43. a
44. c
45. b
46. b

---

*Your wording may be different.

SKILL REVIEW ACTIVITIES

HA-1

Skill Review Activity

SCANNING

Scan the article to find the answers to the questions. Write the answers.

    In the 1800s, coffee exports began to dominate Brazil's economy, maintaining this position until the second half of the twentieth century. Today the coffee business is still one of Brazil's leading industries. In fact, Brazil produces nearly three-fifths of the world's coffee.

    Most of the coffee is grown on huge plantations called *fazendas*. They spread out over the eastern slopes of the hills, which rise from the coastal plains. There, the well-drained reddish soil and mild temperatures allow this crop to thrive. Plenty of rain falls from October through March while the coffee is growing, but the rest of the year is sunny and dry.

1. When did coffee begin to dominate Brazil's economy?

   _____

2. How much of the world's coffee does Brazil produce?

   _____

3. What are the huge coffee plantations in Brazil called?

   _____

4. What two conditions in the coffee-growing regions make the coffee crop thrive?

   _____

5. What is the climate like in the coffee-growing regions of Brazil?

   _____

HA-2

Skill Review Activity

SUBSTITUTIONS

For each underlined substitute, write the word or words that it refers to.

1. After cloth was made in factories, <u>it</u> became cheaper to buy.

   _____

2. The soldiers fought hard to win the battle, and victory was <u>theirs</u>.

   _____

3. We are broadcasting live from Tampa for the Super Bowl. The weather <u>here</u> is sunny and dry.

   _____

176

4. The Olympics take place every four years. Athletes from all over compete for their countries. <u>Only the best</u> win gold medals.

_____

5. Many years ago, computers were confined to businesses. Today, computers are found in homes as well as at the office. <u>These machines</u> save time and effort for many people.

_____

6. Our city's crime rate has doubled in the last five years. The mayor simply has to do something about <u>this problem</u>.

_____

7. Mario is happy about the way the President is handling the country's economic problems. His wife <u>is not</u>.

_____

HA-3

Skill Review Activity

CONTEXT CLUES

Read each example. Then choose the correct meaning of the underlined word.

That cave is <u>accessible</u> only by water. It can be reached only by boat.

1. *Accessible* means
   ___a. visible.
   ___b. dangerous.
   ___c. approachable.
   ___d. attractive.

Many solutions work better if you <u>dilute</u> them. For example, you should add water to bleach before pouring it into the clothes washer. It may harm your clothes if you don't.

2. *Dilute* means
   ___a. to make stronger.
   ___b. to pour into the washer.
   ___c. to shake thoroughly.
   ___d. to weaken by adding a liquid.

The stranded motorist stopped a woman walking by. He <u>implored</u> her to give him some money to call a tow truck. Seeing his desperate state, she gave him some change for the phone.

3. *Implored* means
   ___a. begged.
   ___b. threatened.
   ___c. dared.
   ___d. comforted.

177

Tina found the news about the war distressing. I was also <u>perturbed</u> by what I heard.

4. *Perturbed* means
   ___a. thrilled.
   ___b. disturbed.
   ___c. comforted.
   ___d. angered.

Jamal knows how to talk to people. He gets along with everyone, and everyone likes him. His brother, on the other hand, has no <u>tact</u>.

5. *Tact* means
   ___a. enemies.
   ___b. skill in public speaking.
   ___c. skill in dealing with people.
   ___d. ambition.

Already having two pets, Midori found a new home for the stray dog she picked up. As she was about to leave the dog for good, he let out a terrible cry. Midori's heart was breaking. She just couldn't leave him. Her <u>attachment</u> to the animal was just too strong.

6. *Attachment* means
   ___a. dislike.
   ___b. fear.
   ___c. coolness.
   ___d. affection.

HA-4

Skill Review Activity

INFERENCES

Read each paragraph. Choose the best answer for the question that follows it.

Kelly's dog Buster loves sweets, but she doesn't give them to him because they're not healthy for a dog. One day Kelly, expecting some dinner guests, put a box of candy on the table. Then the doorbell rang, and Kelly went to greet her guests. By the time she walked back with her company, the candy was gone.

1. What happened to the candy?
   ___a. The guests ate it.
   ___b. Kelly ate it.
   ___c. It fell to the floor.
   ___d. Buster ate it.

Local health departments play a major role in the struggle against disease germs. Health workers check to make sure food is safe. They also inspect housing to see that no health hazards exist. Public facilities such as parks and other recreational areas are inspected periodically.

2. Health workers would most likely
   ___a. buy books for schools.
   ___b. hire police officers.
   ___c. inspect public swimming pools.
   ___d. help put out fires.

Many people worry about the fate of the African chimpanzee. These animals are hunted to be sold. For every chimpanzee that is taken alive, five to ten die. In the past fifty years, Africans have sold thousands of these animals for use in business and research experiments.

3. What might happen?
   ___a. The chimpanzee might die out.
   ___b. Africans might stop hunting chimpanzees.
   ___c. The chimpanzees might move.
   ___d. Fewer chimpanzees might die.

Some big hospitals use foster grandparents. These volunteers are senior citizens who put on red jackets and visit children in the hospital. Children learn that the red-jacketed visitors will sing to them, read to them, play games with them, and look after them.

4. Foster grandparents will
   ___a. earn high salaries.
   ___b. make a child's hospital stay less fearful.
   ___c. provide medical care.
   ___d. take the place of parents.

People in the late 1700s feared yellow fever, a highly contagious disease that could wipe out a large percent of a city's population. In 1773, this disease struck Philadelphia. By September, it became so widespread that people who died in the streets often stayed where they fell. No one would touch the bodies.

5. Why didn't people touch the bodies?
   ___a. They were too lazy to move the bodies.
   ___b. They thought someone else was going to pick up the bodies.
   ___c. They didn't know the people who had died.
   ___d. They were afraid of catching the disease.

HA-5

Skill Review Activity

MAIN IDEAS

Read each passage. Then choose the main idea.

Each kind of living thing makes up a population. A city lot may have a dandelion population, a squirrel population, and a pigeon population. A population can be large or small. A bee population would be part of an insect population. This, in turn, would be part of the whole population of living things.

1. The main idea is that
   ___a. each living thing makes up a population.
   ___b. a city lot can have three different kinds of populations.
   ___c. a population comes in all different sizes.
   ___d. an insect population is part of the whole population of living things.

The roots of a plant absorb water from the soil. Dissolved in the water are the minerals that plants need to grow. The roots also help keep the plant upright.

The stem supports the plant and also transports liquids to other areas. Food is stored in the stem until it can be used by the plant.

It is in the leaves that the food is made from the energy of the sun. And seeds are produced in the flower. These seeds later become new plants. Each part of the plant has important functions.

2. The main idea is that
   ___a. the roots absorb water and keep the plant upright.
   ___b. the stem supports the plant and transports liquids to other areas.
   ___c. seeds produced in the flower later become new plants.
   ___d. each part of the plant has important but different functions.

The most amazing machine you own is no bigger than your fist. This machine is your heart, working steadily to pump blood throughout your body. When you sit quietly, your heart beats about seventy times a minute. When you're active, it automatically speeds up to take care of the body's increased demands. This amazing machine maintains almost perfect rhythm throughout your entire lifetime.

3. What is the main idea?
   ___a. Your heart pumps slower when you sit than when you're active.
   ___b. The heart is a machine and is no bigger than your fist.
   ___c. The heart pumps and controls blood flow throughout the body.
   ___d. The heart has more functions than any other organ in your body.

Health departments are responsible for seeing that our water is pure. Yet recent studies showed that water supply systems of over eighty American communities did not meet minimum standards.

Community health departments should guard against all health threats. But some communities have only part-time health directors, who do not do a thorough job.

Sometimes citizen support is a problem. If communities do not vote enough money, health institutions cannot do their job.

4. What is the main idea?
   ___a. Health departments do an excellent job and deserve our support.
   ___b. The minimum standards of health departments are very high, so they are rarely met.
   ___c. Many health departments somehow fail, at least in part, to carry out the duties that have been assigned to them.
   ___d. The effectiveness of a health department depends on how many workers it employs.

HA-6

Skill Review Activity

TYPES OF SUPPORTING DETAILS

Read each paragraph. Then choose the correct paragraph pattern used.

There are many things to keep in mind when you are conducting an experiment. First, have a clear statement of what the experiment is testing. Second, be sure that you have all of the necessary materials. Next, proceed to follow the steps of the experiment in the proper sequence. Finally, observe carefully and draw your conclusion.

1. This paragraph uses
   ___a. enumeration.
   ___b. generalization.
   ___c. opinion/reason.
   ___d. question/answer.

How did Native American tribes of the forests live? Since many wild animals found food in forests, the tribes who lived there trapped deer, bear, squirrels, and birds for food. Animal skins and furs were used for clothing. There were nuts, berries, roots, and seeds to gather. The tribes used the wild plants in the forest for medicine. Also, the rains formed lakes where fish could be caught.

2. This paragraph uses
   ___a. enumeration.
   ___b. generalization.
   ___c. opinion/reason.
   ___d. question/answer.

I believe that the former administration had a terrible domestic policy. The economy was left in a sorry shape. Money was poured into defense, but little was given to help the sick and the homeless. More and more cuts were made to education. And little was done to protect our environment.

3. This paragraph uses
   ___a. enumeration.
   ___b. generalization.
   ___c. opinion/reason.
   ___d. question/answer.

Scientists have been developing chemicals that help produce more food for people. For example, new chemical sprays often kill plant-eating insects that old sprays did not. Another example is improved fertilizers that replace soil chemicals previous crops have taken out. In addition, improved medicines keep animals healthy so they will produce meat and other food products.

4. This paragraph uses
   ___a. enumeration.
   ___b. generalization.
   ___c. opinion/reason.
   ___d. question/answer.

Where do you go to learn how to become a clown? You go to the clown college run by the Ringling Brothers and Barnum and Bailey Circus. Out of the six thousand people who show interest in becoming clowns every year, only those with a talent for acting get admitted to the clown college. The new students take lessons in acting, costuming, applying makeup, and performing stunts. Only the best in the class become circus clowns.

5. This paragraph uses
   ___a. enumeration.
   ___b. generalization.
   ___c. opinion/reason.
   ___d. question/answer.

I think that show is the best new comedy of the television season. All of the elements of good comedy are there. The characters are true to life, and the talented actors who portray them have perfect comic timing. The scripts are well written and well directed. The situations are fresh and funny. All of this produces a very enjoyable half hour of television viewing.

6. This paragraph uses
   ___a. enumeration.
   ___b. generalization.
   ___c. opinion/reason.
   ___d. question/answer.

There are many good reasons to own a pet. First, people who live alone own pets for companionship. Pets are loving and easily show affection. Second, some people own pets for protection. A barking dog can discourage would-be burglars. Finally, pets can be good for your health. People can actually lower their blood pressure by petting an animal or watching fish swim around in their tank.

7. This paragraph uses
   ___a. enumeration.
   ___b. generalization.
   ___c. opinion/reason.
   ___d. question/answer.

Systems in the human body keep it working smoothly. For example, the circulatory system consists of blood, the heart, and blood vessels. This system brings needed materials to various body parts. It also collects waste and carries it away. Another example is the respiratory system, which consists of the mouth, nose, and lungs. This system lets the body breathe in oxygen and get rid of wastes.

8. This paragraph uses
   ___a. enumeration.
   ___b. generalization.
   ___c. opinion/reason.
   ___d. question/answer.

HA-7

Skill Review Activity

COMPARISONS

Read the passage and complete the chart that follows. Then use the chart to answer the questions.

Areas where the heat during a short summer does not allow the growth of plants larger than shrubs are widely called "tundra." The tundra consists of the vast area of level land that surrounds the North Pole. Grasslands are plains common to many regions, including North America.

The climate of the tundra is very cold and dry, while grasslands have a mild climate. Both areas, however, have low average rainfall. In addition, while grasses and shrubs grow in both areas, there are no tall trees in either region. This is understandable in the cold tundra, but the reason for a lack of trees in the mild grasslands might not be as obvious. Although the upper soil layers of grasslands are usually moist for several months, the low rainfall at other times does not allow trees to grow.

Some animals seen in the tundra are Arctic foxes, polar bears, and moose. Some grassland animals are foxes, coyotes, and wolves.

	Tundra	Grasslands
1. Location		
2. Climate		
3. Rainfall		
4. Plant life		
5. Animal life		

6. What is the climate like on the tundra?

   _____

7. What kind of plant life is found in the grasslands?

   _____

8. What type of animal is found in both regions?

   _____

9. In what ways are the tundra and the grasslands similar? (Choose **all** the correct answers.)
   ___a. Location
   ___b. Climate
   ___c. Rainfall
   ___d. Plant life

HA-8
SEQUENCE

Skill Review Activity

Read each selection. Be aware of any flashbacks in the selections as you read. Then number each group of events to show the correct sequence.

In 1918, the United States Post Office attempted to use an airplane to carry the mail. To say that things did not go well is an understatement. The very first thing that went wrong was that the plane wouldn't start. This was simply remedied when someone discovered that the plane had no fuel.

Once in the air, the pilot had a problem of another kind; he was lost. He began to follow train tracks, thinking they were going the right way, but unfortunately they weren't. When he landed the plane to ask for directions, he damaged it so badly that he could not take off again. In the end, the mail had to be sent by truck.

1. a._____ The pilot landed to ask directions.
   b._____ The plane would not start because it had no fuel.
   c._____ The mail had to be sent by truck.
   d._____ The plane could not take off again because it was damaged.
   e._____ The pilot began to follow train tracks.

Ginny put the last item into her suitcase. In a few hours, she would be on her way to her childhood home in Italy. She could hardly wait.

Ginny had been born in Italy in 1940, but she had left there as a young woman to come to this country. She remembered that last day at home with her parents many years ago. Her mother had cried as she kissed Ginny good-bye. Her father was dry-eyed, but emotional nonetheless.

After one last look around, Ginny went down to the waiting taxi to go to the airport. She was ready to go home.

2. a._____ Ginny took one last look around.
   b._____ Ginny put the last item in her suitcase.
   c._____ Ginny's mother kissed her good-bye.
   d._____ Ginny went down to the waiting taxi.
   e._____ Ginny came to this country.

HA-9

Skill Review Activity

CAUSE AND EFFECT

Read each paragraph. Write the cause(s) and effect(s) for each one.

Before the printing press was invented, books were copied by hand. It sometimes took months to make a copy of one book. Because of this, books were very expensive.

1. Cause: _____

   Effect: _____

During the Civil War, the blockade of Southern ports was a smart move by the North. The South could not export goods to Europe, nor could it import needed supplies.

2. Cause: _____

   Effects: 1. _____

   2. _____

Tonya stocked up on food. Then she bought a new snow shovel. Last, she put chains on the tires of her car. Earlier, she had heard that a major snowstorm was coming to the area.

3. Cause: _____

   Effects: 1. _____

   2. _____

   3. _____

In 1867, the United States bought Alaska from Russia. Russia had good reasons for selling Alaska. The fur trade was no longer profitable. Also, the Russian government did not want to protect a territory so far away.

4. Causes: 1. _____

   2. _____

   Effect: _____

HA-10

Skill Review Activity

PROBLEM AND SOLUTION

Read each paragraph. Write the problem(s) and solution(s) for each one.

    Barry had to get on his roof to make some repairs, but his roof was high and steep. The tallest ladder he had was only thirty-two feet long and would not reach the roof. Barry decided to borrow Mr. Cheung's ladder, which was forty feet long.

1. Problem: _____

   Solution: _____

    In 1898, President McKinley sent the battleship *Maine* to Cuba. He did this to protect American lives and business interests in Cuba during the Cubans' revolt against their Spanish rulers. As the sleek steel ship steamed into the harbor, Americans breathed a sigh of relief.

2. Problem: _____

   Solution: _____

    Insufficient domestic oil has long troubled the United States. Oil companies have developed new projects to produce more domestic oil. One of these was the huge Alaska pipeline. Off-shore drilling, another project, has oil companies drilling closer to shore and deeper than ever before. And, or course, they are constantly drilling in new places.

3. Problem: _____

   Solutions: 1. _____

              2. _____

              3. _____

    Andreas Vesalius was a famous physician in the 1500s. In 1564, he took a small boat from Jaffa to Italy. The weather had been stormy, knocking the boat around. Food was running low, and many people on board, including Vesalius, were sick. The captain decided to sail for the island of Zante for supplies, care for the sick, and protection from the storms.

4. Problems: 1. _____

             2. _____

             3. _____

   Solution: _____

HA-11

Skill Review Activity

SUMMARIZING

Read each passage and the list of sentences below it. Write *no* beside the sentences that should be left out of a summary. Then number the sentences that should be included in the summary in the order in which they occurred in the passage.

In June of 1971, some scientists were exploring rain forests in the mountains of Mindanao Island, an area that had never been previously explored. To their amazement and delight, they discovered a small tribe of natives. The tribe, called the Tasaday, resided so deep in the forest that no one had come across them before. The Tasaday, who had never seen other people before, graciously welcomed the scientists. The scientists found that the Tasaday had twenty-four members, thirteen of which were children.

The scientists and others who came after introduced the gentle members of this tribe to some of the technology of the modern world. However, the lives of the primitive tribe did not change much as a result. They were happy with the old ways of doing things.

1. _____ The scientists were amazed and delighted at their discovery.

2. _____ Even though the tribe was introduced to the technology of the modern world, their lives did not change much.

3. _____ Thirteen of the twenty-four members of the tribe were children.

4. _____ The Tasaday, who had never seen other people before, graciously welcomed the scientists.

5. _____ In June of 1971, a group of scientists discovered the small Tasaday tribe in the mountains of Mindanao Island.

6. _____ The Tasaday were happy with the old ways of doing things.

Arthur Mitchell was the first African-American dancer in the New York City Ballet. At thirty-five, he retired from the stage and started a school in the African-American community of Harlem.

Mitchell made it easy for the poor to attend classes. He charged only fifty cents a week and taught out of a garage. He also let his students practice in comfortable clothes like cutoff jeans.

The school was a success, and soon Mitchell formed a ballet company. Today the Dance Theatre of Harlem is one of the best dance companies in North America.

7. _____ Arthur Mitchell was the first African-American dancer in the New York City Ballet.

8. _____ Mitchell retired from the stage at the age of thirty-five.

9. _____ The school was a success, and Mitchell soon formed the equally successful Dance Theatre of Harlem.

10. _____ Mitchell charged fifty cents a week and taught out of a garage.

11. _____ Mitchell made it easy for the poor to attend classes.

12. _____ After retiring from the stage, Mitchell started a dance school in Harlem.

HA-12
Skill Review Activity

FACT AND OPINION

Read each sentence. Then write *FC* if it is a fact easily checked, write *FE* if it is a fact needing further explanation, and write *O* if it is a statement of opinion.

1. _____ Clara Barton was the founder of the American Red Cross.

2. _____ November is the best time to visit Florida.

3. _____ Bleach will remove color from fabric.

4. _____ I think we will have a cold winter.

5. _____ Canada is a country of contrasting physical environments.

6. _____ Joining the army is probably one of the best ways to get an education and job training.

7. _____ The anti-slavery reformers did meet with some success before the Civil War.

8. _____ In light, green plants produce oxygen.

9. _____ Chemical fertilizers do more harm than good.

10. _____ Moby Dick is the best American novel ever written.

HA-13
Skill Review Activity

RECOGNIZING BIAS/AUTHOR'S VIEWPOINT

Read the paragraph and choose the best answers to the questions that follow.

The dedicated teachers of the North Hills District have worked hard to make it one of the finest in the country. At the same time, these capable individuals are grossly underpaid. Something should be done about this outrage.

1. This paragraph
   ___a. shows no bias.
   ___b. is biased in favor of the teachers.
   ___c. is biased against the teachers.

2. Which of the following are emotionally loaded words?
   ___a. dedicated, capable, grossly underpaid, outrage
   ___b. country, same time, should be
   ___c. district, worked, individuals, done about

Each of the following statements uses either a half-truth or guilt by association. Write the information called for in each case.

My opponent may be gaining in the polls, but the people of this country will show that they're not fooled by his cheap brand of politics on Election Day.

3. Fact: _____

   Opinion: _____

Before you vote, ask yourself why gangsters have been contributing to the campaign of Mayor Rogers.

4. Negative description: _____

   Subject under suspicion: _____

HA-14

Skill Review Activity

PERSUASION

Read each statement. Then choose the method of persuasion used.

"Don't lose your teeth to gum disease. Floss them every day with Bronson's Dental Floss."

1. Which method of persuasion is used?
   - ___a. Glittering Generalities
   - ___b. Negative Transfer
   - ___c. Name Calling
   - ___d. Bandwagon
   - ___e. Fear

"More people drive the Kayota Ranger than any other import. All those people can't be wrong. Shouldn't you be driving a Kayota Ranger, too?"

2. Which method of persuasion is used?
   - ___a. Glittering Generalities
   - ___b. Negative Transfer
   - ___c. Name Calling
   - ___d. Bandwagon
   - ___e. Fear

"You don't want to read that book. Its author associates with people who belong to a well-known anti-American group."

3. Which method of persuasion is used?
   - ___a. Glittering Generalities
   - ___b. Negative Transfer
   - ___c. Name Calling
   - ___d. Bandwagon
   - ___e. Fear

"Bring back truth, justice, and freedom to our town. Vote for Weaver."

4. Which method of persuasion is used?
   - ___a. Glittering Generalities
   - ___b. Negative Transfer
   - ___c. Name Calling
   - ___d. Bandwagon
   - ___e. Fear

"Those kind of people are lazy and stupid, and they will cause nothing but trouble if we let them into this country."

5. Which method of persuasion is used?
   ___ a. Glittering Generalities
   ___ b. Negative Transfer
   ___ c. Name Calling
   ___ d. Bandwagon
   ___ e. Fear

HA-15

Skill Review Activity

JUDGING RELEVANCE/FINDING PROOF

Suppose you want to find information about African-American heroes in World War II. Read each book title below. Write *R* for each title that would have relevant information. Write *N* for each title that would not have relevant information. And write *?* for each title that might or might not have relevant information.

1. ___ *The Vietnam Story*, by L.C. Wright

2. ___ *A History of Blacks in America*, by Tamara Douglass

3. ___ *Stories of Courage: Black Americans in World War II*, by Jay Walz

4. ___ *Heroes of the Second World War*, by M. Perez

Read the following passage. Then look at the statements below. Write valid for each true statement. Write not valid for each untrue statement. Write the line numbers from the story where you find the proof.

  1   Dorie Miller was an African-American sailor on the battleship *West Virginia*
      stationed at Pearl Harbor in 1941. At that time, African-Americans were not allowed
      to engage in combat, so Miller had no gunnery training. Yet when the Japanese
      attacked on December 7, Miller became a hero.
  5   When he heard the bombing start, Miller ran to the deck. Some of the gunners had
      been hit, and Japanese planes continued their relentless bombing of the area. Without
      giving a thought to his personal safety, Miller grabbed a machine gun and began
      firing, shooting down at least two enemy planes and perhaps as many as six.
      Miller was awarded the Navy Cross because of his courage. By war's end, the navy
 10   changed its policy regarding African-Americans in combat.

Valid or Line
Not Valid Numbers

5. _____ _____ Dorie Miller was the officer in charge of firing the machine guns on the battleship *West Virginia*.

6. _____ _____ Miller shot down more that one enemy plane when Pearl Harbor was attacked.

7. _____ _____ Miller received the Congressional Medal of Honor for his brave deed.

8. _____ _____ By the end of World War II, African-Americans in the navy were allowed to engage in combat.

HA-16

Skill Review Activity

SETTING/TONE/THEME

Read each passage, and choose the best answer for each question.

   He stood on his own goal line waiting for the other team to kick off. It was warm and the sun, then at its peak, gently beat down on him. A whistle blew. Way down the field the kicker began his run toward the ball. As his strong leg struck the ball, it shot into the still blueness and began its upward flight. The receiver moved toward the ball. Ahead of him, his teammates were gathering to protect him. The ball came down and slammed against his chest and into his waiting hands.

1. What is the setting of this passage?
   ___a. At night during a football game
   ___b. Early afternoon during a football game
   ___d. Early evening during a basketball game

   The large white house was very dignified. Venetian blinds of cheery yellow wood were tilted down to keep out the noon sun. There was a porch as broad and warm and welcoming as an embrace. Through her mind flew the thought, "You can always tell the friendliness of a house by its entrance." The welcoming of the wide steps and the big doorway put her fears to rest. She rang the bell. The big door opened, and a large, comfortable woman stood smiling at her.

2. What is the tone of this passage? (Choose **all** the correct answers.)
   ___a. Cheerful   ___d. Troubled
   ___b. Gloomy   ___e. Informational
   ___c. Friendly   ___f. Comforting

   One hot summer's day a fox was strolling through an orchard. He came to a bunch of grapes ripening on a vine that grew over a high branch. "Just the thing to quench my thirst," he thought.
   Drawing back a few paces, he took a run and a jump, and just missed the bunch. Turning around, he made another jump, but he still did not succeed. He jumped again and again for the grapes, but at last he had to give up. He walked away with his nose in the air, saying: "I am sure they are sour."

3. What is the theme of this passage?
   ___a. People are never satisfied with what they have.
   ___b. If at first you don't succeed, try, try again.
   ___c. Do not take what belongs to someone else.
   ___d. It is easy to despise what you cannot have.

HA-17

Skill Review Activity

CHARACTER AND FEELINGS

Read each passage, and choose the best answer for each question.

   Josefina was helping Rosa with her new baby. Josefina was heavy-faced and her eyes were kind, even when her tongue was sharp. Thus her character: good heart, from instinct; wicked mind, from dealings with the hard world.

"If you all get through the cold winter, that will be one of God's little jokes," said Josefina.
"My husband will bring back money form Mexico," said Rosa. But she began to cry.
"I will stay as long as I can," said Josefina. "Get some sleep."

1. What kind of person is Josefina?
    ___a. Foolish but trustworthy
    ___b. Kind but with a sharp tongue
    ___c. Proud and scornful
    ___d. Fearful and awestruck

2. How does Josefina feel about Rosa?
    ___a. She feels sorry for her.
    ___b. She is afraid of her.
    ___c. She hates her.
    ___d. She is indifferent toward her.

Ted read again the telegram he had received from his mother-in-law that morning: "Come home. Jane is not expected to live. Will wire again if necessary. It was a boy."

Ted's hands clenched suddenly. He sat back, closed his eyes, and listened to the sound of the train. Then he heard a porter call his name. It was another telegram.

Ted's throat felt tight and his hands were shaking. "She said she would wire again if—" he thought. He rose from his seat feeling weak, the unopened telegram in his hand.

He made his way to the back of the train. Finally he said, "It's not true! I don't believe it!" Saying so, he tore the unopened telegram into tiny bits and threw the pieces from the end of the train. Immediately he felt better.

He walked back to his car and talked cheerfully to the other passengers about his wife and new baby. As long as he talked, his wife stayed alive for him.

3. What motivates Ted to tear up the telegram?
    ___a. He doesn't want anyone to see it.
    ___b. He has memorized it, so he doesn't need it anymore.
    ___c. He hates his mother-in-law, so he doesn't want to read anything she had written.
    ___d. He is afraid to find out that his wife is dead.

4. What motivates Ted to talk cheerfully to the other passengers about his wife and new baby?
    ___a. He cares more for the baby than he does for his wife.
    ___b. He wants to believe that his wife is still alive.
    ___c. He doesn't want the passengers to know what has happened.
    ___d. He wants the passengers to comfort him in his grief.

HA-18

Skill Review Activity

PLOT

Read each story summary, and choose the best answer for each question.

Jed and Willy, running from the law, are on a cliff. They come to a wide gap a hundred feet across and fifty feet straight down. Below is the river. Suddenly they hear shots and the pounding of horses approaching. The two men decide to take their chances with the river and they jump. Jed and Willy both survive the fall with a few bruises. They then wade to the riverbank and hide in a cave. The sheriff's men give up the search and turn around to go back to town.

1. What is the conflict of this story?
    ___a. Jed wants to give up, but Willy wants to keep running.
    ___b. The outlaws struggle with their consciences after breaking the law.
    ___c. The sheriff wants to continue after the outlaws, but his deputies want to go back to town.
    ___d. The outlaws struggle to escape the law.

2. The climax of this story comes when
    ___a. the outlaws decide to jump into the river.
    ___b. the outlaws find they have a few bruises.
    ___c. the outlaws first break the law.
    ___d. the sheriff takes off after Jed and Willy.

3. What is the conclusion of this story?
    ___a. The sheriff catches Jed and Willy.
    ___b. The outlaws hear shots.
    ___c. The sheriff's men give up the search and head back to town.
    ___d. The outlaws hide from the sheriff.

When Chee's wife dies, her parents take his little girl, as is Navaho custom. Chee desperately wants his daughter back. When he goes to see his in-laws at their trading store, they scorn him and refuse to give up the child. Just as he feels all is lost, Chee gets an idea. He finds a field, works the land, and is rewarded by plentiful crops. He takes bags of food back to the trading store, where his in-laws have fallen on hard times. They accept the food in exchange for the girl. Father and daughter have a happy reunion.

4. What is the conflict of this story?
    ___a. Chee struggles to get over his wife's death.
    ___b. Chee struggles to get his daughter back from his in-laws.
    ___c. Chee's in-laws struggle to overcome hard times.
    ___d. Chee struggles to survive after his crops fail.

5. What is the climax of this story?
    ___a. After working the land and getting plentiful crops, Chee once more approaches his in-laws.
    ___b. Chee's wife dies.
    ___c. Chee's in-laws take his daughter.
    ___d. Chee feels all is lost.

6. What is the conclusion of this story?
    ___a. Chee's in-laws still refuse to give up the girl.
    ___b. Chee devises a plan to get his daughter back.
    ___c. Chee's in-laws fall on hard times.
    ___d. Chee's in-laws take the food in exchange for the girl.

HA-19

Skill Review Activity

SENSORY IMAGES/FIGURATIVE LANGUAGE

Read each passage, and answer each question.

Awake! Awake! Wonderful fawn-eyed One.
When you look upon me I am satisfied, as flowers that drink the dew.
The breath of your mouth is the fragrance of flowers in the morning. . . .

1. What is the simile in this passage?

_____

2. The author uses this simile to show
   ___a. how good he feels when his love looks at him.
   ___b. how peaceful his love looks when sleeping.
   ___c. how the breath of his love pleases him.
   ___d. his indifference toward his love.

3. What is the metaphor in this passage?

   _____

4. Which sense is appealed to by this metaphor?
   ___a. Sight
   ___b. Hearing
   ___c. Touch
   ___d. Taste
   ___e. Smell

The little waves, with their soft white hands,
Efface the footprints in the sands,
And the tide rises, the tide falls.

5. What is the personification in this passage?

   _____

6. This personification contributes to a feeling of
   ___a. gloom.
   ___b. anger.
   ___c. shame.
   ___d. peace.

Yet by the ear it fully knows,
   By the twanging,
   And the clanging,
How the danger ebbs and flows. . . .

7. What are the examples of onomatopoeia in this passage?

   _____

HA-20

Skill Review Activity

QUALITIES IN LITERATURE: SUSPENSE

The passage below contains many plot reversals, where hope for success is offset by reversals that cause fear of failure. Read the passage looking for the plot reversals. Then answer the questions that follow.

   The earthquake had struck in their sleep. After, Pablo lay in agony, but this thoughts were on his wife and his two young daughters. His extreme physical pain was nothing in comparison to the thought of losing his family. He lay still, listening for signs of life among the rubble. He heard nothing.
   He struggled to free himself and felt relieved that at least there was nothing lying on top of his legs. Maybe it wasn't as bad as he thought.

As he freed his upper body enough to sit upright, he realized his mistake. His legs were crushed under tons of concrete and debris, but he could not feel a thing. He fell back and lost consciousness.

When he came to, he heard whimpering. "My family is alive!" he thought. He called out, but there was no answer. Then he felt a wet tongue licking his face. It was just the family dog. But soon a glimmer of hope appeared in Pablo's eyes. He ordered the dog out to go find help.

1. Which of these is a plot reversal in the passage?
    ___a. After feeling relieved that there is nothing lying on top of his legs, Pablo discovers that they are actually crushed.
    ___b. After an earthquake strikes, Pablo is in extreme pain.
    ___c. After listening for signs of life among the rubble, Pablo hears nothing.
    ___d. After the earthquake, Pablo thinks of his wife and two young daughters.

2. Does this reversal create feelings of hope or fear? _____

3. Which of these is a plot reversal in the passage?
    ___a. After finding his legs crushed, Pablo falls into unconsciousness.
    ___b. After the initial disappointment of finding the family dog instead of a member of his family, Pablo decides the dog can be useful in going for help.
    ___c. After sending the family dog out for help, Pablo gives up all hope of being rescued.
    ___d. After thinking his family is still alive, Pablo calls out to them.

4. Does this reversal create feelings of hope or fear? _____

Answer Key

HA-1

1. in the 1800s
2. nearly three-fifths
3. fazendas
4. well-drained reddish soil and mild temperatures
5. plenty of rain from October through March, but sunny and dry the rest of the year

HA-2

1. cloth
2. The soldiers
3. Tampa
4. Athletes
5. computers
6. Our city's crime rate has doubled in the last five years.
7. happy

HA-3

1. c
2. d
3. a
4. b
5. c
6. d

HA-4

1. d
2. c
3. a
4. b
5. d

HA-5

1. a
2. d
3. c
4. c

HA-6

1. a
2. d
3. c
4. b
5. d
6. c
7. a
8. b

HA-7

	Tundra	Grasslands
1. Location	North Pole	many regions, including North America
2. Climate	cold and dry	mild
3. Rainfall	low average	low average
4. Plant life	grasses, shrubs, no tall trees	grasses, shrubs, no tall trees
5. Animal life	Arctic foxes, polar bears, moose	foxes, coyotes, wolves

6. cold and dry
7. grasses, shrubs, no tall trees
8. foxes
9. c, d

HA-8

1. a. 3
   b. 1
   c. 5
   d. 4
   e. 2
2. a. 4
   b. 3
   c. 1
   d. 5
   e. 2

HA-9

1. Cause: It sometimes took months to make a copy of one book.
   Effect: Books were very expensive.
2. Cause: The North made a blockade of Southern ports.
   Effects: 1. The South could not export goods to Europe.
   2. It could not import needed supplies.
3. Cause: Tonya heard that a major snowstorm was coming.
   Effects: 1. She stocked up on food.
   2. She bought a new snow shovel.
   3. She put chains on the tires of her car.
4. Causes: 1. The fur trade was no longer profitable.
   2. The Russian government did not want to protect a territory so far away.
   Effect: Russia sold Alaska to the United States.

195

HA-10

1. Problem: The ladder Barry had would not reach the roof.
   Solution: Barry decided to borrow Mr. Cheung's ladder.
2. Problem: President McKinley wanted to protect American lives and business interests in Cuba during the Cubans' revolt against their Spanish rulers.
   Solution: He sent the battleship *Maine* to Cuba.
3. Problem: insufficient domestic oil
   Solutions: 1. Alaska pipeline
   2. off-shore drilling
   3. drilling in new places
4. Problems: 1. The weather was stormy.
   2. Food was running low.
   3. Many people on board were sick.
   Solution: The captain decided to sail for the island of Zante.

HA-11

1. no
2. 3
3. no
4. 2
5. 1
6. no
7. 1
8. no
9. 4
10. no
11. 3
12. 2

HA-12

1. FC
2. O
3. FC
4. O
5. FE
6. O
7. FE
8. FC
9. O
10. O

HA-13

1. b
2. a
3. Fact: My opponent may be gaining in the polls.
   Opinion: The people of this country will show that they're not fooled by his cheap brand of politics on Election Day.
4. Negative description: gangsters have been contributing to the campaign
   Subject under suspicion: Mayor Rogers

HA-14

1. e
2. d
3. b
4. a
5. c

HA-15

1. N
2. ?
3. R
4. ?

	Valid or Not Valid	Line Numbers	
5.	not valid	3-4	Dorie Miller was the officer in charge of firing the machine guns on the battleship *West Virginia*.
6.	valid	10-12	Miller shot down more that one enemy plane when Pearl Harbor was attacked.
7.	not valid	13-14	Miller received the Congressional Medal of Honor for his brave deed.
8.	valid	14-15	By the end of World War II, African-Americans in the navy were allowed to engage in combat.

HA-16

1. b
2. a, c, f
3. d

HA-17

1. b
2. a
3. d
4. b

HA-18

1. d
2. a
3. c
4. b
5. a
6. d

HA-19

1. When you look upon me I am satisfied, as flowers that drink the dew.
2. a
3. The breath of your mouth is the fragrance of flowers in the morning.
4. e
5. The little waves, with their soft white hands, ...
6. d
7. twanging, clanging

HA-20

1. a
2. fear
3. b
4. hope

CREDITS

HA-1 **REVENGE OF THE BUGS 101** by Frank Kuznik
Copyright 1995 by the National Wildlife Federation. Reprinted with permission from *National Wildlife* magazine's February/March issue.

HA-2 **JAKE** by Gene Hill
Reprinted by permission of *Field and Stream* Magazine.

HA-3 **MYSTERIOUS TALENTS** by William E. Schmidt
Copyright © 1983 by The New York Times Company. Reprinted by permission.

HA-4 **THE GREATEST BRONC BUSTER WHO EVER LIVED** by Jack Burrows
Reprinted by permission of the author.

HA-5 **THE WEED KILLER THAT KILLS PEOPLE** by Andrew C. Revkin
Reprinted by permission of the author. Excerpted from *Science Digest*, June 1983.

HA-8 **INTRODUCING THE MOM AND POP SUPERMARKET** edited by Gerri Hirshey
Reprinted by permission of *Family Circle*.

HA-9 **THE RETURN OF THE PUFFINS** by Ron Winslow
Reprinted by permission of The Sterling Lord Agency, Inc. Copyright © 1983 by Ron Winslow.

HA-11 **A WOMAN'S ICY STRUGGLE** by Susan Butcher
Reprinted by permission of the author.

HA-15 **LETTERS FROM THE PAST** by Lionel Casson
Copyright © 1983 by Lionel Casson. Distributed by Special Features. Reprinted by permission.